HERMENEUTICS AND
HUMAN FINITUDE

HERMENEUTICS AND HUMAN FINITUDE

Toward a Theory of Ethical Understanding

by

P. CHRISTOPHER SMITH

Fordham University Press
New York
1991

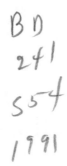

Printed in the United States of America

TO

GEORGE L. KLINE

AND

HANS-GEORG GADAMER,

MENTORS AND FRIENDS

ON MY NOT ALWAYS EASY WAY IN PHILOSOPHY

CONTENTS

ABBREVIATIONS

Frequently cited material appear as listed here. For complete bibliographical information, see the Bibliography.

AV	Alasdair MacIntyre, *After Virtue*
CP	Richard Rorty, *Consequences of Pragmatism*
DD	Hans-Georg Gadamer, *Dialogue and Dialectic*
HD	Hans-George Gadamer, *Hegel's Dialectic*
HL	Hans-Georg Gadamer, "Heidelberg Lectures on Aesthetics"
IGPAP	Hans-Georg Gadamer, *The Idea of the Good in Platonic-Aristotelian Philosophy*
KS I–IV	Hans-Georg Gadamer, *Kleine Schriften*
L I–II	Georg Wilhelm Friedrich Hegel, *Wissenschaft der Logik*
MC	Stuart Hampshire, *Morality and Conflict*
PDE	Hans-Georg Gadamer, *Platos dialektische Ethik*
PhG	Georg Wilhelm Friedrich Hegel, *Phänomenologie des Geistes*
PhR	Georg Wilhelm Friedrich Hegel, *Grundlinien der Philosophie des Rechts*
PI	Ludwig Wittgenstein, *Philosophical Investigations*
PLW	Martin Heidegger, *Platons Lehre von der Wahrheit*
RRF	Edmund Burke, *Reflections on the Revolution in France*
SZ	Martin Heidegger, *Sein und Zeit*
TJ	John Rawls, *A Theory of Justice*
WJWR	Alasdair MacIntyre, *Whose Justice? Which Rationality?*
WM	Hans-Georg Gadamer, *Wahrheit und Methode*

The translations of Plato, Aristotle, Thomas Aquinas, Hegel, Heidegger, and Gadamer are my own.

INTRODUCTION

Lessing has said that if God held all truth in His right hand, and in His left hand the lifelong pursuit of it, he would choose the left hand.

Kierkegaard
Concluding Unscientific Postscript

THIS BOOK IS AN ATTEMPT to show how the theory of interpretation that Hans-Georg Gadamer has developed, his hermeneutics, might be extended to ethics. Gadamer concerns himself primarily with the understanding of texts and works of art. Here, using his exploration of these forms of understanding as a basis, I will be inquiring about the nature of ethical understanding.

Of course, Gadamer comes from a tradition very different from the English-speaking one that, since I am writing about him in English, establishes the framework for my discussion. Consequently my undertaking will involve a kind of translation and what he calls a *Horizontverschmelzung* or "merging of horizons," the horizons, namely, of the traditions of Anglo-American thought, its ethical and moral philosophy in particular, with those of an initially foreign way of thinking. To accomplish this I will begin with areas where Anglo-American thinking, with its familiar topics and approach to these, overlaps with Gadamer's. Then, having gotten a foothold on the new territory, as it were, I will move outward into Gadamer's particular ways of seeing and speaking about things. My goal, accordingly, will not be so much to incorporate Gadamer's approach within the endeavors of Anglo-American thought as the reverse: to widen the concerns of Anglo-American thought, its horizons, so that in the end, newly fructified by graftings from Gadamer's ways of seeing and putting things, it might transcend some of its previous limitations and escape some of the *aporiai* or dead-ends with which it finds itself confronted. Rorty and MacIntyre, it seems to me, have undertaken similar projects.

In Gadamer's case a merging of horizons so conceived is facilitated by a shared attitude: both he and English-speaking philosophers generally, if not entirely, mistrust grand philosophical systems. (Whitehead, of course, is one notable exception here, among others.) Both he and they generally like to take up one thing at a time and probe it carefully, and both are reluctant to combine pieces of inquiry in some sort of comprehensive scheme like Hegel's idealism or Marx's dialectical materialism. For both, there is, on the whole, no single interpretive key for all phenomena, and even the treatment of any single phenomenon remains admittedly incomplete and tentative.

But what joins his thinking with most Anglo-American thought in this respect also divides the two. In the latter, reservations about systematic philosophy show up as skepticism, on the one hand, and, on the other, in the sharp restriction of philosophical investigation to smaller, tractable problems. It shows up in Gadamer, however, quite differently: in his insistence, namely, on human finitude and the limits of human consciousness all the while he continues to take up the traditional issues of speculative philosophy. Hume, who discards speculative philosophy, remains the inescapable father of the prevailing Anglo-American disposition toward philosophy. In contrast, Gadamer comes to his repudiation of systematic philosophy from within the very speculative tradition whose claims to be systematic he calls into question. There can be no doubt, for instance, that Hegel, who is neglected by most twentieth-century English-speaking philosophers, is one of the principal thinkers to whom Gadamer is responding.

At first glance this might not seem to be the case. The standard view would have it that Gadamer derives from Heidegger and Husserl, and the latter is notorious for his obliviousness to Hegel. It is true that Gadamer learned the techniques of careful phenomenological description, the method of craftsman-like piece-by-piece work, from Husserl. But one must keep in mind that Gadamer follows Heidegger in abandoning Husserl's attempts at a systematic founding of phenomenology on the acts or performances (*Leistungen*) of consciousness. And if one asks just where the impulse and model for this rejection come from, the answer has to be sought in Kierkegaard's rejection of Hegel's attempts to "complete the system" of the philosophy of mind and in Heidegger's reception of Kierkegaard. For it is Kierkegaard who insists that, as finite beings, we are "constantly in the process of becoming" and that we therefore never arrive at the point of total absolute knowing, which alone would make comprehensive, systematic philosophy possible. And he insists on this point in response to Hegel.

So does Gadamer. In *Truth and Method* (WM) Gadamer sets out to do what Kierkegaard set out to do in criticizing Hegel, the only difference being that he intends to do it more completely, consistently. In opposition to Hegel, both aim to display that our thinking remains embedded in what will always exceed its grasp. As Heidegger puts it, in any thinking we do we always remain "under way toward" the understanding we seek but never fully attain.

Now, it makes a considerable difference whether one comes to a theory of the limits of human reasoning from outside the speculative tradition—from Hume, for instance—or from within it. For even if in the end one rejects Hegel's overall claim to know systematically, absolutely, and conclusively, one cannot remain untouched by his concerns after having gone through the process of coming to grips with him. *Unlike Hume*, Hegel brings the Greeks to center stage. Heraclitus, Parmenides, Anaxagoras, but above all Plato and Aristotle, with their speculation about mind, and the true, the good, and the beautiful, come alive in Hegel, and their questions remain the questions even of those who ultimately would reject him. Kierkegaard, for instance, though he sought to turn away from these ontological and epistemological concerns to existential ones, in fact raises classical speculative ontological and epistemological questions, as Heidegger's reconversion of Kierkegaard's existentialism into ontology, of the *existentiell* into the *existential*, in *Being and Time* (SZ) makes evident.

In Gadamer, too, the grand questions of classical speculative philosophy are still asked, questions about what truly is (*to ontōs on*), about what is good and bad, *agathos* and *kakos*, and about what is beautiful and ugly or shameful, *kalos* and *aischros*. Gadamer is one of those philosophers of a bygone generation referred to by Richard Rorty, who, unlike today's lawyer-like philosophers, would surely have become classicists had they not become philosophers (CP 221). Consequently, the very thing that might have served as a bridge between Gadamer's way of thinking and the tradition of Anglo-American thought, his rejection of systematic philosophy, also introduces an obstacle for the "merging of horizons" undertaken here. Though there is in Gadamer great caution about treating the subject matters of speculative philosophy—a caution that ought to be well received by English-speaking philosophers—the fact remains that by and large for them any treatment of these things at all remains suspect.

For the better part of a century most Anglo-American philosophy has avoided the speculative tradition. To be sure, scholarship on Plato and Aristotle has continued in Cornford, Ross, Crombie, Vlastos, and others, but in a way that is compatible with analytical philosophy and wholly at odds with the treatment of these thinkers in Hegel and Heidegger, whose interpretations are often simply dismissed. Thus Gadamer's Hegelian-Heideggerian talk of the "equifundamentality" (*Gleichursprünglichkeit*) of Being and not-Being, obliviousness and truth (*lēthē* and *alētheia*), and the "subject matter" (*Sache*) of thought and so forth is sure to stir some of the traditional fears that any speculative philosophy, Gadamer's included, is language on a holiday and that we would be better off staying with things we have a reasonable hope of getting a handle on.

As I have tried to show elsewhere in my translations of his work, however, Gadamer does not abuse his readers with obscure terminology and peculiar ways of putting things. He writes

with unaffected eloquence and lucidity in a superbly literate
German style. Moreover, he writes about things that he makes
plain for all to see. In him there are none of Hegel's thickets of
oddly used words and impenetrably structured sentences. Nor
do we have to contend with any of Heidegger's vatic utterances
about dark quasi-mystical happenings. The remarkable thing
about his work is that he takes up the questions of traditional
speculative philosophy without getting entangled in the violations of natural language that trap many of the others who have
followed Hegel and Heidegger in attempting to deal with them.
If he is right, philosophy does not have to defend itself against
the awesome advances of the natural sciences by abandoning its
initial questions, making its endeavors ever more modest, and
ultimately retreating to logic and language analysis with occasional sallies into the only somewhat wider inquiry of pragmatism. Indeed, we have the best of both worlds in Gadamer's
thought: caution, accuracy, clarity—Husserl's "painstaking
craftsmanship" remains the paradigm for Gadamer's expositions—and that caution, accuracy, and clarity brought to bear
on those speculative themes that have engaged philosophers
from early on: the real, the good, and the beautiful.

My emphasis will be on the second of these: the good, what it
is, and what understanding we have of it. That shifts the accents
in Gadamer's thinking, to be sure, but not in any way that runs
contrary to his overall intentions. In *Truth and Method* (WM)
Gadamer moves from Aristotle's ethical theory to a theory of
interpretation and understanding of artworks. Here that movement is reversed: what Gadamer says about the understanding
of texts and artworks is brought to bear on the understanding
we have of ethical truth.

The result is a provocatively conservative thesis: namely, that
the idea of autonomous moral reasoning, whatever form that
reasoning might take—for example, rule-utilitarianism, contractualism, or, surprisingly, even MacIntyre's return to specific
virtues relative to a concrete historical context—is an abstraction that spins itself out in a vacuum. One would do better,

therefore, to think in terms of making ethical choices on the basis of the authority of tradition, which, as we will see, we interpret with judicious discretion (Aristotle's *phronēsis* or ethical reasonableness) on each given occasion.

There has, of course, been advocacy of the authority of tradition over autonomous reason in English and American thought. Edmund Burke comes to mind immediately. But, despite a Burke renaissance of sorts, advertences to him continue to meet with no small resistance in the English-speaking world. MacIntyre, for example, whose work is in many respects congenial to Gadamer's and whom one might therefore expect to be sympathetic to Burke, summarily dispenses with him. So the "merging of horizons" sought will not be achieved easily on this point.

In extending Gadamer by working out the ethical implications of his hermeneutics, I will argue that, not autonomous individuality, but traditional community with others in language and custom is the starting point for any ethical understanding and any ethical theory. To be more specific, our sense of what is right and wrong, good and bad, fair (*kalos*) and disgraceful (*aischros*), is transmitted to us in the language we have inherited, and that language, sustained as it is by the inexplicit customs we are accustomed to, capacitates us to deliberate well and make ethical choices. Traditional language and custom, I will argue, and not the illusory (Burke: "metaphysical") insights of some sort of pure reason and critical thinking removed from them, are the ground, itself ungrounded, of the ethical. The self-evident objection that such an idea is reactionary and antithetical to the cause of emancipation and justice cannot be taken lightly, and I will devote considerable attention to it.

Since each of the three chapters contains its own introduction to the topics with which it will be concerned, I need not indicate more specifically here what these will be. However, it would be useful, in the way of a general introduction, to say something about the things that are *not* treated in this book. For one thing, in this way I can mark off the special nature of the inquiry I will be pursuing. And, for another, this *via negationis*, as it were, will at the same time provide some preliminary insights into those fundamentals of Gadamer's philosophy of human finitude that will provide the basis here for a theory of ethical understanding.[1] Like rowers we can, with occasional glances over our shoulders toward where we are headed, orient ourselves at first in reference to the things we will be leaving behind.

Anglo-American scholars who, by training, are forewarned about the dangers of speculative philosophy and the kinds of criticism to which that philosophy will be subjected in the English-speaking world have come to expect that any defense of a Continental thinker will give us a well-founded, scientific approach to the problems he or she takes up. Hence, a book such as this one, which attempts to make use of the ideas of a pre-eminent German thinker in English, should, by rights, begin with a clarification of the key concepts, methods, and subject matter of his work. The idea would be that one would learn useful strategies for dealing with specific problems—for example, Husserl's *epochē* or bracketing, Heidegger's *Destruktion*, or Derrida's (very different) deconstruction—that could be applied in continuing research. Gadamer's thought, however, does not lend itself to such an approach. With regard to key concepts, he does have a terminology of sorts; "merging of horizons," "hermeneutic circularity," "historically effected–effective consciousness" are a few of the best-known examples, and I will deal with them as I proceed. But one should keep in mind Gadamer's reservations about terminology and terms in general. These, he maintains, are violations of language insofar as they set artificial limits (*termini*) to the otherwise infinite widening of significances in any natural word and thus quite literally terminate the open-ended range of meanings that it might continue to display to us. If, like J. L. Austin, one thinks of language as a tool to be used in the most effective way, then this termination might be a good thing. One wants to keep one's tools clean and sharp, he says, one's language unequivocal and exact. But if one thinks of language as Gadamer does, that is, as unending veins of significance to be mined in our discursive exchanges with one another, such a fixing of terms is unfortunate, for it diminishes the very richness of language upon which we depend for our insights. Thus, for the most part he avoids it.

Furthermore, given Gadamer's understanding of what language is and his sense of our dependence on it, it is easy to see why he rejects any "method" in the current sense of that word. The prevailing conception of method is an inheritance from Descartes' universalization of geometry. The task for any scientific inquiry, it is said, is to establish secure foundations and then to build upon them, taking no step which they do not warrant. This Cartesian project of founding is behind Husserl's phenomenology and also the early Heidegger's "fundamental ontology." Both of these sought to develop a transcendental philosophy that would ground the significances of reality in the constitutive performances of the human subject.

But, as Gadamer sees it, Heidegger's failure to finish *Being and Time* and his eventual "turn" away from the project of "fundamental ontology" resulted from the recognition that such a project is in fact mistaken. Philosophy, Heidegger discovered, cannot lay down "clear and distinct," certain foundations for a methodical science. Its truths are partial truths given to us as we proceed within indeterminate language bequeathed to us from time out of mind. Gadamer was in close association with Heidegger when the latter came to recognize this and when, as a consequence, he and Husserl parted ways. And herein lies one of the two occasions for Gadamer's own rejection of "methodical" philosophy: first, he sees himself as an expositor of the later Heidegger's thinking. Beyond this, however, and perhaps more decisive, is his experience of two dreadful world wars. These made clear to him that human beings are tragically fallible and that in matters of human conduct, at least, none of us can claim to have the unshakable foundation of clear and distinct insight requisite for securing an edifice of methodical thought.

Nor can it be said that Gadamer's thought has anything to do with problem solving, a point that will be important for our considerations here insofar as heretofore the English-speaking approach to philosophy, and moral philosophy in particular, has largely focused on a kind of reasoning that solves "problems in philosophy" and on a "moral reasoning" that solves "moral problems." Even MacIntyre, who, as we will see, breaks radically with the usual Anglo-American approach to moral philosophy, still concludes the second edition of his *After Virtue* with an attempt to apply his findings about virtue to the solution of problems and defends his choice of Aristotelianism because, viewed pragmatically, it works best.

Thanks in large part to the influence of Wittgenstein, English-speaking philosophers have, to be sure, also devoted their philosophical investigations to "getting clear" about what we mean when we say something, and in doing this they—MacIntyre included—come closer to Gadamer's enterprise, which is aimed at recovery of obscured and lost meanings, not at finding the solutions to problems. Still there is a difference even here. Like Wittgenstein, Gadamer wants to understand meanings, not, however, to understand what *we* as agents mean when we say something in some speech act—and here, as we will see, he departs from English-speaking followers of Wittgenstein such as Austin and Searle—but to understand what something means when *it* is said. His philosophy of human finitude presupposes that whatever human beings might do or say is sustained by something which transcends them and in which they are embedded. Speakers are subordinate, namely, to the language that they speak. The method in "getting clear," or let us say in following the Greek *met-hodos*, the approach via which we proceed, is consequently dialogue. We enter into a discussion of what is expressed or said, of the thing to be understood, in order to come to an understanding of what *it* says and to recover *its* meanings to which we have been oblivious.

It follows that though one might want and expect from Gadamer a set of precisely defined terms and a method of applying them to a circumscribed set of problems—as one correctly expects these things from Husserl, the early Heidegger, and

Derrida—this expectation is misplaced in Gadamer's case. Indeed, it would only distort his thinking to look for these things in it.

There is a final point to be made in regard to the kind of knowing or science we will, and will not, find in Gadamer: not only would it be mistaken to expect from him a method of inference based on a secured starting point or *principium*; it would also be wrong to expect him to arrive at definitive conclusions. For since the language we are probing will always exceed whatever we might find out about it, we never come to the end of either it or our inquiry into it. Indeed, as Kierkegaard puts it, "the system can never be completed." Gadamer's way of saying the same thing is to maintain that the question always takes priority over any provisional answer we might give to it. Inquiry can never be closed off by any answer. Inconclusiveness, *Unabschliessbarkeit*, is intrinsic to it.

Gadamer's model is Plato, who, on his reading of him, maintained the same "doctrines," that is, the theory of unity in indeterminacy, the One and the indeterminate Two, from beginning to end, but never set them forth methodically in our sense of the word, never developed any terminology—though the Latin and English translations might give the illusion that he did—and never came to any definitive conclusions. With good reason: the very principle of indeterminacy, indeterminacy in our dialogue with others and in the "dialogue of the soul with itself," makes it impossible for us either to locate a clear and distinct starting point for any inquiry or ever to arrive at a final answer. Indeterminacy in Plato is thus not a principle from which something may be inferred in the methodical exposition of its consequences, but rather *the* principle that precisely nothing may be inferred with conclusiveness. The One and the indeterminate Two are not the foundations for a coherent deduction, but rather the statement of its impossibility.

But does this reading of Plato not fly in the face of what we learn from the *Phaedo*, for instance? It might appear that the hypothesis of the *eidos* or essence proposed there would indeed enable us to carry out a deduction. Still, when one sees how this "method" actually works, as we will later on, and how facetious Plato is in his apparent applications of it—at the beginning of Socrates' second speech on love in the *Phaedrus*, for instance— one discovers that there is neither certainty about the beginning nor conclusiveness about the end. In the *Phaedrus* one first goes completely astray in determining the *eidos* of love and must start over. And when, in the playful expositions of the *Statesman* and *Sophist*, "conclusions" are drawn, they prove to be only partial insights that are as much a provocation for continued questioning as an answer to the question raised. Most clearly of all, Gadamer points out, the *Parmenides* displays the inevitable concomitance of insight and confusion in which any dialogical inquiry issues.

Like Plato, Gadamer would start in at some point where we already find ourselves under way in our language-constituted understanding of something—ethics will be our concern here— and then pursue what our language shows us about it for a stretch, looking, as it were, first at one aspect it displays and then, sometimes abruptly, turning to another. A discontinuous series of partial insights (Husserl: *Abschattungen*) are reached along the way and that is all. This fact too creates serious obstacles for the "merging of horizons" I am seeking to effect here. For by the usual criteria Gadamer's reasoning and likewise my argumentation in this book must be adjudged "loose." Gadamer does not, and, if he is right, cannot, proceed in "tight" inference of conclusions from set premises.

In what follows I will also be leaving behind the discussion of Gadamer in Europe and the offshoots of this discussion in literary criticism and political philosophy in the English-speaking world. For since this book seeks a "merging of horizons" between Gadamer's and Anglo-American thought, and more specifically a widening of the latter's perspective, it would be diverted from its task were it to treat extensively the differences between Gadamer and the French proponents of other theories of interpretation, for example, Derrida, or the attack on Gadamer's hermeneutics by the German proponents of "critical theory," in particular, Habermas.[2] However, here too at least a brief indication of what the issues of this European discussion are that I am largely neglecting would be useful in providing a preliminary orientation for what follows and in marking off my own endeavor here.

For Derrida, who argues the primacy of the written word, language utterances or "texts," as he calls them, are a self-enclosed, self-referential play generated out of spontaneous subjectivity and referring back to the author but to nothing outside themselves save for other texts. For Gadamer, such an understanding of language represents an extreme version of the mistake Descartes made when he took self-consciousness as his point of departure. (I will have a good deal more to say about this mistake in Chapter 1, Part 4, though in specific reference to Hegel and not Derrida.) If one starts, as Gadamer does, from discussion, which is to say, from our experience of hearing (*Hören*) the word spoken to us and of saying it out loud, it becomes clear that Derrida misrepresents our relationship to language and to the world that it constitutes. For precisely as something that is heard, the spoken word cannot be set in view before us (Heidegger: *vorgestellt*) the way something seen can be. Hence, the spoken word inherently resists any giving any appearance of being an object for a subject and of originating in a subject. In hearing and speaking, it cannot be said that a subject spontaneously generates a self-referential world of significances. And only a curiously abstracted viewpoint could make it seem that something like that happens in writing, though the modern phenomenon of silent reading might explain how such an abstraction, which substitutes seeing for hearing in the experience of language, might occur.[3] On the contrary, in hearing and speaking we draw upon an inheritance of ways of saying things and making sense of them, ways that we have heard from others who speak the same language and who dwell in the shared world that it constitutes. The point, to which this book will often return, is that language and the world it shapes are not "mine," not my "positing," "performance," or "act"; rather "I" belong to (*gehöre zu*) them. Hence, whatever *I* say, far from being self-enclosed, always points beyond itself to what *we* could say, the unsaid, or the "virtuality of language as a whole," as Gadamer calls it.

The issues are quite different in regard to the exchange between Gadamer and the proponents of critical theory, Habermas in particular. For both Habermas and Gadamer come from the same tradition, albeit different branches. Both, that is to say, bear the stamp of Hegel, though for Habermas, the social theorist, Hegel is viewed retrospectively through Marx while for Gadamer, the classicist, he is viewed starting from the standpoint of the ancients, Plato and Aristotle (see HD 5–34, "Hegel and the Dialectic of the Ancient Philosophers"). Habermas faults Gadamer for naïvely taking statements and arguments put forth in the political realm at face value and for overlooking the fact that class interests and ideology actually compel people to say what they do, thereby distorting the truth of what they say and blocking a rational exchange of ideas. This circumstance, he argues, cannot be remedied simply by staying with what is said, as Gadamer proposes to do. Rather, in critical reflection upon what is said, one must unveil the cause of the distortions and enlighten the interlocutors, who would otherwise be ignorant of it. Only in this way can rational communication and discourse be made possible.

Gadamer's ingenious response to this seemingly convincing argument is to point out that Habermas misunderstands the nature of true discussion. In his effort to overcome ideological communicative impediments and to re-establish an open forum of rational debate among emancipated individuals, Habermas takes as his paradigm for discourse the therapist–patient interchange in psychiatry. But, Gadamer argues, this is not the normal circumstance of discussion; for it presupposes that one of the interlocutors is free from distortion—has the superterrestrial intellectual purity of the angels in the *Summa theologica*, as Gadamer wryly observes (KS IV 133)—and that the other is not. Discussion, on the other hand, and particularly that discussion about the good which Habermas has in mind, proceeds on a very different assumption. Both partners, and only here can we speak of partners, acknowledge the relativity and finitude of their viewpoints and the possibility of idiosyncrasy; and both are willing to detach themselves sufficiently from the things said, to submit these to the test of self-validation or self-falsification in ongoing discourse. This willingness presupposes that neither purports to see through what the other is saying to an ideology, neurosis, or whatever, that prompts him or her to say it. And, indeed, nothing is more destructive of good discussion or more maddening, for that matter, than to have one of the partners remove himself or herself from the prerequisite equality of the interlocutors in their mutual submission to the self-unfolding of the subject matter under discussion. Precisely this crippling of discussion occurs, however, if either one switches from listening to what was said to critically analyzing why the other said it. As Gadamer puts it, even if I argue a point heatedly, I have a right to expect counter-arguments in response and not a depth-psychological treatment of my emotions (KS IV 126).

To be sure, it could obviously be objected that the therapeutic discussion is not to be taken as discussion itself, but only as a necessary preparation for it. The discussion Gadamer envisions presupposes the soundness of mind of the partners, and the therapeutic exchange brings about this soundness. After all, one cannot have a discussion with someone who says what he or she does compulsively. Since Gadamer takes Socrates' art of conducting a discussion as his model, and since discussion will be critical to our own considerations of how ethical understanding is reached, a comparison between this art and psychiatry is instructive here. Socrates thought of himself as a soul (*psychē*) doctor (*iatros*); hence, it might appear that his idea of dialogue is the same as Habermas' psychiatric one. In fact it is not.

As noted, Gadamer points out that the psychoanalytic discussion assumes the disparity of the participants: one is liberated from distortion; the other is not and seeks to be emancipated.

But there is no disparity like this in Socrates' relationship to his interlocutors. *Both* submit themselves to the logic of the subject matter. *Both* are patients (*pathontes*) insofar as they yield to the *pathos tōn logōn*, the experience, to paraphrase Austin, of what words do with us. Socrates' famous *docta ignorantia* or learned ignorance is not some ruse that an all-knowing therapist might use to overcome the intransigence of the person he is treating. On the contrary, acknowledgment that one does not know makes genuine discussion possible to begin with, insofar as it establishes the equality of the interlocutors in their submission of themselves to what is said and their willingness to let go of their merely private beliefs should they prove to be that. *Both* partners must have surmounted obstinacy if they are to follow where the discussion might lead them.

Now, it is true that Socrates is often ahead of his partners in this regard. He knows that he does *not* know, whereas they tenaciously assert that they do. The Socratic *elenchos*, or refutation, his irony and stingray laming of his interlocutors, may be viewed accordingly as preparatory for discussion, as propaedeutic, or "protreptic," as Gadamer calls it, referring to the turning (*trephein*) of the soul it is meant to induce. And is this preparation not the same thing as the psychiatrist's attempt to emancipate the patient from obstructions to rational discourse in his *psychē* by making him aware of them?

Closer examination reveals some essential differences. Though Socrates often displays others' deformities of mind to the audience, which is to say, to the readers of the dialogues, and though his concern in what he says to his interlocutors is indeed to cure the diseased soul and restore it to its proper excellence or *aretē*, he is never an analyst who reduces what they say to some deformity of mind that caused them to say it. Whatever is said is examined and tested for what *it* contains. To understand it (as we will see in Chapter 2) we do need to know the occasion for its being said, who said it, that is, and what he was responding to when he said it. But this notwithstanding, the primary task remains to understand, to get clear about, what was said and not to understand the speaker or what compelled him to say it. Socrates himself never switches from listening to what was said to analysis of some quirk, propensity, or other characteristic in the personality of the speaker that would "explain" why he said it.

He is indeed concerned with righting the warped soul, but his "therapy" is to induce recollection and recovery of the shared good that transcends anything someone might stubbornly believe to be his private advantage, a shared good that nevertheless is somehow still meant in what the other person thinks and says even if he does not see this at first. The recollection (*anamnēsis*) is accomplished by showing how this shared good has displayed itself in what the other has said, a point I will exemplify later using Socrates' discussion with Polus in the *Gorgias* (Chapter 2, Part 4). Socrates' task, consequently, is not at all to enlighten his interlocutors about what causes them to say what they do, but rather to enlighten them about what they are saying.

Socrates would have us examine the *logoi*, the things we say in our discourse with others and with ourselves, would have us detach ourselves from them and submit to their self-exposition in our discussion of them. The goal is to be released from the privacy of belief, from *idiosynkrasia*. Socrates, then, attempts a sort of logotherapy: someone, in being led to follow out the consequences of what he says, is raised to the community of speakers whose language he speaks, and in this way he is emancipated from the tyranny of selfish desire. Put in Kierkegaard's language: Socrates brings about the transition from the aesthetic to the ethical stage of existence. These matters will receive more careful consideration later on.

Granted: I have shown just a few of the directions in which the European debate might take us, and in not pursuing that debate explicitly, I by no means wish to imply that it is inconsequential. On the contrary, it is already evident from what little I have said that the discussion of psychotherapy just by itself raises a host of important issues.

Still, given that my goal is a "merging of horizons," the best way to approach Gadamer is not through this foreign debate but through some of the related Anglo-American discussion. This is not to say at all that my investigations will be restricted to the issues currently being treated in contemporary Anglo-American thought. For, again, the aim is not simply to apply Gadamer's thought to the set of questions to which it has restricted itself, but instead to indicate how, in beginning with shared concerns, English-speaking philosophers might follow Gadamer's lead in recovering the heritage of classical speculative philosophy and widen their perspectives to include its questions—questions in particular about the good, what it is, and how we come to understand it, as such things are discussed in Plato, Aristotle, Aquinas, and Hegel. Since MacIntyre, in raising the question of *aretē* or virtue and in turning to Aristotle for an answer to it, has already broken considerable ground here, I will take his work as my point of departure.

NOTES

1. For more general and inclusive expositions of Gadamer's herme-neutical theory, see Joel Weinsheimer's sympathetic and accurate *Gadamer's Hermeneutics: A Reading of* TRUTH AND METHOD (New Haven, Conn.: Yale University Press, 1985) and Gloria Warnke's *Gadamer: Hermeneutics, Tradition, and Reason* (Stanford: Stanford University Press, 1987). The latter includes important passages linking Gadamer to Rorty and MacIntyre and begins something of the merging of horizons I am attempting here. In what follows I will deal exten-sively with MacIntyre and will show that behind the similarities be-tween MacIntyre and Gadamer that Warnke correctly points out some serious differences are concealed. Also, as opposed to both these works, I will rely most heavily on Gadamer's interpretation and appropriation of Plato, Aristotle, and Hegel. For true to his hermeneu-tic principles, Gadamer, I think, develops his most original thought in response to the thought of others.

2. Compare, in addition to Warnke, Richard Bernstein, *Beyond*

Objectivism and Relativism: Science, Hermeneutics, and Praxis (Philadelphia: University of Pennsylvania Press, 1983).

3. That such an abstraction would occur is considerably more likely in an optically oriented, predominantly visual culture that derives from Descartes and the Medieval tradition of the *lumen naturale* than in an acoustically oriented, predominantly musical one that derives from Bach and Luther, with his emphasis on hearing the word of God. Stephen Toulmin, incidentally, is an unexpected source of elucidation of the abstraction of the written from the spoken word when he suggests that logic's resorting to abstract, contextless propositions—"frozen statues of statements," he calls them—might have been in part the result of printing, which makes it seem that speech acts outlast their utterance and are separable from it (see *The Uses of Argument* [Cambridge: Cambridge University Press, 1958], p. 181).

1

MacIntyre and the Disarray of Analytical Moral Philosophy

IT IS NOT AT ALL DIFFICULT TO SAY just where Gadamer's hermeneutical theory might be brought to bear on the contemporary discussion of ethics. MacIntyre's *After Virtue* and the controversy it has engendered are the obvious place to look if for no other reason than for the similarity of the issues they have raised to those raised by Gadamer, a similarity that will be made clear as we proceed.[1] In this chapter I wish, first, in a system-immanent exposition, to explore what seem to me to be the relevant arguments MacIntyre makes—relevant insofar as they treat issues that could also be addressed if one started from Gadamer's hermeneutics—and to examine how he has defended himself against the criticisms of these arguments advanced by his analytically minded adversaries. My task here is to make clear that he has not only unsettled the traditional analytical schools of thought but in fact transcended their limitations. Second, I would like to juxtapose MacIntyre's critical treatment of "rationalist" ethics with Hegel's parallel critique of Kant's moral philosophy. Third, using Hegel as a point of departure, I will attempt a system-transcendent critique of MacIntyre—system transcendent to the extent that Hegel, while dealing with many of the same questions as MacIntyre, comes from a very different tradition quite outside the horizons of MacIntyre's discussion. My purpose here will be to show that from the different perspective Hegel gives us MacIntyre's approach also proves restricted and that his endeavor, however much it might break new ground, cannot succeed. Since in his *After Virtue* MacIntyre recurs principally to Aristotle, my critique of him will, of necessity, treat many Aristotelian themes. Fourth, I wish to indicate how Gadamer's hermeneutics, which evolves from within the Hegelian tradition, albeit with significant Heideggerian modifications, might be applied in getting out of the dead-end in which, I think, MacIntyre finds himself. Having paved the way, as it were, with Hegel, I will begin specifying here just what Gadamer's hermeneutical theory is about and what applications it might have in clarifying the nature of ethical knowing and understanding.

For the time being I asked that the reader set aside reservations he or she might have about my frequent reliance on conventional senses of words and ways of putting things—often taken from foreign languages—and reserve any criticisms of that reliance until I have had a chance in Chapter 2 to provide a methodological justification of it. If attempts at such a justification were introduced here, it would only further complicate what is admittedly already complicated enough.

I. MacIntyre's Dispute with Moral Theory in the Analytical Tradition

Some obvious cracks have appeared in the once seemingly unshakable foundations of Anglo-American analytical philosophy. To be sure, business goes on as usual in most of its citadels, but at least some of its proponents have admitted an uneasy feeling that things are starting to give way underneath. In the final chapter of his *The Consequences of Pragmatism* Richard Rorty, for example, characterizes what he considers to be the present circumstances of analytical philosophers—and not without a certain overtone of disillusionment.[2] He submits that its general project, to which a generation of scholars, he among them, had committed themselves—namely, to establish "rational acceptability" in the various areas of human discourse—has in fact proven incapable of realization. And having discovered that the scientific ideal of objective reasonableness and rational demonstration is unattainable, analytical philosophers, he maintains, now find themselves limited to determining the consistency and cogency of differing arguments whose presuppositions and premises themselves remain outside the critical analysis that one applies to these arguments. The ideal had been first to establish starting points, *principia*, that are self-evident and incontestable, and second to reason logically and cogently from them. But it turns out that any starting point is inevitably relative to the perspective of the person basing an argument on it and thus could never measure up to the mathematical ideal of a universally self-evident *principium*. What can be realized of the original analytical ideal, therefore, is only its second part: the goal of logical, cogent reasoning. In Rorty's view "universal rationality" has consequently given way to particular reasonableness relative to a context, and to lawyer-like argument for or against the "case" one finds oneself charged to defend or prosecute. And under these circumstances analytical philosophy becomes a "theory of inference." Instead of "truth," the concern of today's analytical philosopher, he tells us, is soundness—the soundness of any given argument whatever its particular starting point may be.

It follows that whereas philosophers before the advent of analytical philosophy might have been expected to have become humanist scholars, perhaps classicists, had they not become philosophers, and during the period of analytical philosophy's ascendancy, to have become physicists or mathematicians, we now might well expect them to have become lawyers. For it is that special acuity typical of a lawyer, an eye for implications and inconsistencies, that allows contemporary philosophers either to identify or build sound arguments or to spot weaknesses in someone else's.

And, indeed, Rorty's observations on the proximity of the

contemporary analytical philosopher to the lawyer would seem to be substantiated by the peculiarly litigious, forensic quality of contemporary philosophical debate. Even the contemporary philosophical theory of argumentation—or "reasoning" as Steven Toulmin, for one, calls it—is replete with the language of law: one makes *claims* and supports them with *grounds* linked to the claims by *warrants*. And one does all of this in a *forum*, which is to say, in the Roman version of the Greek *agora* where legal argument, as we know it, got its start.[3]

In short, if Rorty is right, analytical philosophers have seen that the mathematical model of reasoning from clear and distinct, indubitable premises to true conclusions can no longer be said to apply. They have recognized that since any reasoning occurs in a particular context and is valid only relative to that context, there are no starting points apart from situational contingencies. Or, in the words of MacIntyre—another of those grown skeptical about the enterprise and hopes of analytical philosophy—analytical philosophy has now concluded that there are no grounds for belief in universal principles. The Cartesian *a priori* has been expelled, he says, and consequently we may speak now only of "rational superiority" (AV 268ff.). We may speak only of "truths," in other words, that are better or worse relative to the circumstances in which they are put forth. And, he maintains, the language in which these relative truths are stated cannot therefore consist in propositions with "timeless meaning" like those of the mathematical sciences.

Now, MacIntyre makes his arguments in specific reference to moral theory, and it is moral theory that is to be our concern here. He advances his idea of "rational superiority" in opposition to William Frankena, for one, who, along with traditional analytical philosophers, would still maintain that it is the task of moral philosophy to determine, not "rational superiority," which is to say, only consistency and coherence relative to a context, but universal rationality and universal truth. Precisely such a rationality and truth as that, however, MacIntyre finds chimerical. There is, he asserts, no "morality as such," no morality *a priori*, and should somebody attempt to deduce one, that deduction would only end up displaying the contingency of its assumed universal principles, much as Kant's supposedly *a priori* moral theory proves to be but a justification of Northern European Protestant morality (AV 266).

If, on the other hand, one follows MacIntyre and takes as one's standard, not rationality, but "rational superiority," one could carry out moral theorizing in much the same way Rorty proposes one might carry out any kind of philosophical theorizing: instead of chasing after the illusion of absolute truth, one might better content oneself with evaluating the coherence of a moral theory relative to the particular context in which it occurs, relative, that is, to what MacIntyre calls its "practice."

What in Rorty may be said to derive from American pragmatism would seem in MacIntyre to have more of its origins in the later Wittgenstein.[4] Morality, MacIntyre says, is always to be treated as it is "embodied" in "forms of activity" (AV 265) (Wittgenstein: *Lebensformen*). Consequently, our task—something like the therapy proposed by Wittgenstein—should be to uncover where the language of moral theory is not "in order," which is to say, to uncover where there are inconsistencies in moral argument of the sort Rorty suggests analytical philosophical acuity is able to discern, but also, and more to the point, to uncover, as Wittgenstein would have said, where our moral utterances have gone on a holiday and are idling or spinning free of the form of activity or historical moral practice in which they might once have made sense.

And in general I would submit that it is Wittgenstein's own self-criticism, as much as any revival of pragmatism, that began the undermining of analytical philosophy that both Rorty and MacIntyre perceive. If one argues, as Wittgenstein does in the *Philosophical Investigations*, that language does not primarily assign significances to a reality in objective detachment from that reality, but, with the exception perhaps of the language of the mathematical sciences, has significance only as it functions within given forms of life, each with its appropriate "language games," it stands to reason that one could no longer have recourse to any standards of truth that transcend situational contingency. The starting points or *principia* for *any* argument—not only *principia ethica*—would be relative to a particular context, and not universal.

MacIntyre, of course, adds to Wittgenstein's analysis (and Rorty's [see AV 267]) a special emphasis on the historicity of any context or form of life. But that alone does not make MacIntyre into some sort of Continental "Hegelian," for instance, rather than a mainstream Anglo-American philosopher of language within the tradition of the later Wittgenstein. On the contrary, even if he should claim Hegel as a paradigm,[5] MacIntyre's project remains a variation on late Wittgensteinian language analysis; where moral language is in "disorder" it should be displayed as such, and the conditions of its being "in order" are to be specified.

MacIntyre's application of this Wittgensteinian therapy to our moral discourse is not without striking and convincing results. The language of morality, he ascertains at the opening of *After Virtue*, is in a "state of grave disorder": "What we possess . . . are the fragments of a conceptual scheme, parts which now lack those contexts from which their significance derived. We possess indeed simulacra of morality, we continue to use many of the key expressions. But we have—very largely if not entirely—lost our comprehension, both theoretical and practical, of morality" (AV 2).

That is a telling diagnosis for which MacIntyre could find a good deal of support in twentieth-century literature as well as in the philosophers (for example, Sartre) and sociologists (for example, Goffman) whom he cites. In one of the parables from the *Castle*, Kafka, for instance, tells us that "there are now only couriers who hurry about the world, shouting to each other—since there are no kings—messages that have become meaningless." And one might also think of Yeats's "centre" that cannot "hold," and of Nietzsche's "madman" who proclaims that God is dead and that the highest values have consequently lost their value. Certainly one of the accomplishments of *After Virtue* is to have brought this existential circumstance to light within the framework of Wittgensteinian analysis. Thus it may be said that in a way MacIntyre has brought about a fusion of the analytical and literary–historical approaches to philosophy that Rorty sees inevitably going their separate ways. MacIntyre is presumably one of those analytically trained philosophers whom Rorty finds "putting out feelers" to other disciplines in the humanities (CP 225–27).

And MacIntyre's very telling diagnosis is followed by a depiction, no less telling, of the pre-eminent symptom of this language "disorder," namely, the "interminability" of contemporary moral debate. He produces a number of familiar alternative moral arguments to exemplify his point that contemporary moral language provides us with many diverse starting points on which arguments may be constructed, arguments in each case logically valid, but nonetheless leading to mutually exclusive conclusions, since these starting points are remnants from very different, incompatible traditions. The result is a "conceptual incommensurability of the rival arguments" which makes the resolution of the differences between them impossible. Traditional analytical philosophy, in Frankena, for instance, remains committed to finding rational criteria transcending the relativity and particularity of these arguments, to finding precisely those *principia ethica*, as it were, which would permit the resolution of these disputes. But if MacIntyre is right, such attempts—appeals to intuited goods, rules, rights, and so forth—are destined to miscarry, for there are no such things as intuited goods, rules, and rights, any more than there are "unicorns" (AV 69).

Indeed, the appeals to these supposedly universal rational standards are so transparent that philosophers *must* eventually see through them. Those who make them will only pave the way for a Nietzschean unmasking: appeals to purportedly objective standards will be exposed as the disguises in which idiosyncratic volition, will, parades itself. One might add that this unmasking (or "hermeneutics of suspicion," as Paul Ricoeur calls it) could also take the form of exposing one's "class interests" as it does in Marxist critique, or of exposing one's psychological disturbances as it does in Freudian psychoanalysis, or of exposing one's communicative distortions as it does in Habermas' adaptation of the psychoanalytic model to political discourse. Whatever form it might take, it characteristically disregards the meaning of what one says and turns instead to what is supposed to have caused the person to say what he or she did. What one says is treated as a mere clue to that which is taken to be of real interest.

Within the English-speaking world such unmasking in ethics has generally taken the somewhat less radical form of "emotivism" (AV 6–22). Instead of being subjected to some sort of depth analysis that would expose their pretenses, moral utterances are simply dismissed as "*nothing but* expressions of preference, expressions of attitude or feeling" (AV 12), which is to say that they are held not to have any cognitive meaning to be "suspected" in the first place. That assumption has a consequence that is repugnant to all analytical philosophy, even to the reduced analytical philosophy based on jurisprudential acuity that Rorty proposes; emotivism, MacIntyre maintains, "entails the obliteration of any genuine distinction between manipulative and non-manipulative social relations" (AV 23). Consequently it says that when I make moral statements, what I am really doing is "adducing whatever influences or considerations will in fact be effective on this or that occasion" (AV 24). Emotivism would have it that any transition from assertions that state what *is* to assertions that state what *is good* necessarily takes us out of the realm of cognitive utterances. Put in J. L. Austin's terms: we might say that such assertions' "constative" value is nil—they establish no state of affairs—and consequently our attention must be devoted entirely to their "performative" value, namely, what the person who asserts them wants to get done with them. Truth, even relative truth, is therefore of no concern here. And thus moral utterances are no longer to be evaluated even with regard to mere logical consistency, but solely with regard to persuasive efficacy. Rorty, who clings to a vestige of rationality however weakened its claim may be, would surely resist the idea, but perhaps we have stumbled upon the real nature of the lawyer's special acuity to which Rorty appeals: knowing not so much how to make logically consistent arguments as how to make convincing ones, regardless of whether the conclusions have been validly inferred (are consistent) or not. That knowledge is mere rhetorical skill, and if *that* has become the defining characteristic of today's philosopher, philosophy has in fact reverted to the very sophism from which its founder, Plato, had tried to save it. Indeed, though lacking the same vehemence, Rorty's anti-Platonism and attraction to Derrida are nonetheless often more reminiscent of the value nihilism of a Callicles or Thrasymachus than of any of the radical pragmatists to whom he might lay claim.

MacIntyre points out that in the circumstances in which emotivism flourishes a double deception is being practiced, a self-deception and, at the same time, a deception of others. Each puts forward his or her views as if they were impersonal, as if they transcended any particular interest, and were in fact objectively, universally true. And all who join in the argument with these views act as if they accepted that this is how they are intended. Yet at the same time no one really takes what is said to be anything more than advocacy of the self-interest of the one saying it—this even if only a Nietzsche, it seems, is willing to come right out and say so. Tacitly everyone assumes that everyone is a sophist, but all are reluctant to admit it, even to themselves. (Rorty, it seems, is typical insofar as he is not quite ready to draw the radical, Nietzschean consequences of his position.)

But there is, MacIntyre asserts, an alternative to Nietzsche's unmasking. The utterance "X is good" only loses its constative validity, he maintains, once there is no longer a teleological context in which to say it. If, for instance, there is the *telos* of navigating a ship across the sea, one can indeed establish (*constater*) whether someone is or is not a good captain, or in a different context of "practice," whether someone is a good strategist, doctor, or shipwright. Of course here we are talking about trades or crafts (*technai*), but the same sort of excellences can be established within a teleological socio-political practice. And in this case we would speak of a good man or woman as one who has a virtue (*aretē*), and our assertion would be cognitive, not emotive, and hence constative, not just performative. That is not to say that moral assertions would be universally true apart from the particular situation in which they are said—Frankena's aspirations here are unattainable and perhaps not even desirable—but neither would moral assertions be reducible to sophistic, manipulative attempts to persuade. They would be "in order" within the forms of life and language games in which they are properly said. Having sensed the illusoriness of analytical philosophy's endeavor to "determine [universal] rationality" for the area of moral utterances, MacIntyre proposes Wittgensteinian therapy for the contemporary "disorder" in moral talk: once that disorder has been diagnosed as language on a holiday, as language apart from any context in which it might once have made sense, moral language should be returned to the "forms of activity" in which it is properly "embodied." The way out of the modern moral confusion and the unconfessed cynicism of emotivism is to be found, not in chimerical intuited goods, purely rational rules, or rights, but in a return to the virtues as these have appeared in their diverse historical contexts.

So far, then, Wittgenstein and the ordinary language philosophy that grew out of his later works (Austin, Searle, and others) would seem to have provided the framework for MacIntyre's approach. But MacIntyre adds a new dimension to Wittgenstein of which we must now take note: though Wittgenstein did acknowledge that languages grow in time—from older complex and tangled "inner cities" to the newer "regularized suburbs" of the language of the modern sciences—his diagnoses of language "disorders" do not focus on the temporality of language contexts or "games," as he calls them. The disorders identified are not, as it were, the result of using bygone inner-city language after one has moved to the new suburbs. But in MacIntyre's analysis, the disorders in our moral language are precisely of that sort, and, consequently, to understand our present confusion we must see how our circumstances came to be historically. We must see what has changed in them over time, thereby introducing incoherences in our moral talk. We continue to use moral language from the past which fails us, first, MacIntyre argues, because it is an inconsistent amalgam of different incompatible moral languages, and, more important, because the world in which we now use it has, over time, ceased to provide a context for the proper functioning of any moral language at all.

MacIntyre's introduction of historicity leads him to a "scheme of moral development" or, more accurately, "moral decline." To begin with, he says, there are circumstances in which moral language and practice do indeed "embody genuine objective and impersonal standards" susceptible of "rational justification." That stage is followed by another in which "the project of providing rational justifications . . . continuously breaks down," leading to the third in which emotivist theories gain "implicit acceptance because . . . claims to objectivity and impersonality cannot be made good" (AV 18–19).

In the first stage a teleological context still exists, which MacIntyre amplifies, on the one hand, as a "practice" and, on the other, as a "narrative" setting, "narrative" implying that in this setting a human being grows over time from what he or she is potentially (Aristotle: *dynamei*), but not yet, to having an excellence in actuality (Aristotle: *energeiai*), for instance, from not yet being a sea captain to actually being one. When MacIntyre thinks of "practices," what he has in mind are joint enterprises, on the one hand, navigation, chess, and physics, for example, and, on the other, families, kinships, communities, and the like, in which the self is defined by the role that a man or woman comes to play in such historically developing social entities. In just these circumstances where "she is good" designates an excellence or virtue relative to the context of an enterprise or of a family, kinship, or community, such moral judgments can be given rational, impersonal, objective justification. For instance, in the context and "narrative setting" of the navigational arts one can say, rationally, impersonally, objectively, that someone has become, and now is, a good captain. In the second stage the prerequisite context for such judgments begins to come apart, and in the third it no longer exists at all. Instead of a teleological, narrative setting which would give the self a definition at which to aim, we have an empty space for "individuals" "who see in the social world nothing but a meeting place for individual wills . . . and who understand that world solely as an arena for the achievement of their own satisfaction" (AV 25). The goals (*telē*) here have been reduced to either pleasure or power or both. And save for a mere sophistic cleverness (*deinotēs*) (see EN VI) in the pursuit of these goals, there are no excellences, no virtues, left; the "individual" is a "democratised self which has no necessary social content and no necessary social identity" and which consequently "can assume any role or take any point of view, because it *is* in and for itself nothing" (AV 32)—or, in the apt language of Robert Musil, we might say that what we have now is the "Mann ohne Eigenschaften."[6]

The "practices" constitutive of the first stage are defined by MacIntyre as forms of "socially established cooperative human activity" with "goods internal to that form of activity" (AV 187). Though it is not made entirely clear just what the distinguishing features of a practice as such are supposed to be, presumably "cooperative" and "social" here indicate that, in the first place, we are dealing, not with skilled individual activities, say bricklaying, but with a cooperative interlinking of skilled activities, say architecture—a joint undertaking, in other words, in which someone's activity is defined in reference to the activity of others collectively. Practices, then, are not simply the sum of individual activities going on in them. On the contrary, the individual activities, whatever they may be, are first defined by the practice as a whole. I cannot be a father or mother, for instance, were it not for the family that gives these roles their determinate form. In practices community precedes individuality, and thus MacIntyre can say that "the making and sustaining of family life" and, in general, "the creation and sustaining of human communities—of households, cities, nations—is generally taken to be a practice" (AV 187–88).

A second characteristic of a practice essential to MacIntyre's argument is that it is devoted to "internal" as opposed to "external" goods. One could engage in the practice for the sake of whatever the goals of that practice are—building a cathedral or establishing a family—but especially if the community of the practice weakens, one could begin to engage in a practice for the sake of something external to it, for example, "prestige, status and money" (AV 188). And to the extent that the pursuit of external goods supplants the pursuit of internal goods, which is exactly what happens as the "moral decline" progresses, the conditions in which the virtues can exist will be destroyed, the conditions, that is to say, in which it remains possible to give "objective justification" for moral judgments. "In the realm of practices the authority of both goods and standards operates in such a way as to rule out all subjectivist and emotivist analyses of judgment. De gustibus *est* disputandum" (AV 190). But in the realm where external goods are pursued, de gustibus *non* disputandum. For there good and bad have become purely "emotive."

And just that, MacIntyre asserts, is the circumstance in which we now find ourselves, a circumstance that traditional analytical philosophy is incapable of surmounting, however much it might try and however persistently it might cling to its belief in the applicability of critical reason in solving moral problems. Indeed, given the non-historical approach it takes, it cannot even recognize what has happened—as the brilliant opening pages of *After Virtue* display so convincingly. And though it does not know it, in the end its purported moral reasoning amounts to nothing more than "interminable" disputation.

2. A Parallel Critique: Hegel and "Kantian" Moral Theory

But here a question arises concerning this extraordinarily illuminating exposition: Has MacIntyre himself in fact found a way of doing moral philosophy that will lead beyond the impasse at which contemporary analytical moral philosophy now finds itself? And if not, as I think is the case, is there another approach that has more promise of being a way beyond it? In answer to these questions I would like to draw a comparison with another thinker faced with a problem similar to MacIntyre's, and with his quite different attempt to surmount it, namely, Hegel and his endeavor to get beyond the limitations of Kantian thought, Kantian moral thought in particular.

Hegel too, of course, takes an historical approach. In Hegel's language the stages in the history of moral decline which MacIntyre characterizes as a transition from a world of practices to a world of the pursuit of external goods appears as a transition from *Sittlichkeit*[7] to Civil Society. The former, embodied above all in the *family* and *polis*, rests upon customary, immemorial ethical standards in accordance with which each does what he or she ought and can justify what he or she does. In the later Civil Society, the origins of which Hegel traces to Rome in his *Phenomenology* and which he calls there the Condition of Right—or Legal Status, as his *Rechtszustand* is sometimes translated—each individual pursues the satisfaction of wants (MacIntyre: "external goods") under the regulation of external law. In *Sittlichkeit* each has an understanding of what he himself or she herself is insofar as his or her role is given determinate shape by the community of which he or she is a part. In the Condition of Right and Civil Society, on the other hand, the self has become a juridical "person" equal (*gleich*) to all other persons before the law and thereby stripped of any defining characteristics or qualities (see note 6 above on Musil). *Gleich* in Hegel means equal, to be sure, but also "alike" as in *gleich wie ein Ei dem anderen* (alike as two peas in a pod).

In his analysis of virtue in Athens, MacIntyre elaborates on the dialectic between family virtue and civic virtue as this dialectic is displayed in Sophocles' characters Antigone and Creon, who, he shows, exemplify rival allegiances to incompatible goods. It is remarkable that in availing himself of this example of moral "incoherence" MacIntyre does not allude to Hegel's splendid exposition of the same phenomenon, exemplified in the very same characters of Sophocles' (see PhG 330ff., "The Ethical Action"). And it is also remarkable, given the striking similarity between his line of argument and Hegel's, that he would not have included Hegel's account of the result of this dialectic: the transition to the Condition of Right as exemplified in the Roman Empire.

MacIntyre considers only two possible outcomes: that the conflicting virtues of family and *polis* could be reconciled in a "total harmonious scheme of human life" or that they could remain irreconcilably heterogeneous and, consequently, any attempt to reconcile them would end in totalitarian repression of human liberty. He sees Plato and Aristotle arguing for the first possibility and Isaiah Berlin (and indeed anyone who focuses on rights, e.g., Ronald Dworkin) arguing for the inevitability of the second. His own preferences and hopes, of course, are the first outcome. Indeed, one might say that his book is devoted to demonstrating that since rights are devoid of any real moral content and thus bound to be unmasked as unjustifiable, the only hope of finding a morality that can be justified lies in a return to the conditions of virtue. The strength of Hegel's analysis, as I will argue, consists in his simultaneous justification of both the positions MacIntyre sees as excluding each other: if Hegel is right, one can neither preserve the innocence of *Sittlichkeit* while denying the reality of Civil Society and the Condition of Right, nor disregard the content of *Sittlichkeit* in the hopes of substituting for it the purely formal structures of right. Rather, as Hegel saw, the outcome will have to be a state which simultaneously maintains spheres of *Sittlichkeit* and right within itself. Hence, ideally, *Sittlichkeit* and abstract right ought not to be in conflict with each other even though we have no historical example of their not having been. That is to say, in the first place, that any abstract system of right that wholly eradicates traditional ethical structures leads to an evil such as the Reign of Terror in France (see PhG 414ff.). But that is also to say that those ethical patterns which have perpetuated legal injustices ought to be modified so that they no longer do so.

In tending exclusively toward Plato's and Aristotle's resolution of the dialectic or "incoherency" in *Sittlichkeit* and in dismissing the Condition of Right altogether, MacIntyre runs a grave risk. Hegel, for one, saw that any naïve return from the Condition of Right to a contrived *Sittlichkeit*, naïve insofar as it denies the validity and necessity of the sphere of right, would open the way to totalitarian perversions of the state. These perversions, while appealing to patriotic virtue and the good of the country as a whole, are in fact committed entirely to the individualistic pursuit of the "external goods" of power, privilege, and wealth (as later, in Louis Philippe's *Enrichissez vous*), and in the end completely disregard the right and law that alone can restrain that pursuit. See Hegel's exposition of the disintegration of Legal Status in what we today would call fascism (PhG 345ff. on Nero's Rome).

Whatever the reason for MacIntyre's neglect of it, Hegel's formulation, it seems to me, brings important things to light that remain unilluminated in MacIntyre. Consequently, it would be useful at this point to examine Hegel's dialectical exposition of *Sittlichkeit*, first, in general, and then, in particular, as it is manifested in the family, in which, after all, the Antigone–Creon conflict originates. MacIntyre, as we know, considers the family a basic example of a "practice" (AV 187), and for Hegel the family is the very foundation of *Sittlichkeit*. So we have every reason to expect a meaningful convergence here. For purposes of our analysis I will combine Hegel's treatment of *Sittlichkeit* and the family as it occurs in two different dialectical sequences: following the transition from Morality to *Sittlichkeit* in the

Philosophy of Right and following the transition from Reason to Spirit in the *Phenomenology of Mind*.

To understand *Sittlichkeit* as it appears in the *Philosophy of Right*, we must first know something of the phenomenon that precedes it there, Morality. (In the exposition of the *Phenome-nology* Morality comes after *Sittlichkeit*, not before it. Hence Morality can be viewed as privation [Aristotle: *sterēsis*] in two senses: Morality is "not yet" *Sittlichkeit* and also "no longer" *Sittlichkeit*.[8]) What Hegel calls Morality (wherever it might oc-cur) is the unsuccessful attempt to overcome a double alienation: the individual consciousness finds itself estranged from all other individual consciousnesses, on the one hand, and estranged from all world, on the other. Consequently it devotes itself to overcoming the particularity of its actions, to making them universal, hoping in this way to unite itself with all others in a communal world. We could say, then, that Morality has seen through what the *Phenomenology* calls the "intellectual animal realm and its deception" (PhG 285ff.) and what MacIntyre for his part calls the social conditions of emotivism; it reacts to precisely those circumstances in which individuals behave and argue as if what they do and say transcends their particularity, as if their actions and words have universal validity, validity for the intellectual community of them all, when in fact they are thereby deceiving others as well as themselves. For the real significance of what they say remains exactly what they do not say and pretend to have left behind, namely, their particular animal nature, their drives, interests, and inclinations. Thus, the moral consciousness realizes that, though they feign otherwise, what they say is not universal and rational at all, but a mere expression of individual caprice (*Willkür*).

Morality's response to this circumstance is the same response we have seen in the attempts of analytical philosophy, Fran-kena's, for example, to create a purely rational ethics that transcends everything particular, to create, in other words, an *a priori* universal ethics purified of situational particularity. When he thinks of Morality, Hegel, of course, has Kant in mind, but the goal of a rational ethics is certainly not unique to Kant. The "Kantian" argument—one that would be shared by Frankena—is that my moral principles should be such that I can say they are precisely not mine, but true for everyone, in just the way that the Pythagorean law is not an individual's, Pythagoras', but true universally. Reason, rationality, consists in rising to precisely such *universal* truth as this, and the hope of Morality is that morals could be put on that kind of a foundation. Frankena sees even Socrates engaging in such a project.[9] Whether that is an artificial superimposition of his own viewpoint on Socrates' will need to be investigated in a later chapter. Here it important only to note that, as Frankena sees it, anyone who does or ever did moral philosophy aims at rising above particularity to universality. In that, he is a true "Kantian" and a good example of what Hegel means by Morality.

However well-intentioned, Hegel argues, the result of such efforts is an "empty formalism" (PhR § 135). An *a priori* Morality can indeed provide a form that transcends all particularity—Frankena refers to this form as the principle of universalizability—but it cannot provide any content. As a moral consciousness, the most I can do is to "test" the law (*nomos*) that I give myself (*autōi*) for consistency (cf. Hegel on *Gesetzprüfende Vernunft* [PhG 306ff.]), but I still do not know what I actually ought to do in the real world. The empty universal "ought" which I derive autonomously, on the one hand, and the "is" of the real world, on the other, remain hopelessly split apart here, and the moral consciousness continues in the estrangement from the world which plagued it from the start.

Put in MacIntyre's language: we could say that the Morality "fails," but the reason why it "fails" in Hegel is not the one MacIntyre gives. Compare AV, Chapter 5, "Why the Enlightenment Project of Justifying Morality Had to Fail." Significantly, in MacIntyre's view it is not the project of Morality itself that fails but the project of *justifying* it. Put another way: in Hegel the problem with Morality is not at all a problem of inconsistency, i.e., that it holds to incoherent fragments of bygone moral languages and cannot justify its views because of the anachronism and consequent contradictoriness in its starting points. The problem for Hegel, in other words, is not that Morality's language is "in disorder." Indeed, it should be noted that the criteria of consistency and coherence that MacIntyre uses to identify this disorder are the criteria of an *analytical* philosophy that Hegel rejects from the start. Instead Hegel finds Morality as such a failure.

Of course, it could be argued that I am playing with words here and that "morality" in MacIntyre is not the limited term Morality is in Hegel. And certainly a good deal of what Hegel refers to as "the ethical" is included in what MacIntyre means by moral and morality. Still, in choosing the word Morality and particularly in setting it in juxtaposition with *Sittlichkeit*, Hegel is not so much coining a term as bringing to light the abstraction that is characteristic of all morality as such. For Hegel does have a remarkable ear for what is in a word. And indeed "morality" is a peculiarly modern term that, as MacIntyre himself observes (AV 38), makes no sense, for instance, in the Greek world. As Hegel sees it, it is a word that has a function only once the Greek world of *Sittlichkeit* has been lost. And certainly Hegel is right when he senses that the German *gesittet* and *sittlich*, with their emphasis on *Sitte* or custom (*ethos, ēthos*), can render the Greek *ēthikos* with much less distortion than *moralisch* or the English moral. Hence, the argument in Hegel is not that morality *could* be justified if, and only if, a consistent teleological setting still existed in which human beings could achieve their excellences, but rather that Morality as such is a one-sided abstraction and by itself a mere exercise in reasoning that must eventually pass over into something existentially concrete. However reasonable one may be, one cannot derive the content of ethics, communal norms (*nomoi, Sitten*), just by giving and testing laws for consistency by oneself *a priori*, i.e., apart from the given world in which one always already finds oneself. It is the essence of Morality, however, that it tries to derive its content in exactly this autonomous way. When Hegel character-

izes Morality as "empty formalism," he is saying that it necessarily lacks *sittliche Substanz*, ethical substance, and consequently must negate itself. Its reasoning or understanding is
what Hegel calls elsewhere "tabellarischer Verstand," which is
to say that it produces a table of contents but no contents (PhG
44). The issue, then, is whether or not MacIntyre's use of
"morality" covertly perpetuates the abstraction Hegel associ-
ates with the word. I think it does, but that remains to be
demonstrated.

Now, in Hegel, at any rate, the concretion, of which Morality
is the abstraction, is *Sittlichkeit* and in particular *Sittlichkeit* as
that is displayed in the family. Here, according to Hegel, the
consciousness' disposition toward the law as an autonomous
and critical outsider to it is indeed transcended and with it the
"empty formality" of such "critical," "rational" thinking. In
Sittlichkeit we are no longer (or not yet) dealing with a thought
construct, an "imperative which only *ought* to be" (PhG 310),
but with an ethical reality which *is*. Consciousness here finds
itself "in the ethical substance" (PhG 312; emphasis added),
which is to say that its relationship to the laws (*nomoi*) is no
longer (or not yet) that of someone who detachedly surveys
what lies clearly in view before him, but rather that of someone
who is already under way within laws that have been there from
time *out of mind*: "They *are* and nothing more than that—that
constitutes the relationship of consciousness [to them]. That is
the way they hold for Sophocles' Antigone: as *unwritten* and
never deceiving justice: 'Not now indeed or yesterday, but
always there, it lives, and whence it came no one knows' " (PhG
311).

> They *are*. If I ask whence they arose and narrow them down to
> their origin, I have set myself beyond them, for from then on it is
> I who am the universal, while they are the conditioned and
> limited. If they are to be legitimated in my insight, I have already
> set swaying the steadiness intrinsic to them, and I regard them as
> something which is perhaps true for me but also as perhaps not

true. The ethical frame of mind consists precisely in holding fast
and unerringly to what is right and refraining from setting it in
motion in any way, shaking it, or deriving it [PhG 311].

Everything in our own "critical" and "rational" tradition
leads us to balk at Hegel's argument here, for he appears to be
representing blind, unreasoned conformity to even the most
senseless and unjust practices. Indeed, it seems that he is
speaking, not of another kind of reasoning to be distinguished
from Morality's external reason, but of the abrogation of any
sort of reasoning at all. But such a reading of this passage is
mistaken for two reasons. In the first place, in complementing
Morality with *Sittlichkeit* in order to provide the ethical substance that Morality lacks, Hegel does not discard Morality.
Though a naïve *Sittlichkeit* "before" Morality does not apply to
them, Morality's tests of equality before the law and universalizability must nevertheless be applied. For as we will see,
ultimately participants in *Sittlichkeit* are always also to be respected as persons in Civil Society and their rights concerning
personal dignity, satisfaction of needs, and property, to be
observed. Here Morality obtains: "Morality has its proper place
in this sphere . . ." (PhR § 207). Again, in arguing this way
Hegel is stronger than MacIntyre, who seems to abandon the
realm of universal right altogether.

In the second place, within *Sittlichkeit* itself there are indeed
reasoning and justification. I do what I do deliberately at the end
of a course of deliberation in which I adduce grounds to myself
and others for my choice. (See Part 4 below on *bouleuesthai* and
prohairesis in Aristotle.) The point that Hegel is making is not
that I act unthinkingly with no grounds, but rather that as
opposed to thinking in mathematics in my thinking here I cannot
get back to a point of presuppositionless unprejudicedness, to
some sort of self-evident axiom. I can never come up with a first
ground, a *causa sui*, as it were, ungrounded by anything other
than itself. The reasons I bring to mind in my deliberations will
be sustained precisely by other reasons that I do not and cannot

bring to mind. In ethical deliberation, in other words, the foundations of my reasoning cannot be raised to the level of conscious reflection and brought into question themselves. In part, at least, they must remain tacitly presupposed, for the thoughts that come to mind in any ethical deliberation remain embedded in truths from time *out* of mind, and to want to raise these too to the level of explicit consciousness would be to displace myself from participation in the tradition that alone makes possible the thoughts that I have *in* mind explicitly. To draw an analogy with language to which we will often recur, if I think in any part of a language, if I draw upon it in a course of thought, which it alone makes possible, I must leave most of the foundations of that language inexplicit and untouched. I have no extra-linguistic, Archimedean point from which to reflect on them. Consequently, I must "uncritically" presuppose them. Otherwise, I would find myself in the patently ridiculous situation of Russell's hypothetical languageless village elders who wish to set about naming a fox a fox and a sheep a sheep, but who have no language in which to arrive at these conventions. Hegel is getting at something like this when he says that in ethical (*sittliches*) thinking one cannot bring its origins into view. And is this not what Rorty and MacIntyre, for example, have in fact shown to be the case?

We should take careful note of the change in epistemological structure here. As opposed to a moral reasoning that would pattern itself on mathematics (Spinoza, of course, is the paradigm here), ethical consciousness does not have a "critical" or "analytical" vantage point outside of what is given to it. Its own consciousness is not at all the "condition of the possibility" (Kant) of ethical truth and knowledge. It itself does not constitute the ethical norms of which it is aware; rather, it finds itself conditioned by, constituted by, them. Consequently, it has no overview; it always finds itself already under way *within* norms that exceed the horizons of its insight and awareness. (The Heideggerian language—*je . . . schon, sich befindet, unterwegs in*—is not at all misplaced here, as we will see shortly when we come to Gadamer's appropriation of it in his discussion of ethical [*sittliches*] understanding.)

Put another way: ethical consciousness, says Hegel, does not engage in Morality's "Raisonnieren" (PhG 312). Hegel avails himself of this word imported from the French to designate a superficial, rationalistic way of thinking that no longer participates in the subject matter it would conceptualize. *Raisonnieren* is the same sort of thing Hegel characterizes in the "Preface" to the *Phenomenology* and in the *Logic* as "external reflection." What he has in mind is a mathematical, analytical kind of thinking which does not think from within, and in accordance with, the intrinsic self-unfolding process of the thing it is thinking of; rather, from outside, it constructs extrinsic static forms into which it then inserts bits and pieces of the subject matter, as it has arbitrarily broken this subject matter down or "analyzed" it. It is the nature of a mathematical proof, say the Pythagorean theorem, that I do not grasp the proof by tracing the logic internal to the thought or concept of a right triangle as such:

> The movement of the mathematical proof does not belong to its object [e.g., the right triangle]; it is a doing which is *external* to the subject matter. Thus it is not in the nature of a right triangle to break itself down in the way [its analysis is] presented in the construction necessary for proving the proposition that expresses the ratio of its parts. The production of the result is in its entirety the proceeding of cognition and the means it uses [PhG 35].

This same *Raisonnieren* or external reflection analyzes the physical world mathematically into static units of extended material in empty space, and here too—just as in formal logic, one might add—cognition constructs for itself an external form in separation from the movement intrinsic to the things themselves. Significantly, just as *Raisonnieren* reduces the flourishing live world to units at points in its external schematization of physical space (*physis*, like *natura*, originally referred to birth and growth), Morality reduces people and their life-world to equal and qualitatively indifferent units located in its external schematization of social space—hence Musil's metaphors (see note 6 above and Heidegger's SZ III B and C on Descartes' reduction of the world we dwell in to the world as *res extensae*). And in this as well as in its abstract formality Morality shows itself to be external reflection too. *Sittlichkeit*, in contrast, comes before (or after) such externality. It knows itself to be within the dictates of ethical norms as these have come down to it from time immemorial, and it does not construe them according to rational forms external to them. Put another way: in *Sittlichkeit*, as opposed to Morality, I do not prove to myself what I have to do; that would be to import the mathematical, Cartesian idea of rationality falsely into ethics. Rather in my deliberations, what I have to do proves, shows, itself to be what is fitting, just, and right from within the circumstances in which I find myself. The process of deliberation is thus a "getting clear," as Wittgensteinians like to say, yet it is not the "agent" self that effects this clarity but the "things themselves." As I think of them, they become clear *to* me.

Has MacIntyre understood this distinction? Or is his analysis of *aretē* just that, an analysis, which is to say, a perpetuation of the critical, external reflection characteristic of the very analytical philosophy he would call into question? His own success or failure turns, I would contend, on the answer we will give to this question. To be sure, MacIntyre does reject the ideal of proof as "barren" for philosophy (AV 259), but as we will see in the third section of this chapter, he does not have Hegel's understanding of why this is so and, even if much of what he says would seem to preclude it, still speaks himself of "standing back" from disputes and settling them by "appropriate rational procedures" (AV 260). That, at least, would seem to be exactly the language of *Raisonnieren* and external reflection.

For Hegel, at any rate, *Sittlichkeit* is "das an- und für sich seiende Allgemeine": as opposed to the particular whim (*Willkür*) of a private person it is what is common (*gemein*) to all (*all*) of us, what we all have in common in a given community. It exists not only *für sich* in our thought, as do the principles of Morality, but in the social reality *an sich*. Hence, in it the estrangement between particular individual selves is transcended as is the estrangement between self and world. Ethical (*sittliche*) laws are not something alien and external to our consciousness; rather they are "that in which it lives as an element undifferentiated from itself" (PhR § 147). In the community of the family, for instance, my private whims, inclinations, and mere natural drives (*Triebe*) are transcended in fulfillment of duties (*Pflichten*) that are now quite literally second nature to me: "But in its simple identity with the individuals' reality, the ethical displays itself to be their universal way of acting, common to them all—as custom [*Sitte*]—and the habit of it manifests itself as a second nature that replaces the first merely natural will" (PhR § 151).

In this way Hegel can proceed from duty to virtue (*Tugend*) and from there to *Rechtschaffenheit* or what we might call rectitude, propriety, or even justice: "The ethical, inasmuch as it is reflected in an individual's character as it is determined by nature, is virtue. And virtue, inasmuch as it displays nothing other than the appropriateness of the individual in his conforming to the duties pertaining to his circumstances, is rectitude or propriety [*Rechtschaffenheit*]" (PhR § 150).

We should note carefully that here too the emphasis is different from MacIntyre's, for virtue itself is not central to Hegel's exposition of *Sittlichkeit*, but duty, what is due, what ought to be done. To be sure, *Rechtschaffenheit* appears here as a generalization of virtue. In German usage the word *rechtschaffen* is very close to *anständig* (a word meaning decent and honorable, to which we will return in Chapter 3), and *pflichtbewusst* or "conscious of duty." It is said of someone who both knows and does what is right (*recht*), which is to say in Greek, of someone who knows and does *to dikaion*, what is just. *Rechtschaffenheit*, in other words, is that sense for the just which Plato and Aristotle call *dikaiosynē* and Aristotle, the *sympasa aretē*, the composite virtue (see Plato's discussion of justice as the central virtue in the *Republic*). It is important to note that in singling out this virtue of *Rechtschaffenheit* as central to all the others, Hegel shifts the emphasis away from any virtue itself to duty and what is right (*Recht*), thereby bringing specific obligations to the fore such as Polynices' right to be buried and Antigone's duty to bury him. It remains to be seen if in fact Aristotle does not do the same thing in his treatment of the virtues by always directing us to *to deon*, *hōs dei*, *hote dei*, and so forth. I will argue subsequently that like Hegel Aristotle avoids the abstraction of form from specific content in his exposition of ethical thought. For both, what is ethical is indissociable from the concrete, particular circumstances in which one finds oneself and is to be defined neither by rights in the abstract *nor by virtues in the abstract*.

Now, MacIntyre too, as we know, seeks to avoid the very same disjunction of abstract universal "ought" and concrete particular "is" that Hegel finds characteristic of Morality. But MacIntyre finds that disjunction inevitable only in a moral theory based on adherence to some sort of rationally deduced universal rights or rules. His proposal, consequently, is to turn away from any deontologism, any theory of universal obligation, and to reestablish moral theory on the basis of virtue as such, which he defines as "an acquired human quality the possession and exercise of which tends to enable us to achieve those goods which are internal to practices and the lack of which effectively prevents us from achieving any such goods" (AV 191). But is such a formal "definition" essentially different from the formal "definition" of virtue that makes of it the characteristic trait of obedience to rationally derived rules? And is it immune to the criticisms that MacIntyre himself directs toward virtue defined as mere obedience to rules? Granted: any such definition, as MacIntyre himself acknowledges, is intended only as "a partial and first account" (AV 201)—perhaps like Aristotle's definition of virtue as hitting the mean between the extremes of excess and deficiency in the *pathē*, for example, in fear or sensuous desire. But the question remains whether MacIntyre, given his overall analytical approach, could ever succeed in filling his definition out in such a way that would permit him to transcend Morality in Hegel's sense. Indeed, it could be argued that a return to virtue, if the mode of thinking in which that return takes place remains analytical, critical, "external reflection," does nothing to bridge the gap between autonomous reason *für sich*, on the one side, and the real social world *an sich*, on the other, with its actual obligations—nothing, that is, to overcome the problem of abstraction and alienation that Morality faces. A mere shift to virtue would not suffice.

Hegel, certainly, would find perpetuated in MacIntyre's "definition" of virtue exactly that "empty formality" characteristic of Morality; for we have here a form in which any content could be inserted at will, "external reflection's" analytical "test" of consistency being the only one that could be applied. The ethical, in contrast, can be defined only in regard to real obligations, real duties, and rights. It can be defined, that is, only in regard to what is right (*das Rechte* or, in Greek, *to dikaion*), and this, Hegel says (and on occasion MacIntyre too!), cannot be deduced in abstraction; rather, again, it is that within which I always find myself already under way and, accordingly, can only be established through participation in the specific traditional community of which I find myself to be a part: "What a human being must do, what the duties are that he has to fulfill to be virtuous, is easy to say in an ethical community: he must do nothing other than what, given his circumstances, is shown to him, stated to him, known to him" (PhR § 150).

Just how such real obligations arise, as opposed to formal rights or for that matter formal virtues, can be shown by taking the family as an example and beginning with marriage. In marriage, as Hegel puts it, a natural, physical coupling of opposite sexes of the species is transformed into something spiritual: in marriage, love between the sexes (*Geschlechterliebe*) is raised (*aufgehoben*) into ethical love (*sittliche Liebe*), which is not to say that natural love is eliminated by the spiritual, but rather that it is suffused with it. Indeed, *Sittlichkeit* in general consists, as we have seen, in precisely such a transformation. In *Sittlichkeit* the individual's natural drives are superseded; the accidentality of his or her passions, transcended. What Hegel calls spiritual here, *geistig*, can be understood quite simply: the love of a husband and wife for each other contains, certainly, the element of sexual attraction, but if that love is ethical love, its foundation is not sexual, not what is physical or sensual, but a commitment and sense of obligation to each other in which mind (*Geist*) prevails over "matter" much as when someone rouses himself from drowsiness, or pulls himself together when he is on the verge of being overwhelmed by fears or desires. In ethical love, in other words, the partners want to do what they do, not just because their physical nature so inclines them, but because they *know* it is right. The distinction and transition here is one that Kierkegaard displays splendidly in his contrasting of aesthetic enamoration and marital love in *Either/Or*.

Marriage, accordingly, *is not a matter of satisfying individual needs or wants*; the decision to marry is an ethical decision precisely insofar as it is based not on the satisfaction of the partners' desire for each other and least of all on the advantage or gain each of the partners might expect to attain, but on the duty of each to stand by the other (*Beihilfe*), on sharing (*Gemeinsamkeit*), and, above all, on trust, faith, and confidence (*Zutrauen*). That is what is meant when Hegel says that the decision to marry is spiritual and that it is based upon ethical, not natural, love.

As is so often the case, just what Hegel is getting at is displayed in the particular word he chooses to characterize it, in this instance, *Zutrauen*. The stem, *trauen*, which has to do with the related English words trust and truth, appears in a number of other German words, for example, *vertrauen*, *anvertrauen*, and even *Trauung*. *Vertrauen* means to trust that someone can and will fulfill an obligation, and *vertraut* means familiar and hence known as a confidential friend or even a close family member. *Anvertrauen* means to confide in, and *Trauung* is a word for marriage, which is to say, literally, an "entrusting" of the partners to each other. If one sounds out the semantic range of these words, one sees that Hegel means by ethical love something very close to *philia*, and indeed his choice of marriage to exemplify the ethical finds its correlate in Plato and especially in Aristotle's treatment of what might be called friendship, namely *philia*, but love just as well, insofar as the Greek *philos* means beloved and dear. Aristotle, it will be noted, includes familial love, love between parents, between parent and child, between brothers and sisters, in his exposition of *philia*. He has no difficulty at all in using *philia*—for example, in the phrase *hē syngenikē philia*—to speak of family relationships that we would scarcely be able to call friendship in English, in particular the relationship of a mother to her infant.

Hegel, it may be assumed, chooses familial love above all other forms of *Liebe* or *philia* because it best displays the transcendence of natural or sexual love in the sense of duty the sexes feel for each other. His most poignant example is the love of the sister Antigone for her brother Polynices. Though she is his sexual opposite, her love for him as a blood brother can be nonetheless a more purely spiritual love and be more purely founded in ethical duty than other natural relationships, say that of husband and wife. Here, we might say, natural love transforms itself, and the transformation is even more complete, the love even more sublimely spiritual, that anything possible between husband and wife. For in her love for her brother there is no satisfaction of desire and no advantage derived whatever.

On the other hand, that Hegel singles out the family and familial love in no way excludes from *Sittlichkeit* the dimension of *philia* or *Liebe* as friendship, the bond between friends who are not relatives. In his analysis of Plato's *Lysis* Gadamer makes clear what the intrinsic connection is between family love and *philia* as a relationship between friends: it emerges in the *Lysis*, he says, that in the highest form of friendship someone is never dear (*philos*) because of the pleasure or advantage that he or she provides (DD 16)—an argument that is taken up by Aristotle in the books on friendship central to his *Nicomachean Ethics*. In what, then, does true *philia* consist? The key, Gadamer suggests, lies in the Greek *oikeion*; the dear, beloved friend, *ho philos*, is *oikeios*:

> It [*oikeios*] is an ordinary expression for relatives and house friends, i.e., for all who belong to the household. *Oikos*, household, thus has the broad sense of an economic [*ökonomische*] unit such as the Greek household characteristically was. But *oikeion* is just as much an expression for that place where one feels at home, where one belongs, and where everything is familiar [*vertraut*] [DD 18].

To oikeion, in other words, is everything that belongs to the household, and *hoi oikeioi* are those people who belong to it.

To be sure, like any historical community the traditional household has in large part also been not so much a practice as what MacIntyre calls an "institution," that is, an organization dedicated to the pursuit of "external goods," of advantage and wealth (AV 194). And more than by any *philia* its members were bound to each other, often involuntarily and unjustly, by rules dictated by the interests of those dominating it. Still insofar as household members are bound by kinship, there is another dimension of the relationship besides that of such need satisfaction. As kin, at least, they are precisely not private persons obligated to each other, either by force or by contract, in an advantageous or disadvantageous exchange of services and property. Rather they are related to each other by the obligations that fall to each as the particular member of the household to which they belong, as mother, father, daughter, son, and so forth, and, by extension, as friend of the family. In German, Gadamer points out, *hoi oikeioi* are *die Angehörigen*, those who belong (DD 18), and they do *was sich gehört*, what "belongs," which is to say, what is fitting, what is due, or, as Aristotle likes to put it, *ha dei*, which is to say, what is required not by force or contract, but rather by familial obligation such as that of Antigone to bury her brother. Hegel would say they do what is *recht*: they do what is right by each other, which, translated back into Plato's and Aristotle's Greek, would be *to dikaion*. Friendship thus emerges as an extension of family relationships. The friend becomes a member of the family, and consequently where family cultures and kinship are still strong, the family friend is even called "Cousin" or "Aunt."

Since what is ethical hinges on transforming physical needs and in thereby transcending pleasure, power, and advantage, and indeed transcending the entire realm concerned with the mere satisfaction of these "needs," a major part of the obligations in Hegel's paradigm of the family has to do with piety and with sanctifying what would otherwise be mere natural processes, eating, copulation, birth, death, etc., and thereby raising these to the level of spirit in any of the various ways in which various cultures accomplish this. The family, Hegel says, dedicates itself to the Penates. It is on this basis that Antigone's duty to extend the religious rites of burial to her brother and his right to be buried are to be understood; his death is to be made more than the spiritless deterioration of a carcass. But there are obligations of the parents to the children, for instance, that are not immediately understandable as a function of piety, though they too have to do with elevating the merely natural to the spiritual. In the modern European family, Hegel contends, children "have the right to be nourished and brought up from the common wealth of the family" (PhR § 174). "Upbringing" (*Erziehung*) is to be taken in the wide sense of raising the child from the level of mere natural drives into an ethical community founded on "love, trust, and obedience" (PhR § 175). Thus the family provides a teleological setting in which, if we were to use MacIntyre's language, a human being can progress from "untutored human nature" as it is to "man-as-he-could-be-if-he-realised-his-*telos*" (AV 54).

And as we have seen, the family *qua* family also emerges in Hegel as what MacIntyre would call a practice devoted not to external, but to internal goods. Still Hegel's emphasis on specific duties and rights that correspond to these, rather than on virtue as such, leads him in a quite different direction from MacIntyre's. Though a virtue, piety, for example, is important to Hegel not primarily as a character trait, but because of the concrete, specific obligations it entails—Polynices has a *right* to be buried, and Antigone, a *duty* to bury him—these concrete obligations are what provide the ethical substance of Antigone's action, not the formal virtue of piety as such.

Thus for Hegel, within *Sittlichkeit* every right, such as Polynices' to a burial, is the correlate of a duty, namely, his sister's to bury him. And these rights, just like the duties correlative to them and the customs (*Sitten*) enjoining these rights and duties, are neither some sort of *a priori* rational self-evident truths like axioms in geometry, nor the abstract fictions MacIntyre perceives all rights to be. Rather they are actual, immemorial imperatives of *Sittlichkeit* in a given community. Neither these rights and duties nor the *Sitten* from which they derive are pure rational "oughts" existing in abstraction from what "is." Hence, the mathematical model of situationless universal knowledge and demonstration is entirely misplaced here. It would be senseless to ask for a demonstration or proof *more geometrico* why parents within a given culture are obligated to bring up their children, for they stand in a relationship to the ethical truth that they should in an entirely different way from the way in which a geometrician, for instance, stands in relationship to the axioms, theorems, and correlates of geometry; and the justification or account of their actions that they give must also be a different kind which we will have to elaborate later on. The truths of geometry are not traditions from time out of mind. Hence *they* can be either intuited or deduced autonomously. *They* can be demonstrated. Ethical truths, in contrast, cannot be. That they cannot does not mean, however, that they are all mere fictions for which no justification is possible. They could all be "exposed" as mere unjustifiable fictions, as happens in emotivism, only when they are wrongly conflated with mathematical, self-evident, timeless truths and an inappropriate criterion is applied to them. *It becomes clear that to avoid precisely this kind of mistake one must distinguish between different kinds of truth and, correspondingly, different kinds of knowing or understanding.*

Now, since contracts between private persons have to do with the satisfaction of untransformed physical needs, Hegel insists that insofar as the marriage establishes an *ethical* community it cannot be considered a contract between private persons. Consequently as long as the marriage remains intact, the rights of those whom it joins are not to be confused with legal rights pertaining to persons who enter into contractual obligations. Hegel thus distinguishes sharply between a right based on what *is* right according to the dictates of *Sittlichkeit* and a right an individual *has* in Civil Society. In Civil Society the bonds between people are contractual, and all individuals are equal as "persons" before the law. For in Civil Society we have a system both connecting and protecting individuals who pursue the satisfaction of their natural needs—cooperatively, on the one hand, and competitively, on the other.

It now emerges that there are in fact two sides to the family: internally the family is an ethical community bound by the *ethical* duties and rights that pertain to its members; externally the family is a legal person with *legal* rights concerning persons and property, and exists in the "system of need satisfaction" (*System der Bedürfnisbefriedigung*) connecting it to other persons with property. Along with MacIntyre we could say that the family is consequently both a practice and an "institution" (AV 194), that is, both a practice devoted to internal goods and an institution devoted to obtaining external goods. Insofar as the family is an ethical community, it neither consists of persons (*personae*) nor has property (*res*). But to the outside Civil Society the family itself is a private person with property, and each of its members is a potential private person. Consequently, another important part of upbringing is to capacitate the children to enter Civil Society as persons who can compete for its material goods and who can then marry, thereby forming, from the point of view of Civil Society, one legal person with common property where before there were two persons each with his own property. That means that the partners in a marriage, and not only their children, are potential private persons insofar as in circumstances of "total alienation" they can be divorced and thereby revert to their former status as persons in Civil Society (PhR § 176).

Hegel's point here is that human beings necessarily lead a precarious dual existence; in their relationship to one another as members of an ethical community, say a family, they are threatened with the loss of their ethical understanding of themselves and one another when the legal relationships of their other existence in Civil Society intrude. Civil Society, says Hegel, is *verlorene Sittlichkeit*, the ethical lost (PhR § 184). And indeed, what Hegel means by alienation and the loss that it entails may perhaps be demonstrated best by the shift from ethical love to the distanced, cool civility that takes place in a failed marriage. In civility each acknowledges the other, no longer as a partner in the "practice" of the family, but instead as a partner in a merely contractual obligation to maintain the family as what MacIntyre calls an institution, or something Hegel refers to at the end of his discussion of Civil Society as a corporation or joint venture. In these circumstances the spouses have come to view each other and even themselves as private persons with their own private property. They no longer sense that they belong to (*zugehören*) the same ethical community; rather each views the other from the outside and as an outsider. Incipient dissolution of the ethical community of the family evidences itself in a division and exchange of services and property characteristic of the system of need satisfaction in Civil Society (in modern parlance, "I'll take the kids to the dentist if you'll get the dinner ready") and more advanced dissolution in outright distribution of personal possessions ("I'll take the antique silver vase and you can have the stereo system"). And in these circumstances the meaning of a right and of what is right changes dramatically: the observance of rights here is a way of ensuring that force or even violence does not determine how and to what extent the needs of each are satisfied. And given the dissolution of familiar affinity (*philia*) between those who have now become estranged private "individuals," it is often only the existence of an outside instance of authority, the courts and agencies of law enforcement, that can ensure that rights in the legal sense are respected. For those who were *philoi*, beloved to each other, have now become *echthroi*, that is to say, alien to each other and even hostile; and if hostilities are to be avoided, they have no choice now but to acknowledge their new relationship to each other as equals before the law, that is, as "persons" in the Condition of Right or Legal Status (*Rechtszustand*) (PhG 342–46). Certainly the Condition of Right is preferable to the only alternative to it at this point, Hobbes's war of all against all. But that there is nonetheless a tragic and painful loss here, a loss that transcends matters of *personae et res*, however bitterly these may be contested, is something everyone senses.

In his trenchant exposition in the *Phenomenology* of the transition from *Sittlichkeit* to the Condition of Right, Hegel uses as his example, not our modern experience of divorce, of course, but the breakup of the ancient pagan family. But that example is no less effective in displaying just what the loss of *Sittlichkeit* consists in—a loss, it should be noted, to which the whole of MacIntyre's *After Virtue* may be said to respond, although MacIntyre understands it quite differently from Hegel. In the Condition of Right, Hegel says, the ethical substance common to all, the "universal," as he calls it, has splintered, leaving atomic individuals, all equal and all alike (*gleich*), which is to say that each is a "person" and "recognized" by all as such (PhG 342–43). Kant would say that all are now acknowledged as "ends in themselves," and Dworkin, as "human beings who are capable of forming and acting on intelligent conceptions of how their lives should be lived" and who are to be treated with "equal concern and respect."[10] What Hegel sees that Kantians and Dworkin do not, however, is that these determinations of the individual, though valid and essential, are only formal and unable to provide anything like the "ethical substance" that at this point they completely displace: "Thus [by itself] in its reality this empty unit of the person is an accidental existence, a process and doing which has nothing essential about it at all and which come to nothing of lasting consistency" (PhG 344). "On the contrary precisely when right obtains [in isolation from *Sittlichkeit*], the consciousness of right thus experiences the loss of its reality and its complete inessentiality" (PhG 345). It is given to a "skeptical confusion of consciousness, a glib negativity, which, taking no shape at all, strays errantly from one contingent way of being and thinking to another, dissolving all of them in its own absolute independence and self-sufficiency [*Selbstständigkeit*] and experiencing thereby its own insufficiency, its vacuity" (PhG 344).

The problem here is one with which emancipation movements are often confronted. In the effort to achieve the rights that as persons everyone in the Condition of Right ought to enjoy, e.g., life, liberty, and property, emancipation often seems to require the annihilation of an entire system of *Sittlichkeit* that perpetuated the violations of these rights. To eliminate the injustices and inequities of the patriarchal family, for instance, the family as such might have to be eliminated—perhaps even the bourgeois society that produced it—and with it, familial roles, rights, and obligations as we have known them. But if that annihilation is in fact entire, there is then nothing left to give concrete definition to the liberated person who emerges. As Stuart Hampshire points out, the triumph of liberation is therefore not always unequivocally beneficial. The equality gained and inequity overcome must sometimes be weighed against the loss of a "way of life" and of the character roles that it defined (MC 6).[11]

For should a "way of life" be wholly destroyed, we would be left with MacIntyre's "democratised self which has no necessary social content and no necessary social identity" and which, in "flitting evanescently" from one role and one point of view to another, can take any of them (AV 32). Or, put another way, we have Musil's "man without qualities." The *Gleichheit* of the person entails, of course, precisely that equality upon which Dworkin, for example, builds his theory of rights, but in Hegel's German word, as we know, one also hears that in the pure realm of legal right every person is just like every other, the same, *gleich*, which is to say that as a mere "person" freed from any embeddedness in any ethical tradition, I no longer have any intrinsic distinguishing characteristics. As a "person" the self has been reduced to a qualityless quantity, a numerical unit, an "Eins," says Hegel.

Hence the meaning of *a* right for this "empty unit of the person" must be correspondingly empty of content and purely formal. In an ethical community, as we have seen, there is no such thing as a right in the abstract; there are only concrete rights which concern what is specifically due to a member of the community, given the specific part he or she plays in it. To children are due sustenance and upbringing; to a dead soldier, burial by his sister; and so forth. Specific rights here are thus qualitatively different from one another. In the Condition of Right by itself, on the other hand, there exists only the person's formal right to be acknowledged and respected as the like of every other person, as the equal of every other. (Dworkin, I think, says as much in the citation above.) Since persons are qualitatively indifferent, so, too, is their right to be recognized as "rational agents," or however else one might attempt to characterize these legal persons who by definition have no characteristics that would distinguish them from one another; they are all "gleich." It follows that my rights as a person can be rights only to what can be subsumed under the qualitatively indifferent quantifiable category of what is "mine" (PhG 344), a category into which anything at all may be inserted as content, for instance, "I'll take the antique silver vase and you can have the stereo system."

Thus, for example, when the ethical community of a family breaks up, what was a relationship between husband and wife becomes a relationship between equal persons mediated by property. As a person I no longer have qualities or characteristics (*Eigenschaften*) to you; nor do you, as a person, have qualities or characteristics to me. Therefore nothing is due to either of us other than how much is mine and how much is yours. As Hegel puts it, in our thinking of each other, the *Eigenschaften* once given to us by the community of which we were a part have been replaced by *Eigentum* (property).

It is to Marx, of course, to whom we owe the development of this idea, of which Hegel gives us only the outlines here. "The real content," says Hegel, "what the 'mine' is determined to be—be that content an external possession or inner wealth or poverty of mind and character as well—is not contained in this empty form and is of no concern to it. The content thus belongs to a power all its own, something different from the formal universal ['mine'], namely, coincidence and caprice" (PhG 344–45). Marx would maintain that relationships between human beings, say of husband and wife to each other, become relationships between things, a silver vase to a stereo sytem, once these have taken on a capricious power all their own. He argues that alienation between human beings is the result of property exchange. Hegel argues, convincingly I think, that the converse is true: the mere relationship of property exchange is the result of alienation, the loss of *Sittlichkeit*.[12]

3. THE INSUFFICIENCY OF MACINTYRE'S ALTERNATIVE TO ANALYTICAL MORAL THEORY

Certainly MacIntyre is fully aware of the phenomena we have been discussing here,[13] but Hegel's analysis of them, it seems to me, is better for two reasons. In the first place, although Hegel, like MacIntyre, is conscious of the deficiencies in the Condition of Right, of what has gotten lost in it, and of its inability to make up for what has gotten lost, unlike MacIntyre, he does not overlook the necessity and validity of legal right for that dimension of our existence that has to do with our individual personality and with the satisfaction of our individual, personal needs.

There is a place for legal right, in other words, where we are engaged in the pursuit of "external goods," and in Hegel a justification for the Condition of Right or Legal Status can be and is given. In MacIntyre, on the other hand, it is not.

That is a serious weakness, for ultimately the realms of *Sittlichkeit* and Legal Status function only in dialectical conjunction with each other. Though, as Hampshire has shown, the two realms of our existence are not always compatible and conflicts between them not always resolvable, ideally neither should be in violation of the other. On the one hand, a one-sided emphasis on just, contractual relationships between persons ought not to be allowed to hollow out the substance of ethical practices as it seems to, for example, in Locke, Rawls, Nozick, and the entire Anglo-American liberal tradition. That, MacIntyre senses properly. But neither should ethical practices be unjust in their results for the persons *qua* persons involved in them, and, as we have seen, anyone involved in an ethical practice is, if viewed from the perspective of Civil Society, at the same time a person. Hence, though a wide indeterminacy exists in just how to proceed, ethical practices ought to be balanced in some way against the abstract juridical standards of equality and universalizability. Kant was correct about that. The standards of abstract right should provide some guarantee for the dignity and inviolability of the individual in any ethical community, a guarantee that MacIntyre forfeits when he jettisons legal right altogether.

In treating the distinction between internal and external goods, MacIntyre provides the illuminating though not entirely unproblematical example of a child who is taught to play chess with the inducement of money and who with time then becomes sufficiently engrossed in the game that he begins to play it for its own sake. MacIntyre sees this shift as a precondition for the restoration of the self-identity and virtue that are lost when institutions replace practices and the competitive pursuit of external goods replaces the cooperative pursuit of internal goods. (Apparently two dedicated chess players would, on this account, not be competing with each other!) MacIntyre's primary, if not exclusive, concern is with "good" insofar as it may be said of human beings displaying excellences or virtues in the cooperative pursuit of internal goods. And, to be sure, "right" (*ius*) does not have its application here. Hegel's *dialectical* exposition of the social world shows, however, that a one-sided concern with virtue and a disregard of right are naïve and dangerous. For as MacIntyre himself sees, all practices are inextricably tied to the institutions that sustain them (AV 194). In Hegel's terms all members of ethical communities must inevitably also enter into relationships of Civil Society. They are inevitably legal persons as well as husbands, wives, or whatever, and they will inevitably be involved in Civil Society's "system of need satisfaction." The chess player, for example, will *need* to eat between games and that will eventually put him in a civil, institutional, relationship with providers of food outside the circle of his partners in chess. MacIntyre's concern is that these inevitable institutional relationships not be allowed to undercut the virtues exemplified in practices, a concern that, if we may extrapolate from the critical tone of the transition from *Sittlichkeit* to abstract right in the *Phenomenology*, Hegel seems to share. But if the *Philosophy of Right* is any indication, Hegel, unlike MacIntyre, also insists that civil or institutional relationships, precisely given their inevitability, must be regulated by right.

There have been, as we know, various utopian attempts to circumvent their inevitability by internalizing the system of need satisfaction within the practices of an ethical community—Marxism and monasticism among them. The first is a notorious failure, as MacIntyre himself observes: "as Marxists move towards power they always tend to become Weberians," he says (AV 261), meaning that they will always end up maneuvering for power to acquire external goods. Another way of putting this point would be to say that instead of Civil Society's being taken up into the community—instead of the bourgeois state's "withering away," as Marx and Lenin liked to project it—the community is absorbed in the system of need satisfaction of Civil

Society, but a civil society not only divorced from any system of *Sittlichkeit*, but now without any system of right to govern it. This fact alone, incidentally, gives the lie to Marx's critique of Hegel's *Philosophy of Right*.

In his *Philosophy of Right* Hegel tries to show how the reciprocity between *Sittlichkeit* and Legal Status may be stabilized. Whatever his success, this much is clear: legal rights, equality before the law, cannot be dispensed with as fictitious "unicorns." Families do break up and their members then assume the status of right for each other that they always had for Civil Society. If for no other reason, that happens as soon as the children come of "legal age." But if the proper balance can be struck, precisely these children will, in addition to taking their place in Civil Society, form new families in which *Sittlichkeit* will be maintained and passed on to subsequent generations. Accordingly, though Legal Status and legal rights are indeed bereft of ethical content and can, in the absence of ethical content, provide no substitute for it, they have their justification in the realm where they obtain. Morality, which attempts to substitute formal right for *Sittlichkeit*, necessarily fails. But as collectivist experiments have demonstrated, a contrived *Sittlichkeit* is no substitute for formal right either.[14]

But second, and more central to our ethical–epistemological considerations here, in MacIntyre's own attempt to get beyond the same alienation as Hegel finds in Legal Status, and to get beyond the same abstraction as Hegel finds in Morality, MacIntyre in fact remains within the way of thinking characteristic of Morality, remains, that is, in its "external reflection" and *Raisonnieren*. He never completes the necessary ontological and epistemological differentiation between the analytical, critical thinking characteristic of Morality and the actual deliberation and discretion of *Sittlichkeit* from within its given situation. In short, he never gets clear about the distinct reality, being, and truth of substantive ethical duties and rights and consequently never gets clear either about the particular kind of knowledge and understanding that the ethical man or woman has of these truths.

As we have already seen, his definition of virtue *in general* displays the formality characteristic of Morality. Unlike Hegel, who stresses the substantive content of *Sittlichkeit* and the particular obligations and rights with which a given ethical virtue, say piety, is bound up, MacIntyre reviews particular virtues in the pagan and Christian traditions in order ultimately to focus on virtue in the abstract. Once his review is completed, he offers his "partial and tentative definition of a virtue" (AV 191) in which he treats virtue as a general form which would be presupposed by *any* practice (see the full citation from AV 191 above).

Now, one might hope that MacIntyre would go on beyond this formal, preliminary treatment of virtue, but these hopes are not really fulfilled. Indeed, indicative of MacIntyre's perpetuation of the formal thinking characteristic of Morality is his exposition of the presumably specific virtue of justice, which, along with truthfulness and courage, he finds to be "virtues in the light of which we have to characterise ourselves and others, *whatever our private moral standpoint or our society's particular codes may be*" (AV 192; emphasis added). Like the other two, then, "justice" emerges here as an *a priori*, Kantian "condition of the possibility" of any practice, a form presupposed by, and existing prior to, any specific content. "Justice," says MacIntyre, "requires that we treat others in respect of merit or desert according to uniform and impersonal standards . . ." (AV 192). That definition is a curious, but symptomatic mélange of *Sittlichkeit* and Morality. On the one hand, it does include a trace of *what is due* to someone as a member of a given, concrete ethical community, and in this regard MacIntyre scores telling points against the theories of justice advanced by Rawls and Nozick, both of which neglect people's "just deserts," given who they are in their community (AV 246ff.). For insofar as it alludes to merit and desert, justice (*dikē*) here would seem to imply *to dikaion*, or what is right, given the qualitatively diverse obligations and rights that pertain to the practice of that community. And yet MacIntyre's own definition of justice also seems to presuppose that in being just to someone, I in fact no longer stand in the relationship to that individual which defines an ethical community, the relationship, namely, of *Liebe*, *philia*, which is to say, of familiarity and friendship. As he sees it, in justice all intimacy gives way to impartiality, and my relationship to the other becomes precisely that of the Condition of Right: I treat him or her, not, for instance, as I would a brother or sister, friend or neighbor, but "according to uniform and impersonal standards." That much, at least, is the language, the "empty formality," of Morality and Civil Society. Indeed, justice emerges here precisely as a kind of *civility*. When Antigone strews earth upon her brother, she has done justice by him, the justice of *Sittlichkeit*. But obviously that justice, based on the intimacy of those beloved to each other, cannot be what MacIntyre means here.

Consequently, his definition of justice, which we would expect to pertain to the domain of concrete ethical practices, in fact comes remarkably close to Dworkin's definition of the right to be treated equally and to another analytical philosopher's, Alan Gewirth's, definition of the right to the "necessary goods of freedom and well-being," rights that we have seen pertain to Legal Status and that by themselves cannot provide ethical content. And one wonders if the argument MacIntyre uses against Gewirth—which is a good deal more forceful than the "unicorn" argument he glibly advances against Dworkin—could not be turned against MacIntyre himself, namely, that "the existence of particular types of social institution or practice is a necessary condition for the notion of a claim to the possession of a right being an intelligible type of human performance" (AV 67). Would that not hold for a virtue, say justice, as well as a right? Of course, the answer here, and, in fact, any evaluation of MacIntyre's criticism of Gewirth, requires a distinction that MacIntyre has not made: namely, between legal and ethical rights and legal and ethical justice.

We shall set aside for the next chapter the question whether the language of "speech act" philosophy ("intelligible type of human performance") does not set traps of its own. Let us turn instead to the point that MacIntyre succeeds in making here: namely, that specific ethical rights always exist relative to concrete ethical circumstances. It would follow from this that if Gewirth is indeed attempting to deduce rights in abstraction from any concrete circumstances, as MacIntyre thinks he is, his attempt must inevitably miscarry. But is it not the same with MacIntyre's attempt to define justice? That it is just for Antigone to "bury" her brother could never be deduced from the abstract "uniform and impersonal standards" that MacIntyre believes underlie justice. The fact that MacIntyre shifts the emphasis from rights to virtues does nothing to address the problem.

In MacIntyre's conception of justice there is a serious confusion of ethical rights and ethical justice with rights and justice in what Hegel calls Civil Society in his *Philosophy of Right* and the Condition of Right or Legal Status in his *Phenomenology*. Or, using MacIntyre's own way of speaking, we could say that a distinction is missing between justice insofar as it pertains to the pursuits of goods internal to practices and justice insofar as it pertains to goods external to them.

That there is a distinction of this sort is evident not only to Hegel, but to Plato and Aristotle. If one looks at the discussion of justice in Plato's dialogues, for example, in the *Republic* and particularly in the *Gorgias*, one is struck by the sophist interlocutors' utter incomprehension of what Socrates has in mind when he speaks of justice. It is as if he is talking of oranges and they of apples. The disparate understandings of justice here come from shifts back and forth in the sense of a range of words: *dikē*, *dikaios*, *to dikaion*, *dikaiosynē*, all of which have an ambivalence in them that the Latin *ius*, *iustitia*, and, consequently, our own "justice" no longer adequately convey. The Greek words have one sense within an ethical community and another within the Greek adumbration of what Hegel will call the Condition of Right or Legal Status. (The full-fledged Condition of Right presupposes the "experience," as Hegel would put it, of the Roman Empire, the likes of which, of course, was wholly unknown to the Greeks of Plato's and Aristotle's time. See note 15 below.)

Dikē in one of its senses means custom (German: *Sitte*), what is customary, the way things are done, and consequently what is right, i.e., the right way of doing something. Within this semantic field the adjective *dikaios* refers to a deed that is right in the sense of being called for, and is also said of someone who does things rightly, someone who fulfills his or her specific obligations and does what is to be done, *to deon*. Here *to dikaion*, the substantivized adjective, means what is right, and *dikaiosynē* identifies the character trait or virtue of someone who is *dikaios*. The opposite trait is *adikia*, but *adikia* in another sense refers not to a character trait but to a deed that is wrong, an injustice. *Adikia* here is thus the opposite of *to dikaion*.

In another range of their meaning, however, *dikē* and *to dikaion* mean at least implicitly what we, after the Roman Empire, would call legal justice (*ius, iustitia*), and, if we may depend upon Aristotle's sensitivity to how people spoke Greek (*pōs legetai*), mean justice regarding "the distributions [*dianomai*] of honor, wealth, and such things as are to be allocated among those sharing in the community [*politeia*]" (EN 1130B 31). At another point (1130B 3) Aristotle adds security or safety (*sōtēria*) to honor and wealth and indicates that there is something in all of them deserving of the same name, whatever that name might be, since they all have to do with gain (*kerdos*). As is well known from Aristotle's *Ethics*, *adikia* in this realm turns on distribution: on the one hand, *adikia* here consists in an inequitable (*anisos*) distribution, and, on the other, in the character trait or vice opposite to the virtue of *dikaiosynē*, which here has come to mean equity. And it is somewhere in this sphere, I would suggest, that justice as MacIntyre means it is to be located. Its opposite, *adikia*, is, as MacIntyre himself observes, not so much wanting to gain too much as wanting too much to gain—namely, *pleonexia* (AV 137).

It is clear, I think, that even if all this continues to take place within what remains an ethical community (*politeia*) of neighbors and kinfolk, we have taken at least an initial step away from the familial realm of *Sittlichkeit* toward Hegel's "system of need satisfaction." Indeed, alongside distributive justice Aristotle specifically introduces a correlative rectificatory (*diorthōtikon*) justice which concerns voluntary business transactions such as selling, buying, lending at interest, and leasing as well as an assorted list of "involuntary" transactions involving not only money but honor and security, e.g., theft, assault. And as a matter of fact Aristotle devotes the bulk of his analysis of justice in the *Ethics* to this second range of the meaning of justice and its cognates, namely, to the realm in which goods and services are exchanged with persons to whom one is bound not so much by *philia* or *Liebe* as by contractual obligations, where debts are incurred and where what in a later (Roman) culture will be called *iniuria*, injury to persons (*personae*) and damage to, and loss of, property (*res*), must be redressed.

But that Aristotle is no less deaf than Plato to the fundamental *ethical* significance of *dikē* and its cognates is made clear by the distinctions with which he opens Book V. There is, he says, a sense in which justice (*dikaiosynē*) is the composite of all virtue, is "perfect virtue" (*teleia aretē*) (1039ʙ 25), insofar as it may be said that one virtue is displayed in someone's conforming to the dictates of *andreia, sōphrosynē, praotēs* (courage, temperance, gentleness), etc. (1029ʙ 20ff.). *Dikaiosynē* here has nothing to do with gain. And correspondingly, Aristotle continues, there is a sense of injustice (*adikia*) that also has nothing to do with gain and is consequently *not* called *pleonektein* or taking more than one's share, e.g., the *adikia* of *deilia, chalepotēs*, and *aneleutheria* (cowardice, harshness, illiberality). In these the injustice consists instead in not behaving in a way that is fitting and right, not behaving *hōs dei* (1030ᴀ 15ff.). Or again, he says, if two men commit adultery, one for the sake of gaining something (*kerdainein*) and the other out of desire, only the first is unjust in the narrow sense of *pleonexia* (1029ᴀ 24). And by the same reasoning we may conclude that the other would be unjust in the opposed sense of having done what is unseemly, indecent, despicable, wrong—presumably out of a vice that is a composite of *akolasia, chaunotēs, aphilotemia, anaischyntia* (intemperance, vanity, disreputableness, shamelessness).

Now, insofar as *these* vices and virtues are based on a particular communal practice and on the bonds of *philia* which sustain it, injustice here, in the sense of the composite of all vice and, correspondingly, justice, in the sense of the composite of all virtue (*sympasa aretē*), do indeed depend on specific social circumstances for their content. Thus unlike injustice and justice in regard to *personae et res*, what they forbid and the obligations they enjoin cannot be determined universally in detachment from a particular situation, but only from within that situation in which one finds oneself under way. That is what Aristotle is getting at when he says that the ethical decision or choice (*prohairesis*) ultimately rests with one's perception or sense (*aisthēsis*) of what is demanded on each occasion (EN 1109B 24).

It can be stated generally only that when one chooses well, chooses justly or rightly with regard to any of the virtues of which justice is the composite, one will find oneself somewhere in between extremes (though just where cannot be said) and that one will have chosen first and above all what is *kalon* (noble, fine, decent), second, what is *sympheron* (beneficial), and third, and least of all, what is *hedu* (pleasant) (EN 1104B 30ff.). Being virtuous or good (*agathos*) is in Aristotle's eyes *kalagathia*, and just this fusion of what is *kalon* and what is *agathon*, we must assume, provides the rough outlines of that composite virtue in which one of the two senses of justice would consist. Significantly nothing more exact (*akribes*) can be said generally about the substance of this or any other virtue, for they contain simply too much aberration and indeterminacy (*planē*) given the ever-varying circumstances in which they have their place (EN 1094B 13ff.).

Thus in his elaboration of the *kalagathia* of any virtue, what is *kalos* about it, and even in his discussion of the all-encompassing virtue of justice, Aristotle is in no way establishing some sort of universal, abstract definition of what a virtue is or what our obligations are, but instead only using specific contemporary virtues to display the analogousness (*analogia*) (EN 1096B 28) in what we are doing within particular situations each time we fulfill a specific communal obligation or exhibit a particular virtue. He does this in the hopes only that consideration of this analogousness might be of help in "hitting the mark" more accurately when we are called upon to carry on our own deliberations and make our decisions (*prohaireseis*) on specific occasions. (See IGPAP 163 on Aristotle's metaphor of the archer.) Hence his project is a very different one from Kant's—as Kant himself stresses.[15] Aristotle's frequent and deliberately indeterminate references to "what is fitting," "the things that are fitting," "as it is fitting," "when it is fitting" (*to deon, ha dei, hōs dei, hote dei*), and so forth are meant to indicate that no precise content can be established *a priori* apart from particular given occasions. Put another way: there is no good in itself, no *form* or idea of the good, as Aristotle argues against his Platonizing colleagues (EN 1096A 12ff.), but merely an analogous structure in specific goods, each of which is good is a different way from the other (*allo . . . allou*: the one in its way, the other in another) (cf. IGPAP 155). Thus what is actually fitting can be determined not by some sort of abstract universal reasoning (*epistēmē*) in detachment from the particularity of one's world and one's self, but only by concrete *phronēsis*, by reasonable good sense or discretion within the situation in which one happens to find oneself.

We might say, then, that, given the obvious failure of the "Kantian" project to put ethics on the foundation of universal *a priori* reasoning, MacIntyre has good reason to go back to Aristotle in his efforts to find a possible way to do ethics. Or should we say, given the failure of the "Kantian" project to put *morality* on that foundation—and avail ourselves of Hegel's critical exposition of Kant and of Hegel's distinction between Morality and *Sittlichkeit*? But if we do say this, the question raised by our examination of MacIntyre's understanding of justice becomes all the more acute: namely, whether MacIntyre really succeeds in recovering the Aristotelian inheritance, or whether, instead, MacIntyre actually remains caught in the "Kantian" formalistic project—even if he himself acknowledges that it is a flight of intellectual fancy that has taken leave of the only thing on which it might have grounded itself, that is, concrete historical circumstances, traditions, or "narratives," as he calls them, within which we find ourselves under way.

Put another way: has MacIntyre really established just what special sort of reasoning ethical reasoning, or what Aristotle calls deliberating (*bouleuesthai*), is? And has he succeeded in distinguishing ethical reasonableness or *phronēsis* from other forms of intelligence?

There is no denying that in distancing himself critically from traditional analytical moral philosophy he has taken some important steps in this direction. A comparison of his understanding of ethical reasoning with Frankena's will suffice to illustrate the point. Frankena, at the beginning of his *Ethics*, gives us the outlines of precisely the kind of "Kantian" moral reasoning that MacIntyre would call into question. In analyzing Socrates' justification of his decision in the *Crito* to remain in prison and not to escape, and in taking that justification as a paradigm for all moral reasoning, Frankena discerns what he believes to be three distinguishing features of moral reasoning. First, he says, there is the need "to get our facts straight and to keep our minds clear. Questions like this can and should be settled by reason." Second, he says, we cannot appeal to what other people generally think; rather "we must think for ourselves." And third, "The only question we need to answer is whether what is proposed is right or wrong." The "Kantian" project is evident in all three points: reason, universal reason, is to be our guide. We are to reason autonomously, and we are to base our decision on what our reason shows us to be right in principle and right *a priori*: "In this pattern of moral reasoning one determines what one should do in a particular situation by reference to certain general principles or rules, which one takes as premises from which to deduce a particular conclusion by a kind of practical syllogism, as Aristotle called it. One takes general principles and applies them to individual situations."[16]

Now, MacIntyre too adverts to Aristotle's practical syllogism (AV 161–62), but his exposition of it is different in many important ways. In the first place, he finds that it presupposes "wants and goals" of the "agent" making the decision which are "not expressed" in his reasoning. For "[w]ithout these there would be no context for the reasoning, and the major and minor premises could not adequately determine what kind of thing the agent is to do." In the second place, we have the major premise which tells us that something is "good for or needed by a so-and-so"; in the third place, a minor premise based on a "perceptual judgment" which asserts that the case in question "is an instance or occasion of the requisite kind"; and, finally, the action the "agent" takes.[17] Significantly, on MacIntyre's understanding of it, this ethical reasoning, unlike geometrical reasoning, for instance, takes place within a context of tacitly accepted goods which themselves are not raised to the level of consciousness here, but which instead might be said to be there from time *out of mind*.[18] Significantly too, the "agent" is not just anyone, not an abstract moral reasoner, not a "person" stripped of distinguishing characteristics and hence the like and equal of every other "person," but a particular "so-and-so," a man or woman with specific characteristics—again not in question here—that define what would be good for him or her to do. Despite the word "agent" with its Kantian rationalist overtones, we *are* moving here in the realm Hegel calls *Sittlichkeit*, and not Morality: "For the judgments which provide the agent's practical reasoning with premises *will include judgments as to what it is good for someone like him to do and to be*; and an agent's capacity to make and to act upon such judgments will depend upon what intellectual and moral virtues and vices compose his or her character" (AV 162; emphasis added)—and, we might add, though of course MacIntyre does not explicitly say so, will depend upon what obligations and rights fall to someone of that character in whatever the world may be in which he or she find themselves. Plainly, far from being autonomous and reasoning "for ourselves," the reasoner here does indeed depend on what other people of that world have thought and continue to think. Precisely that collective tradition of thinking provides the tacit basis and context of his or her own thinking. Hence MacIntyre can say that moral reasoning is grounded in what I am, and that "What I am . . . is in key part what I inherit, a specific past that is present to some degree in my present," and consequently, he adds, "all reasoning takes place within the context of some traditional mode of thought . . ." (AV 221–22).

What MacIntyre calls the "narrative form of embedding" is central here: "the individual's search for his or her good is generally and characteristically conducted within a context defined by those traditions of which the individual's life is a part" and our actions are "made intelligible in terms of the larger and longer history of a number of traditions" (AV 222). This "embedding" implies that, contrary to what Frankena maintains, practical reasoning is based, not on "the knowledge of a set of generalisations or maxims which may provide our practical inferences with major premises," but on what MacIntyre calls a "capacity for judgment" in selecting and applying general principles to particular situations (AV 223). Ethical reasoning, in other words, would appear to be deliberation based on what Aristotle calls *phronēsis*, which MacIntyre's "capacity for judgment" could very easily and accurately translate.

And, as in Aristotle, such *phronēsis* or "capacity for judgment" would, it seems, be acquired not through any training in abstract reasoning, but only through a sort of habituation and apprenticeship, an education (Aristotle: *paideia*; Hegel: *Bildung*, *Erziehung*) to the "embeddedness" in the tradition of which MacIntyre speaks. Goods, MacIntyre says,

> can only be discovered by entering into those relationships which constitute communities whose central bond is a shared vision of

and understanding of goods. To cut oneself off from shared activity in which one has initially to learn obediently as an apprentice learns, to isolate oneself from the communities which find their point and purpose in such activities, will be to debar oneself from finding any good outside of oneself [AV 258].

The result of cutting oneself off, he adds, will be "moral solipsism" (AV 258), which is MacIntyre's apt epithet for the moral reasoning, proposed by Kant and Kantians like Frankena, that is based on the autonomous individual. MacIntyre, then, does indeed recognize the inevitable contextuality of any ethical reasoning, and in this he is true both to Aristotle on *phronēsis* and deliberation and to Hegel on *sittliches* or ethical knowing.

But even if he has made notable advances beyond the "Kantians," the question remains whether he has carried through on his insights and elaborated the structure of ethical understanding and the ontological status of its subject matter and truth sufficiently to distinguish ethical understanding from analytical philosophy's moral reasoning. In opposition to those who would sharply differentiate between history, on the one hand, and critical philosophical analysis, on the other—Frankena for one might be meant, but possibly also Rorty, who distinguishes between philosophy as "story telling" and philosophy as a theory of inference—MacIntyre does indeed point out that "the subject matters of moral philosophy at least—the evaluative and normative concepts, maxims, arguments and judgments about which the moral philosopher enquires—are nowhere to be found except as embodied in the historical lives of particular social groups and so possessing the distinctive characteristics of historical existence" (AV 265). For that reason, he maintains, one cannot approach that subject matter, as Frankena would, by trying to determine the universal, trans-historical "appropriate criteria for rationality and truth . . . in that particular area" (AV 265), the criteria, that is to say, of self-evident timeless principles and correct inference from them. Instead one must view all ethical arguments historically and assess the conclusions arrived at as historical results. The "story"—MacIntyre would say, the "narrative"—and the inferences drawn as it unfolds cannot be treated separately, but only in conjunction with each other. MacIntyre seems on the verge of saying that to understand an ethical truth, we must in some way or other already be or have become participants in the "narrative history" in which it displays itself, of saying that we could understand it only from *within* the tradition in which it exists. And had he acknowledged this necessity, he would indeed have gotten beyond the impasse of analytical moral philosophy.

But he takes another route. He argues that since there are "no grounds for belief in universal principles," making intelligible how a theory came to be advanced, when, and under what circumstances is essential to any *critical* evaluation of it as "rationally superior" to its "rivals" (AV 268). No theory is universally, absolutely best, but only the "best so far" or best "to date," the best, that is, not outside of, but in, history.

Important as the advances that he has made may be, it seems to me that at this point MacIntyre gets diverted from the fundamental epistemological and ontological inquiry that his insights into our "embeddedness" in the historical traditions of ethical truths should have induced him to pursue. He turns here to a radical pragmatist theory that he superimposes on the tradition of the later Wittgenstein and language analysis. For he now argues that just as Newtonian physics prevailed as "rationally superior" to its "rivals" at the time because "it was able to *solve problems* in areas in which those predecessors and rivals could by their own standards of scientific progress make no progress" (AV 268; emphasis added), so too his version of Aristotelianism can be seen to be "rationally superior" to its contemporary "libertarian," "individualist," "emotivist" rivals, and to be the best theory "to date." "Best" here evidently refers to what James would call "cash value," and as such it implies less a regard for historical, traditional ethical truth by which I feel myself sustained than a concern for immediate practicality. Indeed, in disregard of whatever tradition I might find myself, in setting it aside as a possibly prejudicial encumbrance, I am now to judge autonomously what means will serve "best" to solve the problem at hand. As we will see in the next section, this is not the thinking of *phronēsis* at all but of *technē*.

Even though it might introduce historicity—pragmatic truths, after all, are not eternal verities but historically evolving adjustments to shifting circumstances—the pragmatism to which MacIntyre and a good number of other analytically trained philosophers have turned is not sufficient to overcome the "abstraction" in analytical thought, not sufficient to move it beyond what I would call its "critical" disposition and what Hegel called its *Raisonnieren* and external reflection. As Frankena quite properly notes, MacIntyre's own arguments against emotivism "are drawn from analytical philosophy" (compare AV 265), which is to say that the arguments themselves are assumed not to be embedded in history at all. They themselves are not known to be the outcome of any evolving tradition. That they are not is made evident by the obvious difference between Newtonian physics and MacIntyre's new proposal for moral theory: Newtonian physics prevailed over rivals continuous with it in history—namely, its immediate Galilean and Aristotelian predecessors and contemporary Cartesianism—and the dispute with them was accordingly carried on from within an evolving tradition, not from an absolute stance outside it. MacIntyre, in contrast, plays off Aristotelianism against Nietzscheanism as if he were a detached observer surveying a past in which he is no longer a participant and by which he is no longer conditioned. Anachronistically, he selects those past theories which, from his critical position outside them, he assesses to be "rationally superior" and the "best" he can find "to date." If one thinks about it, his project is hardly less astonishing than if someone were to propose that we disregard the English language we have inherited and try to speak in some other tongue, let us say, ancient Greek. For while thinking in some sort of artificial language that unlike either English or Greek is not the outcome of any historical language but absolved from the "embeddedness" in any of them, we can, so the argument runs, critically conclude that for solving the moral problems with which we are confronted Greek is the "best" language "to date."

The fact is, however, that we never can remove ourselves from our inherited ethical language in order to make such a critical evaluation. And we can avail ourselves of Greek, and of Aristotelianism, for that matter, only insofar as we continue to participate in the historical language tradition of which they are constitutive, only insofar, that is, as they have been carried over (trans-lated) into the idiom in which we are at home and within which we continue to be under way, and only insofar as we have thereby succeeded in maintaining our continuity with them. In *After Virtue* there is no indication that MacIntyre is aware of the momentous consequences for our conceptions of truth and method that are thereby implied.

To be sure, in the subsequent *Whose Justice? Which Rationality?* there is again the promise that MacIntyre will get clear about the consequences of this ineliminable embeddedness in the ethical language we speak. In a penultimate chapter, whose title, "Tradition and Translation," is strongly reminiscent of Gadamer's theory of interpretive understanding, MacIntyre tells us of the native speaker's "knowing how to go on *and to go further*" (WJWR 382 and 383; emphasis added) that he or she displays by the transference of a word into new contexts or by what in standard rhetoric is called metaphor or, literally, from the Greek *metapherein*, "carrying over" a sense. with this addition to Wittgenstein's "knowing how to go on" MacIntyre wants to point out that he who knows "white" from inside the language and whose reasoning is not that of the external grammarian, knows not just when to repeat those units of language in which "white" has already been applied, those stock phrases, but also knows how to *extend* "white" in saying things like " 'Snow is white and so are the members of the Ku Klux Klan, and white with fear is what they were in snow-covered Arkansas last Friday' " (WJWR 382). MacIntyre is on to something here, for precisely this "poetic," meta-phorical ability underlies me-

tonomy ("Man does not live by *bread* alone"), anthimeria
("*Knee* thy way to mercy"), eponymy (as in "quixotic") and
indeed the entire unending process of word- and concept-for-
mation. (See WM 406ff., on *Übertragung* [transference, trans-
lation], *Begriffsbildung* [concept formation] and the "grundsätz-
liche Metaphorik der Sprache" [the fundamental metaphorics of
language].)

Significantly, this linguistic knowledge—as opposed to the
grammarians'—is not rule governed; rather, it is knowledge of
how to break the rule or at least reconstrue it given the new
occasion. Hence, like ethical knowing this knowing cannot be
taught. It is only to be acquired by practice *within* an evolving
tradition of speaking that, as Gadamer and MacIntyre both say,
is historically constituted and historically constitutive (see note
1 above). There are no schemata, no set grammatical, syntacti-
cal, or semantical rules, that I could acquire as an outsider and
that would enable me just to step in and start playing this
language game. Knowing how to go on further is not knowledge
of anything formal or general like that. Instead it is knowledge I
have acquired by always already (Heidegger: *je schon, immer
schon*) having been under way in the language. Grammar books
are makeshift guides for outsiders, for people learning what *can*
be taught of a language. Only participants in the tradition of its
ways of speaking can know what cannot be, namely, how to
transfer, translate, meanings from one context to a new one.

We should note too that such metaphorical reasoning proceeds not via situation-transcendent, static universals in some
kind of from–to demonstration (Aristotle: *apodeixis*), but by
analogy of shifting particular to shifting particular. Never in
deliberating (Aristotle: *bouleuesthai*) about what to say does the
speaker remove himself from the ongoing process and history of
speaking, of which he is a part, to an eidetic chart or schema of
what is occurring. As a child experiences trains, coming into
and leaving the station, from the platform and with no recourse
to a schedule, and sees each one as like the others but also as
new, so too for the native speaker familiar words come into play

anew each time and acquire additional senses on each occasion. Reasoning here proceeds, not by static rules, but from what was similar on previous occasions for using the word to what is new and different here and now. As we will see, reasoning here is like the judge's reliance on precedent that is guided not by intellection (*nous*) of unchanging essences, but by perception (*aisthēsis*) of particulars and the special prudence (*phronēsis*) of jurisprudence (*dikastē phronēsis*). (See WM 301).

And something of this same kind of knowing also seems to be present in MacIntyre's account of ethical reasoning, at least as it occurs in Homer. Here (WJWR 12ff.) MacIntyre seems to find the same *Sittlichkeit* Hegel does, the same continuing to be under way within an ongoing event with recourse not to any transcendent universal truths, but only to a particular truth from time out of mind to be concretized each time anew. With regard to Homer's protagonists MacIntyre writes:

> Thinking well (*eu phronein*) or soundly (*saophronein*) is a matter of reminding oneself or another of what *aretē* and *dikē* require. . . . He [Odysseus] conducts a dialogue with himself or rather with his *thumos*. . . . Odysseus reminds himself, or rather his *thumos*, of what he knows: whoever is *agathos* as a warrior, rather than *kakos*, stands fast; and it would be natural enough for us to say of him that he gives himself a reason for acting as he does. But this could be misleading if it suggested that Homer was ascribing to Odysseus a process of reasoning. Odysseus makes no inferences. What he does is to call to mind what he knows in order to counteract the effect upon his *thumos* of a disturbing passion, fear [WJWR 15–16],

and

> what is required of one in one's role is to give what is due to those others occupying roles that stand in determinate relation to one's own, king to kinsman or subject, swineherd to master or fellow servant, wife to husband and other kin, host to stranger and so on . . . [WJWR 20].

Contrary to MacIntyre I would argue that there is indeed reasoning here—the reasoning of deliberation or taking counsel with oneself—but I agree that the model of inference does not fit. Odysseus does not say, All A are B, this is an A, therefore B. Rather he brings to mind, reminds himself of, the obligations of *aretē* and *dikē* his warrior role enjoins; he brings to mind more clearly what he always already knew as a participant in a tradition from time out of mind. MacIntyre stresses that he thinks in this way to counteract a "disturbing fear," and that the dialogue is between himself and his distracting *thumos*. That is surely true. But to say that this is all that occurs is unnecessarily reductive. There is also *bouleuesthai* in his dialogue, a taking counsel with himself about something that could go one way or the other and that is "susceptible of being otherwise," as Aristotle says of the proper matters for *bouleuesthai* (EN 1139A 5ff.). This is not to say that there is demonstration here or *apodeixis*. MacIntyre is right in saying that for Odysseus any syllogistic demonstration is subsequent and concerns only the means to attain what deliberation had already revealed to be the *telos* or good (WJWR 19). For in the deliberation itself Odysseus does not remove himself from the occasion in order to view it in the light of transcendent universal principles and to reason from them to the particular situation in which he happens to find himself. Rather, he reminds himself of what it has meant previously to be a warrior and to stand fast and extends these meanings to his present circumstance. He reckons (Aristotle: *logizetai*) what to do now by analogy with precedents in the past. Let us say with Gadamer that he *reaches an understanding* of what it means to be a warrior now by *interpreting* it again and anew for the present occasion.

It should be re-emphasized that this kind of reasoning cannot be taught in the way, let us say, that mathematics can be, for it makes no use of teachable universal forms to be applied to particular circumstances. For example, a judge in adjudicating in the Anglo-American legal tradition knows how to reckon by precedent in a way that a later judge in that tradition will find reckonable when availing himself of the first judge's reasoning as a precedent for his own reasoning. Or a speaker in a language knows how to extend the usage of a word metaphorically in a way that another speaker would find comprehensible in further extending that usage himself. But neither of these could provide an outsider to their traditions, judicial and linguistic, with a "form" that would enable him just to join in and "go on and go further" by himself. Only long practice, at first guided in apprenticeship with experienced judges or native speakers, would make this extension possible. (Hence, MacIntyre rightly distinguishes between phrasebook knowledge of a language and a "second first language" that can be acquired only by living in a culture for a certain length of time [WJWR 374].)

However, it is an indication of the ascendancy of analytical philosophy and its "external reflection" in MacIntyre that in the end he does not recognize the unteachability of deliberative reasoning that has no static logic to be taught in distinction from demonstrative reasoning that does. For not only the subsequent demonstrative reasoning about means to the end, but also Odysseus' deliberations themselves would seem in MacIntyre to have some sort of static form, even if not that of syllogistic logic. "Central to every culture," he says,

> is a shared schema of greater or lesser complexity by means of which each agent is able to render the actions of others intelligible so that he or she knows how to respond to them. This schema is not necessarily ever explicitly articulated by agents themselves, and even when it is so articulated, they may make mistakes and misunderstand what it is that they do in understanding others. But an external observer, particularly one coming from an alien culture, cannot hope to understand action and transaction except in terms of such an interpretative schema [WJWR 22].

Of particular interest here is MacIntyre's conflation of the thinking of the "external observer" with the thinking of the participant in a culture. Here, in contrast to what he says later about native speakers, *both* participant and external observer are said to have recourse to an interpretive schema, the only difference being that in the case of the participant it is not always an explicit one. In this conflation, I would contend, MacIntyre persists in the stance of external reflection, and he even projects that stance upon all ethical reasoners. His conception of their "rationality" is the conception of analytical philosophy.

Of course, it seems at first glance that in stressing different rationalities *Whose Justice? Which Rationality?* would in fact develop an account of the special nature of deliberative reasoning prior to its subsumption in Spinoza under the demonstrative reasoning *more geometrico* of external reflection, that it would elaborate, so to speak, an ethical epistemology or even several ethical epistemologies. Unfortunately, however, MacIntyre consistently confuses ethical reasoning with the Enlightenment's autonomous demonstrative reasoning, confuses it, that is to say, with what Hegel has termed Morality. He thereby abandons any effort to give us an account of the process of ethical understanding and interpretation, such as we find these displayed in Homer, for instance. He passes over their special epistemology in order to get at the reasoning, not of a participant under way in truths from time out of mind, but of an "agent" concerning what he or she is to do.

Consequently, the versions of reasoning he does expatiate upon (not Homer's but Aristotle's, Augustine's, Aquinas', and Hume's) all turn out on his reading to be variations on the logic of *apodeixis* from premises to a conclusion. The variation is not the kind of reasoning but only the different content to be inserted in the premises and conclusions:

> In some ancient and medieval accounts the agent reasons from premises about what the good for agents of his or her kind is, conjoined with premises about his or her situation, to conclusions which are actions; in some modern accounts the agent reasons from premises about what he or she wants, conjoined with

premises about how what he or she wants is to be obtained, to conclusions which are decisions or intentions to act in a particular way; and in some early modern accounts the agent, motivated to satisfy some desire, selects according to some rational criterion an action as a means to the satisfaction of that desire [WJWR 20].

The argument here is strongly reminscent of Rorty, who maintains that not attainment of universal truth but rather internal consistency and coherence of arguments from contingent truths to variable conclusions must be the criterion of acceptability.

Despite himself, then, MacIntyre remains very much in the post-analytic, neo-pragmatist tradition and not at all in the Aristotelian tradition he chooses in *After Virtue* or the Augustinian tradition he says he is in in *Whose Justice? Which Rationality?* (p. 19). When MacIntyre speaks of "socially embodied" as opposed to "socially disembodied" reason (WJWR 398), he is not, it turns out, distinguishing between reasoning that is under way within a tradition of truths from time out of mind and the very different kind of external, formal reasoning that retrospectively establishes the formal pattern of what is analyzes. He is simply saying that to understand any application of that formal pattern, which he assumes to be constant from society to society, we must acknowledge the contingency and variation in its content from society to society.

Intriguing—even tantalizing—in this regard is his treatment of dialectic, for here too MacIntyre appears to be on the verge of getting behind apodictic reasoning to something like the dialogical process of taking counsel in which an understanding is reached. After all, *dialegesthai*, from which dialectic derives, means talking something through or out (*dia*) in order to reach an agreement. In Gadamer's language it is *Sichverständigen* or making ourselves clear and reaching an understanding. This is a process that is guided by *Verständnis* or the understanding someone has for another's point of view, and that ends in *Sichverstehen*, our understanding one another in some matter.

But at this point the peculiarly litigious quality of the analytical philosophy out of which MacIntyre writes (Rorty: today's analytical philosophers might best have become lawyers) wreaks its havoc. For though the model is supposed to be conversation (WJWR 398) (Gadamer: *Gespräch*), it is in fact advocacy and contention.

There are, MacIntyre tells us, two ways of arriving at the *archai* or starting points from which we may then proceed to demonstrate consequences. One is *epagōgē* or induction and the other is dialectic or "that process in which a particular thesis or theory justifies itself over against its rivals through its superior ability in withstanding the most cogent objections from different points of view" (WJWR 91). As opposed to a dialogical getting clear about what something means for us here and now, as opposed, that is, to a *dialegesthai* that goes hand in hand with *bouleuesthai*, dialectic emerges in MacIntyre as the adversarial contest and clash in which one "claim" "emerges victorious" over the "challenges" of its "rivals."

To be sure, in *Whose Justice? Which Rationality?* MacIntyre often speaks of "enquiry" in conjunction with the kind of reasoning he assigns to dialectic, and he is right to do so, for in the end talking something through is surely more asking questions successfully than successfully defending claims. But MacIntyre's polemical language of law courts, contest, and war subverts this insight and throws discursive investigation back into sophistic refutation. Inquiry is obliterated insofar as questions are perceived as challenges and what might have been a process of shared discovery devolves into assertion and counter-assertion, one to be the victor, the other the vanquished. In this version of dialectic there is no understanding shown and no understanding reached. (See WJWR 118 and Chapter 20, "Contested Justices, Contested Rationalities," pp. 389ff., which concludes MacIntyre's exposition.)

Hence, MacIntyre is surely right when he points out that what would be shared in genuine deliberation and talking something through would not be "universal standards of rationality"

(WJWR 400) but rather a particular language and tradition. But neither would it be language and tradition that we autonomously choose because it provides the "best answer to be proposed so far" (WJWR 358). Instead it would be a language and tradition in which we discover ourselves to have always already been under way—as MacIntyre himself at other times seems to recognize. For we cannot answer questions about "justice and practical rationality," he says, "from a standpoint external to all tradition," and the way we do answer these questions "will depend in key part upon what the language is which we share with those together with whom we ask them questions and to what point the history of our own linguistic community has brought us" (WJWR 369). Again, MacIntyre comes tantalizingly close to Gadamer's *Verstehen* with the "authority" of tradition (WM 261ff.) when he writes (WJWR 394) of the "shock of recognition" we have when we encounter "seminal texts" of our own tradition and say "*this* is not only . . . what I now take to be true but in some measure what I *have always taken to be true*" (emphasis added). And when MacIntyre speaks in the same place of the "imagination whereby the individual is able to place him- or herself imaginatively within the scheme of belief *inhabited* by those whose allegiance is to the rival tradition" (WJWR 394; emphasis added), surely this is indeed what Gadamer, building upon Aristotle's *synesis*, calls *Verständnis* (WM 306).

But in this last quotation the fundamental error that blocks MacIntyre's insight and perpetuates the prejudices of the Enlightenment intrudes. For in effect he has split apart two simultaneous *momenta* of the same thing, *Verstehen* and *Verständnis*, creating the appearance that I would first find myself in the language shared with my friends and then alienate myself into the language of my "rivals." This is to presuppose that there is a chasm between myself and the other and that what is foreign must be inimical. It is to presuppose that "[t]he multiplicity of traditions does not afford a multiplicity of perspectives among which we can move, but a multiplicity of antagonistic commit-ments, between which only conflict, rational or nonrational, is possible" (WJWR 368). But in fact self-recognition always emerges in the encounter with what is at first foreign too. As an interpreter and translator of what another says to me—and when, if I want to understand, do I ever cease to be these things?—I do not become some sort of spy who, all the while plotting my return to the homeland, temporarily dons the linguistic garb of the enemy so that I can see how he does things and smuggle out what might be useful to me back home. On the contrary, in interpretation and translation the horizons of my world and the horizons of the other's world come to overlap, to fuse, and what was just mine and just his becomes ours. (See Gadamer on *Horizontverschmelzung* [WM 289ff.].) Hence it is mistaken to divorce understanding something said to me in my own language from translating something from a foreign language in the way MacIntyre divorces them.

Whenever anyone says something to me and I do not entirely understand it, it becomes our task to get clear about what was meant. The process of reaching an understanding is the process of carrying over what he has said into what I am saying and carrying over what I have said into what he is saying, so that in the end our talking something out and running it through is a running-together of my world and his in what has become a shared sense or *sensus communis* (WM 16ff.). Thus, though the balance between them shifts as understanding grows, the familiar and the foreign are always concomitant. Recognition of oneself in an other presupposes the initial otherness of that other. In reaching any understanding, what was foreign to begin with then becomes familiar.

MacIntyre, it turns out, misconstrues dialectic as a kind of solving problems or resolving incoherencies and inconsistencies in a given interpretive schema. He construes it, in other words, in the language of a post-analytical neo-pragmatism where the later Wittgenstein is phasing into Quine *et alii*. Thus he speaks of "inadequacies" and "discrepancies" (WJWR 358) between "intelligent thought" or "mind" and its "objects," namely, "the realities of the social and rational world" (WJWR 356). "Mind," he tells us, is taken to be "activity," to be "mind as engaging with the natural and social world in such activities as identification, reidentification, collecting, separating, classifying, and naming and all this by touching, grasping, pointing, breaking down, building up, calling to, answering to, and so on" (WJWR 356). And such "mind" is "adequate to its objects insofar as the expectations which it frames on the basis of these activities are not liable to disappointment" (WJWR 356). When expectations are not met, we have inadequacies and, if these unfulfilled expectations are in regard to central theses in the "scheme of belief," we have an "epistemological crisis."

Here is where dialectic, as MacIntyre conceives of it, comes in: it is only by entertaining the most substantive challenges and objections and by advancing in response to them the "best answer to be proposed so far" that the epistemological crisis is to be overcome. In this way—by the "invention or discovery of new concepts and the framing of some new type or types of theory" (WJWR 362)—we will arrive at a scheme of revised first principles (*archai*) that "have, by surviving the process of dialectical questioning, vindicated themselves as superior to their historical predecessors" (WJWR 360).

Characteristically this invention or discovery is seen, not as our shared coming across or shared uncovering of something already there, but as the spontaneous creativity of an agent in contending with his or her own inconsistencies and incoherences. In this process the "other" serves only as a prod by posing the most challenging questions possible. Hence, there is no reason to speak of understanding here, either of understanding shown for someone else or of reaching and understanding with someone else. "Mind" here is more Cartesian and consciousness more solipsistic than MacIntyre allows it is.

Consequently, MacIntyre also remains more of a "perspectivist" than he allows. Perspectivists, he tells us, "suppose that one could temporarily adopt the standpoint of a tradition and then exchange it for another, as one might wear first one costume and then another" (WJWR 367), and perspectivism, "like relativism, is a doctrine only possible for those who regard themselves as outsiders" (WJWR 368). All this is lamentable *anomie*, he maintains. But has he himself escaped it? What tradition is his own book written out of? What is its "shared language"? Where has his "linguistic community" brought him? He suggests that he has now, or perhaps even before, come to the point at which "it is no longer possible to speak except out of one particular tradition in a way which will involve conflict with rival traditions" (WJWR 401). But was it ever possible? What language was he speaking in before? And were he to continue, he says, he would have to begin writing out of an Aristotelian, Augustinian, Thomistic, Humean, or some other tradition. He submits that in his case it would be the Augustinian (WJWR 10). But is he free to choose? If so, he would be a perspectivist after all. If not, he would have always found himself already under way in the language of Augustinian Christianity and could not just voluntarily switch to it beginning with his next book. And surely his language has not been not Augustinian except perhaps as a most distant of descendants now scarcely recognizable as such.

No, the immediate lineage is much clearer. With its talk of rationality and his critique of authority, MacIntyre's language reveals itself, despite his invocation of tradition, to be the direct descendant of the Enlightment and a fusion of, among others of its children, Kant (in translation), J. S. Mill, Wittgenstein (in translation), and Dewey. Either he falls back into perspectivism or he admits this. His dilemma is like that of the liberal thinkers whose pretensions he so brilliantly exposes. When their illusion of universal truth is shattered, either they must yield to perspectivism and *anomie* as the upshot of their external reflection or they must acknowledge that they are not tradition-free after all but participants in a tradition that they have not chosen and in which they already find themselves under way. In the end it is the word rationality that gives away the tradition MacIntyre participates in. Used in the way it is in his work, it implies that nothing is to be accepted for which we cannot find a reason, a *rational* justification. *Nihil est sine ratione.* Nothing is to be taken on authority; everything must be brought before the court of reason. So MacIntyre, like Mill, speaks of a first stage of society "in which the beliefs, utterances, texts, and persons taken to be authoritative are deferred to unquestioningly" (WJWR 354) and which is to be surpassed in a stage of dialectical, critical "revaluation of authorities" (WJWR 355). For in an epistemological crisis the "weakest form of argument . . . will be the appeal to the authority of established belief, merely as established" (WJWR 359). Even the justification for a belief, even the reason itself, it seems, will have to be given a reason— ad infinitum.

But for everything to be brought before the court of reason in this way, for everything thus to be brought to mind, mind would have to have excerpted itself from its setting in the tradition of things that are given to it from time out of mind by the authority of tradition. And this it cannot do, though it is the fallacy of Enlightenment liberalism to think that it can, a fallacy that MacIntyre repeats. In the end, his attempt to find a "rationality of traditions" is self-contradictory, and hence we must see if there is another rehabilitation of tradition besides MacIntyre's, one that speaks not of its rationality but of its authority and hence not of reason but of understanding. Here inquiry, seeking, a quest, would indeed replace advocacy, cross-examination, refutation, and contention. Though it is Gadamer and not Augustine we will turn to, Augustine might have helped us as he might have helped MacIntyre had he really learned to "go on and go further" in his language. The beginning of Augustine's *Confessions*, for instance, displays precisely the structure of dialectical deliberation that we are looking for: with faith in what is given by authority—in this case, the preacher of the word—Augustine seeks, in questioning, understanding of what has been said for him to hear. "Nisi credideritis non intelligetis": If you have not already believed, you will not understand.

4. Gadamer's Modified Hegelianism as a Way Beyond the Impasse

Viewed in regard to his overall project, the picture I have given up to now of Hegel's thinking on *Sittlichkeit* and ethical understanding (*sittliches Verstehen*) is, of course, incomplete. For Hegel would in fact transcend both *Sittlichkeit* and Morality in an absolute knowing, which, having begun with *Sittlichkeit* and having passed through the loss of it in Morality, synthesizes both in a higher form of consciousness no longer flawed by the naïveté and "immediacy" of *Sittlichkeit* and the abstraction of Morality. Viewed within Hegel's entire system, *Sittlichkeit* emerges as simply inexperienced, which is to say that it has not yet suffered its own inevitable dissolution and negation and has not been through the "hard work of negativity" that awaits it. Only absolute knowledge, which has put this "hard work" behind it, can count as stable. Thus Kant is not in any sense "wrong" in Hegel's eyes, for precisely his Morality, though partial and inadequate too, provides the necessary "mediation" of immediate *Sittlichkeit*. To Hegel, Morality, if viewed in one way, is an abstraction from *Sittlichkeit* and "before" it. But if viewed in another, it represents an irreversible advance beyond *Sittlichkeit* insofar as it is a further stage on the way to an experienced, absolute knowing, fully confident of itself (*selbstbewusst*).

But suppose that while availing ourselves of Hegel's critique of external reasoning and his juxtaposition of *Sittlichkeit* and Morality we were to suspend his overall project, and suppose that, accordingly, we were to suspend the dialectical method he uses to propel us from *Sittlichkeit* through Morality to Absolute Knowledge. Suppose, in other words, that we were to place the whole idea of Absolute Knowledge into question, as Gadamer does, and to ask if such knowing really exists for human beings, who are in fact never absolved from the contingencies and limitations of their particular perspectives. What would result then, I suggest, is a discursive, *un*systematic thinking appropriate for the finite human being, the human being, that is, that Gadamer maintains we are and will always remain. And for such a finite human being *Sittlichkeit* and Morality, *Sittlichkeit* and Civil Society, cannot be viewed from some absolute vantage point from which they might methodically be demonstrated to be logically connected stages, both leading necessarily beyond themselves in the self-unfolding of a systematically unified entirety, namely, Hegel's "whole" (*das Ganze*). Rather, since we are participants *in* the whole that always transcends any of the limited insights of which we are capable, *Sittlichkeit* and Morality can be interpreted only as partial shadings, concomitant and often even conflicting aspects of human social existence, and our finite understanding of them could never surpass the dialectical tension between them in some sort of total comprehension transcending them both. If we were to make this finite understanding, as opposed to Hegel's Absolute Knowledge, our starting point, what we would have, I suggest, is something very close to Gadamer's "hermeneutical" approach.

I say "approach," not "method," for as I have indicated in the Introduction, the predominant modern understanding of method is essentially Cartesian and emphasizes clearly secured, certain insights as starting points (*principia*) and rigorous inference from these. Consequently, it tends to de-emphasize the ongoing and unending process of moving toward these insights and neglects the *hodos* or the "way" to something, which the Greek word *methodos* contains and which would make "approach" perhaps the best translation of it. In ethics, however, a conception of method seems called for in which the Cartesian emphasis would be reversed—not clear and distinct starting points would be stressed, for in ethical reasoning these, as we have seen, are unattainable, but rather the way to the truth, the approach on which we continue to find ourselves under way to ever more inconclusive answers. Inquiry would be given priority over inference; and the question, priority over any answer (see WM 344ff.).

With that we have come to the heart of Gadamer's philosophical enterprise and perhaps the most appropriate place to begin our consideration of its ethical–philosophical implications: the question, namely, of what different kinds of truth there are, and what different kinds of method are appropriate for getting at them—the question, in short, of truth and method, which, I think, MacIntyre fails to address sufficiently. Insofar as it introduced a distinction between the Cartesian method suitable for mathematics and the immanent dialectical self-exposition of the subject matter appropriate for philosophy, Hegel's critique of external reasoning has already highlighted the issue for us of how a particular subject matter is to be approached. But as valuable a step as Hegel's distinction is, Gadamer shows it to be insufficient. We must look further, then, if we are really to get clear about the difference between mathematical knowing and practical knowing, between methodical, systematic understanding and ethical understanding, and if we are to assess properly both the usefulness and the inadequacy of Hegel for specifying the nature of ethical understanding.

Indeed, more than anything in Hegel Gadamer finds Book VI of Aristotle's *Nicomachean Ethics* to be the paradigmatic text for anyone who would undertake an inquiry into the different kinds of understanding (see WM 295ff., "The Hermeneutical Relevance of Aristotle"). For there Aristotle points out explicitly how knowledge of the right thing to do, ethical reasonableness or *phronēsis*, is to be distinguished from scientific knowledge, *epistēmē*, on the one hand, and from knowledge of how to make something, *technē*, on the other. These three are shown to be different in regard to both the kind of reality or truth in relation to which they stand and the way or method one might use to get at that truth (*alētheuein*). To be sure, Gadamer's treatment of these Aristotelian distinctions ultimately aims at extending Aristotle's inquiry beyond these three. He sets about specifying the reality or truth of the artwork and the written text, and his overall task is to elaborate a method for approaching this reality, that is to say, a hermeneutical method or method of interpretation; he intends, in other words, to extend Aristotle's differentiations to yet a fourth kind of entity and to our special kind of understanding of it. But since our concern here is with precisely one of the three forms of knowing which Aristotle does treat, with *phronēsis* or ethical understanding, we need go no further than the *Nicomachean Ethics* does in raising the question concerning truth and method. Just what are the distinctions Aristotle makes? Relying on Gadamer's exposition in *Truth and Method* of Book VI of Aristotle's *Nicomachean Ethics* (WM 295ff.), let us clarify them.

Epistēmē, or scientific knowing, in Aristotle, Gadamer points out, is defined by the fact that the reality or truth it knows cannot be other than it is. Simply put: that reality is constant, always the same, and never was or will be different from what it is. For example, a geometrical figure, a square, in the pure abstract sense in which the geometrician knows it, never was not yet a square and never will no longer be one. Nor can it be square in one respect but not square in another. It is what it is, *ti estin*, constantly, purely, and perfectly. As is obvious, we are dealing here not with any physical square that a carpenter might make, but with a mathematical noetic reality, a truth known by pure intellection or *nous*, as Aristotle calls it. This is not the place to establish the finer nuances of Aristotle's Greek understanding of *nous*, which as a sort of direct "sensing of things" or *aisthēsis* implies a different disposition of the knower to what is known from that found in the Latin translation of the Greek *nous* and *epistēmē* into *intellectus* and *scientia* and, with yet further modifications at the end of Medieval philosophy, into the *res cogitans* of Descartes and the methodical knowledge of the objects of its thought. Whatever shifts might have occurred here, the mathematical model remains pervasive. And this fact makes clear what the appropriate method must be: a clear and distinct insight (Plato: *mathēma*) must be had into first principles, an insight that is known, not just believed or ventured as an opinion. And giving an account of one's knowledge, giving reasons in justification of it (*logon didonai*), means leading back (*epagōgē*) to what can be known in this clear and distinct way, and, conversely, in starting from it, showing, demonstrating, whatever is to be accounted for (*apodeixis*). The method or "way" of science to its truths consists in this back and forth to and from fundamental, invariable certainties.

In *technē*, on the other hand, we are dealing with a reality that did indeed not exist before and that need not necessarily be what it is or, for that matter, even have existed at all. The artifact that the *technitēs* or artisan brings into being could always have turned out differently from the way it happened to. Here, accordingly, we are dealing, not with something that necessarily and constantly is what it is, but rather with a *gignesthai*, a contingent coming-into-being at some particular time and place in the physical world. Carpenters, to be sure, know how to make square things, and to that extent they have insight into what it is to be "square," insight into the *ti estin* of "square," insight into "square" in the abstract. But their knowledge does not consist in that insight alone or even primarily. It is worthwhile in this regard to compare the *Nicomachean Ethics* on the difference between a carpenter's and a geometrician's knowledge of a right angle (EN 1098A 28ff.), a difference brought home to anybody who, lacking all experience, would rely exclusively upon the "theoretical" instruction manual when trying to build something from a kit. Carpenters, since their concern is with producing a square thing here and now, must have a "feel" for the particular circumstances and the peculiarities of the material with which they have to work at a given time. Hence, their understanding of how to make something is in large part a matter of practice, of having the "feel" of it and knowing how to make the right adjustments. The reasons a carpenter gives are, consequently, largely pragmatic: "If that is what you want to do, this is the way it is done; this is the best way to do it." "Try it yourself, following my example, and you'll see"—where "seeing" or knowledge here means getting the hang of it.

Of course, this knowledge can be taught and learned too, but plainly not in the way mathematics is taught and learned. Someone who has a feel for wood and who, knowing how to adjust the material wooden components, succeeds in building a square thing has a very different knowledge and method from someone who sets about "constructing" the double area of whatever is square, of what is "square" in the abstract, on the diagonal. Construction in geometry is precisely not building, though the slave in Plato's *Meno* who is given just this problem of doubling the area of a square starts off thinking of it that way. In his first attempts he does indeed try to build the double area as if the problem were the technical–pragmatic one of hitting on the right means to succeed (see *Meno* 82Aff.). In the manner of a *technitēs* he tries out various extensions of the side—doubling it, extending it half again as much—to see if these will work. None of them does, but the fact that he is not successful is irrelevant since here the actual problem is precisely not pragmatic–technical but noetical–mathematical, and his initial "method" is consequently misplaced. The task Socrates gives him is to recognize the abstract relationships governing what a "square," its "diagonal," and "double" are conceptually and universally. If, on the other hand, his problem had been how to make a square thing twice the size, his success or failure in finding the right means would indeed be crucial; as Aristotle puts it (EN 1140A 20) and Gadamer underscores (WM 299), in contrast to *epistēmē*, *technē* loves *tychē* (chance success) and *tychē* loves *technē*.

Obviously, with *technē* we have come a lot closer to ethical knowing, or *phronēsis*. Neither ethical reasoning nor *technē* proceeds by inferring logical conclusions *more geometrico* from clear and distinct, fixed starting points, that is, from principles that would be available to a mathematical intelligence removed from any situational contingency. Rather, while under way within tacitly accepted presuppositions that are not explicitly brought to mind, ethical reasoning too "hits"—like an experienced archer—upon what is seemly and fitting given the peculiarities of the occasion. And somehow one has the sense that if one mastered the scientific "typical pattern of moral reasoning" that Frankena proposes, for instance, it would be about as useful in making ethical decisions as mastery of geometry would be in building a tool shed, and that Aristotle is right when he says that long apprenticeship in "how it's supposed to be done" is indispensable in matters both of *technē* and of *phronēsis*. But Gadamer, building upon Aristotle's analysis, establishes important differences here, which it is now our task to make clear.

Technē and *phronēsis* are alike, to be sure, insofar as both, unlike *epistēmē*, have to do with things that might be other than they are, things that might or might not exist; *phronēsis* has as its object, so to speak, a choice or *prohairesis*, that is, a giving-preference to one thing over another, and by definition choice implies that things "could go one way or another." That might be said of the choices of means that the *technitēs* makes too. And again, as in *technē*, *phronēsis* as knowledge of the right thing to do is dependent upon the peculiarities of the particular stituation and requires the ability to "size them up" properly. Just such an ability is no doubt part of what Aristotle has in mind when he says that an ethical decision ultimately depends upon the perception (*aisthēsis*) of the one who has to make it (EN 1109b 23). But despite these similarities, the two are actually not at all the same. As applied science, *technē* remains far closer to *epistēmē* than *phronēsis* does, for the carpenter who builds something square is still guided by the fixed idea of what "square" is, its *ti estin*, even if the end product inevitably falls short of the ideal. But in the realm of *phronēsis*, the realm of ethical choices, there is precisely nothing fixed in this way. There is no "idea of the Good."

It is to make just this point, according to Gadamer, that Aristotle draws an analogy here to transactions in the market place where the measure, say a cord of wood, quite legitimately varies depending on whether the one selling or the one buying is doing the measuring—varies, that is, within limits that provide the basis for the understanding that is finally reached. At the start the only thing that can be established is what would be beyond the pale, what would be the outright "extremes" that decency and honesty prohibit. (One wood dealer I know informed me at the beginning of our dealings that a cord would be 128 cubic feet so stacked that a squirrel could get through it, but the cat chasing it could not.[19]) Obviously the "method" of arriving at knowledge, or, better said, understanding, of what is right here is unique and unlike the method of either *epistēmē* or *technē*. For one thing, both of these presuppose that I can put myself at a distance from what I am working with, that is, that I can objectify it. But in reaching an understanding with others, in this case striking a bargain, or, more generally, in reaching an understanding with others or myself about what is right, neither the others nor I am in a position to objectify what is under discussion. For the understanding here will be reached *within* a language in which we are always already under way and which is in fact constitutive of the self I take myself to be and of the consensus with others with whom I happen to live. Gadamer's way of putting this is to say that objectification is impossible here because we are in fact embedded in, and "belong to," the thing that concerns us (cf. WM 297 on *Zugehörigkeit*).

Furthermore, though it has often been debated,[20] *phronēsis* is not just the successful choice of means that the *Nicomachean Ethics* sometimes might lead one to believe it is (e.g., EN 1144A 8ff.):

> Aristotle emphasizes that in general *phronēsis* is concerned with the means, *ta pros to telos* [what contributes to the end], and not with the *telos* [end] itself. It is probably his opposition to Plato's doctrine of the idea of the good that leads him to stress this point in the way he does. But that *phronēsis* is no mere capability of choosing the right means, but is instead an ethical [*sittliche*] *hexis* [disposition] that has the end in mind too, is made unequivocally clear by its place within the system of Aristotle's ethics. Cf. in particular EN Zeta 10 1142B 33, 1140B 13, and 1141B 15 [WM 304].

Gadamer reinforces this argument by pointing out that if *phronēsis* were indeed concerned merely with means, it would make no sense to distinguish it as Aristotle does from *deinotēs* or mere adroitness in finding the right means to any end whatsoever, good or bad (see EN 1144A 24ff. and IGPAP 165–66).

Again the key to the distinction here is that I stand in a completely different relationship to the choices I have to make when they are ethical from my relationship to my choices when they are pragmatic–technical. In the latter case, I myself am not a part of the material I have to deal with and not a part of the product I wish to make. This detachment of "standing back," as it were, makes it possible for me to learn a *technē*, to learn "how it's done," in some course of instruction that simply transmits know-how. But in making ethical choices I am elaborating, not some thing, some object, but a tradition constitutive of the very self that I am and always already was. And, consequently, learning and teaching here, if they are possible at all, are a very different and impenetrable sort of thing—as Plato's *Protagoras* and *Meno* make all too clear. If *technē* is exemplary, any learning means acquiring knowledge that I did not *have* before. But if that is so, in ethical matters I actually do not learn at all; rather I remember, recall, what I already know, the tradition of which I have always *been* a part. In short, I recall what I *am*. (See Chapter 2, Part 4 on Plato's doctrine of *anamnesis*.) Hence the knowledge that allows me to choose the means to the good here is simultaneously foreknowledge (Gadamer: *Vorwissen*) of the good or end, knowledge of the good in which I always already participate.

MacIntyre, it will be recalled, makes essentially the same point in his discussion of the practical syllogism insofar as he stresses the inexplicit dimension of any ethical reasoning, its unquestioned presuppositions;[21] and herein lies the fundamental and clear difference between his and Frankena's interpretation of the practical syllogism. But precisely this distinction between *technē*'s practical choices and *phronēsis*' ethical ones makes MacIntyre's eventual fusion of pragmatism and ethics suspect: MacIntyre's appropriation of Aristotle's ethics as the "best to date" is strikingly like the detached choice a *technitēs* might make concerning, not his self-effectuation, but the effectuation of an artifact of which he himself is not a part. In turning to pragmatism as a way beyond analytical moral philosophy, MacIntyre, it would seem, ends up conflating the distinct methods of *technē* and *phronēsis*.

Indeed, MacIntyre fails to distinguish sufficiently among all three of the ways we have considered here of standing in relationship to a truth, to distinguish, that is, not only between *technē* and *phronēsis* but between each of these and *epistēmē*. *Phronēsis*, he says, is the conjoint actualization of four other faculties: first, of characterizing the particular situation in which one finds oneself; second, of attaining by *epagōgē* and dialectic to first principles for moral reasoning, i.e., to an "adequate concept of the good as such"; third, of understanding oneself and one's role as a participant in a social whole; and, fourth, of reasoning from the general to the particular (WJWR 125–26). *Phronēsis* may also be defined, he says, as *epistēmē*, or knowledge of arguments, plus knowledge of particulars (WJWR 92), and it can go wrong, accordingly, in lacking either knowledge of universals or acquaintanceship with particulars. Direct intuition or *nous* figures on both sides insofar as it apprehends both the unchanging and primary universals from which reasoning will proceed and the irreducible particulars.

Now, in reality this account fits *technē* better than it fits *phronēsis*. For it will be recalled that in *technē* a universal form must be envisioned and then the means found to actualize it in the particular circumstances. Theoretical or epistemic knowing is thus necessary in *technē* although it is not sufficient since familiarity with the singular nature of that wherein the form is to be realized is also required. And clearly in *technē*, though not so clearly in *phronēsis*, error results from either deficient knowledge of the universal form or deficient acquaintanceship with the particular matter at hand. And in regard to the four faculties it is again *technē* rather than *phronēsis* that they seem most adequately to define. The *technitēs* who produces something, be it shoes, ships, or health, must have the knowledge of how to characterize the particular case or problem, must have had some education in the theoretical discipline of ascertaining the universal forms of what it is that is to be produced (as the carpenter must know geometry), must have a sense of how his calling and production fit into the overall enterprise or "practice" of his society, whose goals, we should note here, are not in question for him, and must know how to reason from general principles to particulars. So how, then, would *phronēsis* differ from *technē* on MacIntyre's account?

To be sure, MacIntyre makes a good start in answer to this question by stressing the importance of *epieikeia* for *dikastē phronēsis* or jurisprudence and in fact for *phronēsis* and prudence generally (WJWR 119–21; compare WM 301–302). *Epieikeia* is clearly not a faculty involved in *technē* and its problem-solving. It has to do only with practical reason and the choice of actions and not at all with productive reason and the choice of means to an external end. *Epieikeia*, MacIntyre maintains, means not so much equity as reasonableness, and, far more than "equitable," the adjective *epieikēs* can even mean "good" (EN 1137b 1). *Epieikeia* comes into play where the law does not cover the special case and therefore must be emended. Hence Aristotle speaks in this regard of an *epanorthōma nomou* or rectification of the law (EN 1137b 27). MacIntyre points out, however, that *epieikeia*'s application is not limited to law: "what the judge does in the case where he cannot simply follow and apply a rule provided by a legislator, but has to go beyond that rule in some way, exemplifies what more generally any *phronimos* must from time to time do, not only in order to be just but in order to exemplify any of the virtues adequately" (WJWR 120). Here, then, the *phronēsis* of the *phronimos* or ethically reasonable individual is precisely *not* the application of the general to the particular that MacIntyre had said *phronēsis* implied. Instead it seems to be very much like the power of productive judgment (Kant: *produktive Urteilskraft*) that we saw employed by the native speaker in "knowing how to go on and go further" in adding to the meaning of a word, and that, it will be recalled, is precisely what distinguishes his or her speaking from the *ars grammatica* or merely technical application of the rules of a language. (Compare Gadamer on Kant's *Urteilskraft* and jurisprudence, WM 35–38.)

But somehow this feature of *phronēsis* and *epieikeia* eludes MacIntyre, who, in seeking a translation of the latter passes over some important clues that the word itself gives us. It derives from *eikein* meaning to yield. Hence, the adjective, *epieikēs*, is said of one who can relent and "give way," and *epieikeia* is said to be the trait of one who does not exact the full measure of what is justly due him (compare *Magna Moralia* 1198B 29). Thus originally *epieikeia* means the opposite of legalistic overexactitude; it means clemency, mercy. This is why Aristotle, in coming the closest he ever does to Christian forgiveness of debts, can call the *epieikēs* man "good" and why one common German translation of *epieikeia* is "Gütigkeit." Far from being unyielding, the *epieikēs* man is kind. He does not press his case, an eye for an eye, a tooth for a tooth, but, as Gadamer puts it in his account of *epieikeia*, he "lets up" (*lässt nach*) (WM 301; see also HD 51 on *summum ius – summa iniuria*, "maximum justice – maximum injustice and harm"). As opposed to *akribeia* or exactitude, *epieikeia* is precisely not rigidly achering to the letter of the law, not being a "stickler" for the rules, but "giving way" and allowing one's general principles themselves to be called into question by the uniqueness of the particular case.

Having experienced the exceptionality of every particular case, the *epieikes* individual will see that the form of *ho orthos logos* or right reasoning and argument here can only be stated in a very loose outline. In matters of what is *kalos* and *dikaios*, fair and just, Aristotle tells us, we cannot expect a high level of *akribeia*, for in these there is great indeterminacy (*pollē planē*) (EN 1194B 15). This is to say that here the general principles must be left open and cannot be fixed or established. For to the extent that each new case is an exception to the rule as it has been defined until now, the rule must be adjusted to accommodate it. So the general principle, the good in general, is not static but develops as what it is in each new application of it. Its being or reality is the ongoing open-ended history of its interpretations and not something by itself separate (*chōristos*) from them. MacIntyre overlooks the fact that what he rightly characterizes as this "application of rules to instances, but which is not itself rule-governed" (WJWR 117) entails a kind of reasoning quite distinct from technical or productive reasoning concerning the application of established general rules to a particular problem.

Indeed, in what amounts to a fusion of *epistēmē*, *technē*, and *phronēsis*, he overrides a number of the crucial distinctions Aristotle makes among these kinds of reasoning. In the first place he fails to observe Aristotle's separation of demonstrative epistemic reasoning, which reasons from static, necessary first principles to what they entail, from calculative or deliberative reasoning (*logizesthai, bouleuesthai*), which concerns what is variable and susceptible of going either one way or the other (EN 1139A 3–16). The latter is special to *technē* and *phronēsis*. Since its subject matter, a choice of means or action, is not established as what it is, but is still in question, this *bouleuesthai* or taking counsel proceeds not by inference but by dialogue, by question and answer. Though MacIntyre often refers to "enquiry," he nevertheless makes no clear distinction between demonstrative *epistēmē* and interrogative *technē* and *phronēsis*. For the most part inquiry seems to be relegated in MacIntyre to what he calls dialectic, which is not so much dialogue as the adversarial testing of a thesis against its rivals in order to arrive at *epistēmē*'s first principles (WJWR 91). He acknowledges, to be sure, that Aristotle calls deliberation inquiry (*zetēsis*) (EN 1112B 12–13; WJWR 136), but ends up seeing deliberation as prior to the theoretical or epistemic reasoning from first principles that in turn precedes and combines with *phronēsis* as knowledge of particulars. Deliberation is thereby reduced in MacIntyre to attaining the major premise of the so-called practical syllogism (WJWR 130)—which makes it difficult to see why

Aristotle would say that it is guided by *phronēsis* (EN 1141B 8–11) and issues in choice (EN 1113A 9–13).

Having neglected the distinction between demonstrative *epistēmē* and interrogative *logizesthai* and *bouleuesthai*, MacIntyre goes on to neglect the distinction within *logizesthai* and *bouleuesthai* between productive reasoning that concerns making something and practical reasoning that concerns doing something (EN 1139B 2–6). In productive reasoning one reasons concerning the means to bring about the product one has envisioned. The end product or goal is thus pre-established, and, as we have noted, any error in the choice of means in the production of it will lead to a falling short of what was envisioned, to a deficiency in the actual product. The rational faculty that keeps such deficiencies to a minimum is *deinotēs* or inventiveness in finding the right means to achieve a pre-established end (EN 1144A 23ff.) We should emphasize that *deinotēs* is specifically characterized by Aristotle, in plain distinction from *phronēsis*, as amoral. If the pre-established end is good and noble, *kalos*, the choice of means will be too. If the end is bad, so will the choice of means be (EN 1144A 27–28). The end, however, is not a consideration for mere *deinotēs* and hence, as the word *deinos* (frightening) contained in it indicates, there is even something unsettling about it. *Deinotēs*, then, is the adjunct not of the ethical *phronēsis* but of *technē*.

Practical reason, in contrast, realizes an end not external, but internal, to itself (EN 1139B 2–6). For the end or good is the very activity of making good choices and is therefore achieved in the choosing itself, not by means of it. The adjunct of *phronēsis* that enables this enactment of the good end is thus not the value-free *deinotēs* or inventiveness but *euboulia*, well-advisedness, being of good counsel (EN 1142A 33ff.).

Now, this immanence of the end or good to the practical choice of an action implies an important difference in the structure of phronetic reasoning aided by *euboulia* from technical reason aided by *deinotēs*. For as opposed to *technē*, in *phronēsis* the general principle, in this case what is good, is not and cannot be pre-established. Rather, as we have seen, like the law in Anglo-American jurisprudence, it evolves in coordination with the changing situation. Thus not only the particular situation is variable and indeterminate, as it is in *technē*, but the general rule as well. What the good life is is defined anew in each enactment of it, in each choice of better over worse, noble over base, right over wrong.

Phronēsis's *euboulia* is thus not subsumption of a particular case under a static universal, but inquiry that seeks its answers in the *analogy* of precedent particular cases to the present particular case. As analogical it in fact reasons neither from universal to particular (*apodeixis*) nor from particular to universal (*epagōgē*) but from particular to particular. (Compare in this regard Aristotle's account of reasoning by example in the *Rhetoric* 1357B 25–30.) Thus *phronēsis* involves a very different faculty from either the second or the fourth of those that MacIntyre thought intrinsic to it, different from either that of reasoning to first principles or reasoning from them. For in finding the answer to the question posed in ethical deliberation, there is ultimately no recourse to any transcendent principle but only to particular decisions or choices that precede the present one. The "general principle" here is nothing in itself but only the analogousness of the cases to each other. (Compare in this regard Gadamer's analysis of the *kat' analogian* at EN 1096B 28, IGPAP 152ff.). Again, the good *is* the history of these choices, not something apart from them.

Hence, as we have also noted, unlike *technē* and its *deinotēs* where choices of means or solutions to problems can be inadequate because the pre-established end is only deficiently realized by them in the product and the product is therefore defective, in *phronēsis* and its *euboulia* choices can be good or bad, well- or ill-advised insofar as they add to the reality of our good life by further enacting it or seduce us into eventual *akratia* or powerlessness and ruin our *phronēsis*. The deficiency that results from a bad choice is not in the deed itself but in ourselves, in our capacity to do well the next time. Accordingly, the cardinal virtue is *sōphrosynē*, which is to say, "saving our *phronēsis*."

Insofar as syllogisms belong to demonstrative, not moral, reasoning, Aristotle's recourse to the so-called practical *syllogism* thus proves to be deceptive. For it makes it seem that practical reasoning is, after all, the demonstrative application of a fixed universal to a particular case and hence a matter more of *deinotēs* than of *euboulia*. MacIntyre is misled by precisely this appearance. In the practical syllogism the good is accepted as a given in the major premise, much as health is accepted as a given in the medical *technē*'s prescription of means to achieve it. As there is no deliberation about what health is in applied medicine—one does not deliberate about things that are fixed—so too there is no deliberation about what is good in a practical syllogism. In the minor premise it is established that the means to this good are available, and in the conclusion the agent avails himself of these means. So, to use MacIntyre's example (WJWR 140–41), a hockey player might reason that "Given that it is good for the team to score a goal [major premise] and having perceived that in this case my teammate is in better position to score [minor premise], I pass the puck [conclusion]." Note that there is no question in his mind about whether it is well-advised and good counsel to score. Put another way: *epieikeia* has no place here, for the general principle that it is good to score is seen to be in no need of interpretation or adjustment for these circumstances.

Now, we should note that Aristotle's examples of the practical syllogism are all alike in this and consequently are not illustrations of *euboulia* at all: Sweet food is not good for me, i.e., is not conducive to the pre-established and unquestioned good of my health; this is sweet food; therefore, as a means to the external end of maintaining my health, I do not eat this sweet food. For in the final analysis, Aristotle's concern with the practical syllogism is not at all to illustrate the *orthos logos* or right reasoning of *phronēsis* but the misdirected wrong reasoning of *akratia*. Under the influence of pleasure, the acratic individual insinuates a misplaced minor premise, "But this food tastes pleasant [sweet] [*hedu*]," and then eats it. With closer scrutiny it becomes plain that this reasoning is errant not just because it goes wrong in the minor premise but because from the start it was reasoning in the sophistic way of *deinotēs* rather than the ethical way of *euboulia*. It goes wrong, in other words, not just in heeding the urgings of desire but in reasoning in terms of means to attain the unquestioned object of desire. Such is the result of leaving the good unquestioned—as Socrates saw. (Compare Gadamer on the inadequacy of the practical syllogism to accommodate practical reasoning, IGPAP 164–65.)

In the end, then, MacIntyre's third phronetic ability of understanding who we are in a *polis* or civic practice that defines our calling for us must be more clearly separated not only from theoretial *epistēmē* but also from productive *technē*. It differs from the theoretical in the same way as the knowledge of the player in a game differs from the knowledge of the spectator. For one thing, the spectator has an overview of the whole that the player on the field does not, and, for another, the spectator is not involved in the game except vicariously and is not changed by the course of it in the way that the player is, who, for the duration of the game, at least, has become the execution of his part. As opposed to the spectator, the player *is* what he does in the game. And so too the practical deliberator, as opposed to the theorist, *is* the choices he makes.

However, as well as it works in distinguishing *phronēsis* from *epistēmē*, the player-and-game analogy fails in an important regard in distinguishing *phronēsis* from *technē*—as MacIntyre's example of the hockey player shows us. True, insofar as the hockey player creates his being qua hockey player in the actions he takes, he is different from a *technitēs*, whose actions effect some thing other than himself, and like the ethical deliberator. This notwithstanding, the making of ethical choices is unlike playing a game, for in a game the purpose is fixed and invariable and the "good" not in question. And it is unlike a game insofar as there are no set rules by which it must abide and which, if need be, can be enforced exactingly. For in regard not only to the particular circumstances (*peri ton kath' hekasta*) but to the general rule itself (*tou katholou*), as our discussion of *epieikeia* has already made clear, we must allow for modification (EN 1104A 5–7). Indeed, in ethics, general rules are more like laws that a judge applies with *epieikeia* than the rules of a game that a referee must impose with *akribeia*. Thus in the end Mac-Intyre's "practice" analogy, his sociological extension of Wittgenstein's *Spiel* or game analogy, leads him astray.

But if MacIntyre goes astray, what then is the truly appropriate method of finding out what one has to do, the method of arriving at the right ethical choice? The key here is Aristotle's *bouleuesthai* or giving advice to, consulting with, taking counsel with, oneself. The expression thus indicates that the method of arriving at ethical understanding, the approach to it, is dialogical even if the dialogue here is a "dialogue of the soul with itself" (Plato). And how is this dialogue, this giving of advice to oneself, to be carried out? To understand that, we must be aware of the conditions under which giving advice is possible generally. Giving advice, we would say, is possible only between those who can transcend their individual desires, needs, and advantage and who view things in regard to what is *kalos* and *agathos* in the community in which they participate and which they share with one another. Giving advice, in other words, is possible only between people bound by *philia*:

> The one asking for advice, just like the one who gives it, presupposes that the other is bound to him in friendship. Only friends can give each other advice, which is to say that only advice that is meant in a friendly way makes any sense to the one receiving it. Hence here too we see that the one who shows understanding [in giving advice] does not think of himself as standing detached, apart from the other and of himself as passing judgment, but thinks along with him from within a specific sense of belonging [to the community], and feels himself affected too, so to speak [WM 306].

Thus Aristotle finds that ethical knowing or *phronēsis* goes hand in hand with *synesis* and *gnōme*, with having understanding for the other, showing consideration for him, and being able to "put oneself in his shoes," so to speak.

Generally English translations of the *Nichomachean Ethics*—for example, Thomson-Tredennick and Ross-Urmson—have taken *synesis* to mean only an individual's capacity to comprehend or grasp a situation, a capacity that in itself is not linked to the perspectives of the other people in that situation. But that may be a post-Cartesian superimposition. Of course, *synesis* is often meant simply as a kind of putting together (*synhiemi*) of things in a comprehensible relationship, or "getting the picture," as we might say. That sense of the word is rendered quite adequately with the English "understanding." But Gadamer, building upon the *allou legontos* (when someone else is speaking) at EN 1143A 16 and the concatenation of *synesis* and *gnōmē* in Aristotle's exposition—see also Thucydides 1.75: *zynesis gnōmēs*—argues that *synesis* is not just understanding *of* a situation, but also understanding *for* the view of someone else as he judges that situation, a double meaning that Gadamer's German translation, *Verständnis*, brings out nicely. And Aristotle's use of *synesis* elsewhere would often seem to have this double sense, in the *Politics*, for instance, when he speaks of *synesis politikē* (1291A 28), but most obviously at EN 1161B 27 when he says that parents love their children as soon as they are born but children, their parents only once they have acquired *synesin ē aisthēsin*.

And does *aisthēsis* here mean nothing more than some sort of detached, objective perception divorced from any communal affinity? It seems unlikely in this context. In fact, even in the often-cited EN 1109B 23, *ek tēi aisthēsēi hē krisis* (the decision [lies] with the perception), an *aisthēsis* is probably meant that, far from being a faculty of a private individual, depends on my affinity with others in the community, that is, an *aisthēsis* or perception, not so much from *my* perspective as from *ours*. For the *aisthēsis* referred to is perception of precisely how what is *commonly held* to be appropriate or inappropriate applies in a particular situation. We have an indication here of a crucial difference between mathematical understanding and any kind of ethical understanding. I could come to a mathematical understanding on my own, perhaps, and *aisthēsis* and *synesis* can indeed be used here too. But ethical perception and understanding can be reached only by participation in dialogue with others. Here, accordingly, the Cartesian *cogito* must give way to a *cogitamus*.

The structure of *bouleuesthai*, then, is that of reaching an understanding (Gadamer: *Sichverständigen*), reaching an understanding of what is the right thing to do, that is, on the basis of the understanding I have for the other and he or she has for me. The key to this process is precisely the overcoming of the self-referentiality characteristic of someone who knows an object. For in *bouleuesthai* I think starting not from myself, as I might in considering my pleasure or advantage, but from the community binding me to the other in which both of us knew each other as friends. And that transcendence of self-referentiality, of mere sophistic prudentialism, is present even if the process is one of "advising myself" concerning what is right; to give myself advice concerning an ethical choice I have to understand things from the perspective of the community of kin, friends, and neighbors within which I find myself.

And in what medium does this process of reaching an understanding take place? In what element is this community and its understanding of what is right perpetuated? For Gadamer the answer is clear: dialogue can take place only in the *logos*, in the language I share with the others. Thus ethical truths, an understanding of which I am to reach, are borne by, and couched in, language, and the process of *bouleuesthai* is actually the verbal, dialogical process of bringing them to light in discussion, the back-and-forth of questions asked and tentative answers proposed in our discourse or the *logoi*.

Gadamer makes much of the fact that in Plato's *Phaedo* Socrates abandons the attempt to discover what *is*—that is to say, being or the real—"directly" in natural phenomena, and turns instead to the *logoi*, to what we have to say about things, in order to approach the truth about them (IGPAP 15). And Aristotle's emphasis on *pōs legetai*, on how something is spoken of, is in Gadamer's view the continuation of this turn which Plato announces in the *Phaedo*. Whatever their differences, both Plato and Aristotle are philosophers of what we say, philosophers of the *logos* (utterance) and the *logoi* (discourse or our utterances taken collectively). And not only is what *is*, what is true, what is real, to be gotten at in this "way," but also what *is good*. Our understanding of what is the right thing to do is to be reached only in the medium of the inherited language that we have to talk about it. But this language is not something we have in front of us, objectified and at our disposal. It is not anything that we could "stand back" from and evaluate "critically," evaluate, that is, without carrying on our evaluative discussion *in* it and thereby tacitly presupposing it. Rather, it is something "there" from time out of mind in which we find ourselves under way, and by which we find ourselves sustained in our efforts to reach an understanding of what is right. In short, we learn from Gadamer precisely what we had learned from Hegel concerning *Sittlichkeit* save that Hegel did not stress *language* as the bearer and transmitter of the just and good, "whence it came no one knows" (see the quotation from PhG 311 above).

There is good reason why Hegel does not, indeed cannot, acknowledge our dependency on language. For the inescapable structure of our participation *in* language in fact renders the Hegelian project incapable of fulfillment. The absolute knowledge Hegel seeks must, by definition, be absolved from dependency on anything that might exceed the horizons of its insight. That is to say that absolute knowledge precludes being housed, embedded, *in* anything more than itself which could be said to sustain it. On the contrary, to be absolute it must contain the whole of what it thinks in itself. Everything must lie before it in full presence to its awareness; indeed, it has the total presence of mind and presence to mind that Aristotle reserves for his *theos* (see *Metaphysics*, 1072A 30ff. and Hegel's appropriation of this passage at the end of his *Enzyklopädie*).

But, as Gadamer convincingly argues, knowledge such as that, though possible for a god, is impossible for finite human beings. For us there is never any thinking without language— ordinary, natural, traditional language—at its ground. Even the artificial languages of Wittgenstein's "regularized suburbs" are precisely "suburbs" and have natural language of the "inner city" at their origin. And to acknowledge this dependency on natural language is to accept the unattainability of absolute knowledge, for it is to acknowledge that any human thinking is discursive and runs through thoughts that "come to it" within the medium of language that always surpasses whatever can be thought of at any given time. Whatever is present to mind comes to mind within a language from time out of mind.

In his own effort to overcome "representative thought" (*Vorstellen*), Gadamer *like* Hegel rejects all forms of external reflection that divert subjectivity back into itself and away from the self-explication of the subject matter of thought. For both Gadamer and Hegel thinking starts not from some agent doing the thinking but from what is thought of, the *Sache* or subject matter. Both Gadamer and Hegel want to think of what is, not as an object for subjectivity, not as we re-present it to ourselves, not as it appears secondarily in subjectivity's reflection upon itself in abstraction from the thing as it was originally thought of, but rather as *it* presents *itself* in our thinking of it, with all subjective intrusions—Hegel: *Einfälle* (PhG 72)—into its self-explication "bracketed."

The issue between Gadamer and Hegel lies only in the question of what form the self-exposition of the subject matter will take. Can it have the form of a *Wissenschaft*, of a logical science that orders the self-revelations of the subject matter in a logical sequence of speculative statements (*speculative Sätze*), each one following necessarily from the previous one? Or does Hegel's attempt to systematically explicate the content of thought in this way by use of his dialectical method not somehow obscure a more fundamental level of this subject matter of thought? Gadamer's view is that Hegel's systematization does in fact block the deeper insight. Indeed, insofar as Hegel's exposition aims at being systematic, it fails to transcend Cartesianism after all. For it remains a doing of subjectivity to its object that despite itself remains external to the subject matter. It remains a doing of a consciousness that has somehow reflected itself out of its embeddedness in what sustains it, of a consciousness that has become self-consciousness, a Cartesian *cogito me cogitare*.

As Gadamer views it, the key to Hegel's dialectical methods and his systematization of the self-explication of the subject matter, or the Concept, as Hegel calls it, is to be found in his argument regarding indeterminacy, on the one hand, and externalization, on the other. To begin with, if the exposition of the Concept is to display the necessity Hegel expects it to, and if the exposition is to be systematic rather than a haphazard series of hypotheses such as one finds in Plato's *Parmenides*, for instance, it must begin with what is "immediate," at the point of utter indeterminacy, and move to what is absolutely and completely mediated and determined.[22] In other words, the structure of finite speaking and thinking in a language, as Gadamer describes it, the structure of the definiteness of what we can say and think *within* the indefinite "virtuality" of what remains unsaid and unthought of, is precisely what Hegel seeks to surpass.

As we might expect, given his affinity for the ancient philosophers, Gadamer advances Plato's arguments against Hegel on this point. For in Plato, as the *Philebus* in particular makes clear, the determinate, *to peras*, always remains embedded in the indeterminate, *to apeiron*. And as in fact all the dialogues make clear, for Plato any good outcome (*euporia*) of a dialogical inquiry will accordingly still contain an element of inconclusiveness and impenetrable puzzlement (*aporia*). Finite clarity is reached against a background of persisting confusion (IGPAP 91). Put another way: as opposed to Hegel for Plato—and

Gadamer—*anamnēsis* and *lēthē*, being reminded of something and obliviousness, are inevitably concomitant.

It is characteristic that in Hegel's hands the idea of *anamnēsis* undergoes a radical subjectification (L II 1ff.). His translation is *Erinnerung*, which is natural enough, but he forces on it something not present at all in the Greek, namely, the idea of internalizing something external. For Hegel *Erinnerung* is *Er-innerung*, the *act* of making something "inner." With that Hegel has effectively inverted the referentiality of any remembering as Plato had conceived of it. In Plato's *anamnēsis* what comes to mind comes to us from what, as a whole, remains beyond the horizons of what we could ever have in mind. Consequently, in any knowing I continue to be aimed toward what is "beyond me," as we say, toward what exceeds my grasp. In Hegel, on the other hand, knowing that re-collects itself, or *sich er-innert*, now turns its attention inward on itself, where the whole (*das Ganze*) that is the true (*das Wahre*) is to be found.

It should not be overlooked that in appropriating the German noun *Erinnerung* as internalization of something, Hegel does no small violence to the grammar of the verb from which this noun originates, *sich erinnern*, to say nothing of what he does to the Greek idea of *anamnēsis*. In Hegel's transition from the logic of Being to the logic of Essence we find the following:

> Erst indem das Wissen sich aus dem unmittelbaren Sein erinnert, durch diese Vermittlung findet es das Wesen.

> Only in recalling itself out of Being does knowing, by this mediation, find essence [L II 1].

In customary usage *sich erinnern* does not have the transitive active sense Hegel assigns to it here when he turns the *sich* (itself) into the direct object of the verb. Normally, as in "sich erinnern an etwas," the *sich* functions reflexively, and the *erinnern* is of something (*etwas*) other than the self. Hence grammatically, as German reflexive verbs often do, *sich erin-*

nern, even if the *sich* is accusative, renders a Latin deponent or Greek middle, *reminisci* or *anamimnēikesthai*, namely, to *be* reminded of something. Compare in this regard *Phaedo* 73D, for instance: "τοῦτο δὲ ἐστιν ἀνάμνησις· ὥσπερ καὶ Σιμμίαν τις ἰδὼν πολλάκις Κέβητος ἀνεμνήσθη" (But this is *anamnesis*: just as someone seeing Simmias often *is reminded* of Cebes) (emphasis added). Seen in this way remembering is not something we do to something, even to ourselves, but rather something that happens to us.

It is characteristic of Hegel that he overrides precisely this fact. Indeed, the structure of *Erinnerung des Entäusserten* or recollection and internalization of what consciousness has externalized from itself is basic to the whole circle of Hegel's system. For without the referentiality of all being to self-consciousness, there could be no conclusiveness, but only the "bad infinity" Hegel denies. There could be no "completing the system" (Kierkegaard), there could be no whole (*Ganze*), and consequently there could be no systematic exposition of the "logical necessity" of the subject matter. On the contrary, there could be only fragmentary and finite insights, often in insurmountable contradiction with one another, such as are had, for instance, by the participants in Plato's dialogues. Just this is the price to be paid for acknowledging that as discursive humans and not gods our thinking remains under way *in* the spoken language that sustains and exceeds it.

All this is of the greatest importance for our consideration of ethical (*sittliches*) understanding. For Hegel, who for reasons of his systematic method must suppress our dependency on language, it seems possible to enter into an entirely new cognitive relationship to the ethical norms of *Sittlichkeit*, a relationship in which the *un*conscious not-knowing "whence they came," their being from time *out* of mind, would be overcome. As we know, for his absolute knowing precisely nothing is out of mind, nothing unconscious. But if I am right in my extension to ethical understanding of Gadamer's theory of the "medium of language" as the basis of any non-mathematical understanding, it is clear that this new cognitive relationship Hegel strives for is unattainable. And hence it is clear also that no stance above the conflict between *Sittlichkeit* and Morality is attainable either. There can be no transcendence of the tension between *Sittlichkeit* and Morality in some higher form of thought such as Hegel's absolute knowledge (or in some corresponding higher political reality, that is, Hegel's "state").[23]

This is not to say, on the other hand, that because we cannot go forward beyond the conflict of *Sittlichkeit* and Morality, we either could or should simply revert to a naïve *Sittlichkeit*—to a *Sittlichkeit*, in other words, which has not yet come up against Civil Society and Legal Status and does not continue to be tested by it. There is no returning to the pre-Roman experience of Aristotle, for whom even distributive justice is a function of the community of *philoi*, of kin, friends, and neighbors (see note 19 above), and for whom nothing like a Civil Society and its Legal Status had established itself over against that community, and for whom, consequently, ethics and politics could remain a single continuous field of inquiry, but for whom, as well, the civil rights of women and slaves were not even an issue.[24] Any regression to the naïve simplicity of immediate *Sittlichkeit* represents only the illusory utopianism of, say, a Rousseau, in which the universality of moral thought collapses into insanely idiosyncratic self-righteousness (Hegel: *Eigendünkel*) (see PhG 266ff. on the "Law of the Heart"). On this point Hegel was right.

Nevertheless, precisely while justifying the modern necessity of Civil Society and preserving its rights of the abstract "person," the task of any *ethical* philosophy must at the same time be to understand the special character of *Sittlichkeit*, what its knowing is, so that we might preserve *it* against Civil Society's erosion of its domain—family and neighborhood, kinship and friendship—an erosion whose reflection in our "moral reasoning" is so evident that the claim of Civil Society and Legal Status on us, on the one hand, and our obliviousness to *Sittlichkeit* and its mode of understanding, on the other, could be said to have become almost total. One need only think in this regard of those whom MacIntyre challenges, Gewirth, Dworkin, Rawls, Nozick, and, despite his valiant resistance, MacIntyre himself. For MacIntyre's resistance to have succeeded, his juxtaposition of classical virtue with liberal individualism would have to have been recast as the juxtaposition of the ethical, *sittliches* self with its substantive, qualitatively specific duties and rights, with the moral "person." And the hermeneutical understanding of finite ethical consciousness would have to have been juxtaposed with the analytical reasoning of external reasoning or *Raisonnieren*.[25]

Our task now is to lay bare *Sittlichkeit*'s structure of embeddedness-in or, in Heidegger's language upon which Gadamer builds so extensively, the structure of *immer schon unterwegs sein in*—always being already under way in something, namely, the language that we speak. We have seen that ethical understanding is an instance of such being under way in something, an instance of our participation in the language that we have inherited, that sustains us, and in which we reach our ethical understandings. We must now turn to Gadamer's overall treatment of language itself so that on the basis of the insights we might attain concerning our relationship to language, we may then proceed to give clearer definition to the dialogical process of reaching ethical understanding in language and, more generally, to the idea of a hermeneutical ethics.

NOTES

1. The question of at least an indirect influence of Gadamer's thought upon MacIntyre is an intriguing one. There is no indication of it in *After Virtue* though that book treats many Gadamerian themes as we will see. However in the later *Whose Justice? Which Rationality?*—to which I will refer often and in greater detail further on—there is frequent reference to "tradition-constituted and tradition-constitutive" inquiry (WJWR 9, 10, 354, 390). Of Continental "hermeneutical" philosophers only Derrida receives mention (WJWR 369), but this expression comes so close to the translation of Gadamer's *wirkungs-*

geschichtlich as "historically effected and effective" that one must wonder what influence of Gadamer there might actually have been (see IGPAP 1n1). The idea is certainly Gadamerian.

2. See also Rorty's *Philosophy and the Mirror of Nature* (Princeton, N.J.: Princeton University Press, 1979) and Stanley Rosen, *The Limits of Analysis* (New York: Basic Books, 1980) for further evidence of the weakening of analytical philosophy's self-assurance.

3. A clear prefiguration of Toulmin's turn from the paradigm of science to the jurisprudential model of argumentation, is to be found in his *The Uses of Argument*, a turn that receives further elaboration and definition in his *An Introduction to Reasoning* (New York: Macmillan, 1984).

4. It should be noted, however, that later on in this chapter we will also find obvious traces of James's and Dewey's radical pragmatism in MacIntyre's argument. But this, as I will try to establish subsequently, constitutes not a break with Wittgenstein, but a logical extension of his later thought.

5. MacIntyre's discussion of Hegel is very short indeed, and if neglect is any indication, he gets no further than Rorty, who maintains that Hegel has nothing to add to Kant's treatment of the problem of knowledge. That view must surely strike anyone as puzzling who finds either the "Preface" or the first three chapters of the *Phenomenology of Mind* convincing. It will be one of the major concerns of this chapter, and indeed of this entire book, to show the epistemological importance of Hegel, in particular in regard to ethical understanding, but also in regard to knowledge as a whole. Hegel, perhaps better than anyone else, exposes the limitations of the mathematical reasoning and method of objectification characteristic of the natural sciences, and in so doing displays the complete inapplicability of such a mode of reasoning in any ethical deliberation. Exactly that inapplicability and inappropriateness will be thematized here.

6. "The Man Without Qualities," the title of Robert Musil's major work and devastating display of the dissolution of community in modern society (*Der Mann ohne Eigenschaften* [Hamburg: Rowohlt, 1952]). Musil often uses the metaphor of particles in empty space to display this dissolution, a metaphor that seems strikingly appropriate for us today, who, with evidently no sense of the dissolution of community which our very language reveals, glibly speak of "relationships" in which free individuals might "get close," but "leave each

other space" for "self-actualization." We seem oblivious to the fact that the "intimacy" we seek, as the Latin origin of the word might have made clear, presupposes that each of us could affect and be bound to one another in some "innermost" way and that in fact that bond may precede and determine anything that we could be individually.

Of course the beginnings of this particle or spatial vision of human society are to be found at least as far back as Hobbes, who sees human beings as nothing but atomic individuals variously charged, we might say, with the "positive" desire for glory and power and the "negative" aversion to bodily hurt and death, and who end up in something like the condition of a relatively stable gas if they are sensible, and lucky enough that the negative charge, as it were, predominates in their reaction to one another.

7. For the time being I think it best to leave this word untranslated. Let us say for now only that it is built on *Sitte*, meaning, much as the Greek *ethos*, customary practice or way of doing something. There is no English equivalent of *Sittlichkeit*, but the sense of it will, I trust, emerge in English as we proceed.

8. In the *Phenomenology* the word Morality is reserved for a subsequent discussion of the dialectical transition from Kantian ethics of duty and conscience (*Gewissen*) to what Hegel calls Religion. See "Spirit Sure [*gewiss*] of Itself, Morality," PhG 422ff. But different aspects of the same Kantian ethics are also explored earlier at the end of Hegel's exposition of Reason ("Reason Giving Laws [Autonomously]," PhG 301ff., and "Reason Testing Laws [for Consistency]," PhG 306ff.). Though Kantian ethics is not yet called Morality at that point, the problem with consciousness that Hegel is getting at here too is the problem of Morality, namely, that the precepts it is able to derive are precepts only for it, *für sich*, and do not obtain *an sich* in the world of actual deeds. It is significant that Hegel can "deduce" the same phenomenon in different ways, for example, *Sittlichkeit* from Reason in the *Phenomenology*, but also from Morality in the *Philosophy of Right*. Of course, the projects in these two works are quite distinct, one being to elaborate the phenomena in the dialectic of consciousness and its object, the other being to display the phenomena in Spirit's self-explication in the real world. Still, the fact that there is more than one way to skin a phenomenological cat, as it were, indicates Hegel's own recognition of indeterminacy and variability in his dialectical

logic. (Compare Gadamer on Hegel and "the logical" [*das Logische*], HD 95ff.). For the interpretation of Hegel generally it is important to keep in mind that the "chronology" of a phenomenon or stage of consciousness, the sequence in which it occurs, can be reversed. This is why Hegel can say of Self-Actualizing Reason, for instance, that it can be viewed both as "not yet" *Sittlichkeit* and as "no longer" *Sittlichkeit* (PhG 259). As the difference in the sequences in the *Phenomenology* and the *Philosophy of Right* demonstrate, the same variability of exposition is also true of Morality. Hence, though it does not contribute in any way to either of the different tasks that Hegel was setting himself in his two works, I would argue that my running together of his diverse expositions of *Sittlichkeit* and Morality and appropriation of these expositions for our purposes here does not do violence to them. I am not seeking to make a contribution to Hegel scholarship, but to illucidate phenomena on which I think Hegel has already shed a great deal of light.

9. *Ethics* (Englewood Cliffs, N.J.: Prentice-Hall, 1963), pp. 2–4.

10. *Taking Rights Seriously* (Cambridge: Harvard University Press, 1978), p. 273.

11. We will have many occasions to return to *Morality and Conflict* since this splendid book treats many of the themes treated here, among them the inevitable and unresolvable conflict not only between what we, following Hegel, have called *Sittlichkeit* and Morality, but conflict within *Sittlichkeit* itself, or what Hegel calls the tragic conflict. Hegel takes Antigone and Creon as his illustration of the latter, but conflict internal to *Sittlichkeit* is the motor of much of Greek tragedy. See the *Medea*, for instance. Hegel and MacIntyre look for a resolution of both these kinds of conflict in some higher order. Hampshire argues effectively, however, that they are mistaken to do so; for such conflicts will always exist, and as finite human beings we can never hope to escape them. This thesis will be argued here also.

12. The relevance to contemporary American society of Hegel's elaboration of *Sittlichkeit* and its dissolution in the "system of need satisfaction," Civil Society and Legal Status, is made amply clear in *Habits of the Heart* (New York: Harper & Row, 1986) by Robert Bellah and others, a book that treats a number of themes that will concern us here, among them the importance of language to ethical understanding and the inexplicit dimension of ethical reasoning in the predispositions of thought or "habits of the heart." Relying not on Hegel but princi-

pally on de Tocqueville and writing from the standpoint more of empirical sociology than of philosophical theory, the authors neverthe-less present a nearly perfect exemplification of Hegel's argument—Hegel played out in modern dress, as it were. And they thereby bring home in just what sense a life of Morality in Civil Society is indeed *"Sittlichkeit* lost." What they aptly refer to as "communities of memory"—namely, ethical communities held together by kinship and a shared heritage transmitting accustomed and accepted duties and particular, not abstract, rights—they see disintegrating as ethnic and familial ties yield more and more to the imperatives of need satisfac-tion. Community, taken as a "moral ecology" or "web of moral understanding that ties people together" (pp. 40–41 and 335), is, they display, being increasingly displaced by *contractual* relationships be-tween insular individuals tied to one another only by the needs they are able to satisfy for, and expect to have satisfied by, one another. See pp. 128–30 on the "therapeutic contractualism" that "denies all forms of obligation and replaces them with the ideal of honest com-munication [of feelings] among self-actualized individuals" (p. 101). The constrictive authority of any tradition is jettisoned, allowing com-plete autonomy of persons who now enter into transactions with one another using cost-benefit analysis as the sole measure of good and bad. In this modern example of Hegel's Civil Society, technical and bureaucratic rationality supplants the "specificity of concrete commit-ments," i.e., specific rights and duties (p. 152). Plainly we are in the province of radical utilitarianism here. For any sense of obligation has been eliminated, and the authors thus speak of the asocial atom that replaces the participant in the moral order. What is lost is above all any sense of a shared good, a destiny or purpose at which a community with a memory of its past might aim in the future. "Utilitarian" and "expressive" individualists have, it seems, neither recollection nor expectation, but only discontinuous experiences of the present.

13. In a quite different way but one that is by no means incompatible with Hegel's thinking on the split of *Sittlichkeit* and Morality, Mac-Intyre's *Whose Justice? Which Rationality?* explicates a dialectical split in the idea of *dikē* or justice by starting from the Homeric duality of *aretē* as excellence at what one does and *aretē* as being victorious in the *agōn* or conflict. Later, in the *polis* or community, this Homeric duality develops into a split between the "goods of excellence" and the "goods of effectiveness" and into justice defined in terms of each

respectively (WJWR 35ff.). With regard to the goods of effectiveness, MacIntyre writes, ". . . each person can only hope to be effective in trying to obtain what he or she *wants*, whatever it is, if he or she enters into certain kinds of cooperation with others. . . . What the rules of justice will have to prescribe is reciprocity, and what is to be accounted as reciprocity, what is to be exchanged for what, will depend on what each party brings to that bargaining situation of which the rules of justice are the outcome" (WJWR 36; emphasis added). Clearly we are dealing here with the realm of need satisfaction (Hegel's *Bedürfnisbefriedigung*) and the Condition of Right or Legal Status. And clearly too we are dealing with it in distinction from the excellences or *aretai* some would display in the realm of *Sittlichkeit*. But MacIntyre does not assign this split the central significance it receives in Hegel. If he had, Hume's theory of practical rationality and justice (see WJWR 260ff.) and the liberalism that follows it in MacIntyre's exposition would have been portrayed as the predominance of the justice of effectiveness to the exclusion and even elimination of the justice of excellence. Such an idea, however, is quite far from MacIntyre's understanding of Hume.

14. One hears a great deal about solidarity nowadays, as if it might be a form of *philia*, in fact *the* form of *philia* available to us now that traditional communities seemed to have pretty well vanished. The question that must be asked about this word and its predecessor, *fraternité*, is whether the solidarity of the oppressed in resisting their oppressors, or of those who have joined together in competition with another person or group of persons for some gain, is the same sort of thing as the *philia* that exists between blood brothers and sisters in a family, or between friends. or between members of a neighborhood or *polis*. I would suggest that MacIntyre's distinction between the pursuit of internal and external goods and Hegel's, between *Sittlichkeit* and the Condition of Right, provide a basis for us to make distinctions between *philia* and this solidarity that is supposed to substitute for it. Solidarity would seem to be the feeling or esprit de corps of those engaged in a joint effort to win from someone else some external good or gain (Aristotle: *kerdos*), be that profits for a company, a military advantage for an army, or fair wages in a general strike. Solidarity, then, would be the subjective feeling of those mobilized as a corporate "person" in conflict with another corporate "person" for advantages and the satisfaction of needs—a conflict usually and, at best, certainly,

under the rule of law or the Condition of Right. This is not to deny that between those engaged on one side of the conflict comradeship and friendship may develop of the sort, for instance, that Aristotle describes between those who love each other for their excellence and virtue. Significantly, however, these friendships will persist after the conflict is over, for they were never dependent on it for their existence. That solidarity, on the other hand, evaporates at the end of the conflict is made evident by the course taken by revolutions: once the revolution is over and the initial oppressor overthrown, solidarity can be perpetuated only by a new real or fictional enemy, the "reactionaries" who threaten the *gains* of the revolution.

By contrast, *philia* underlies a web of traditional obligations and loyalties defining what is to be done and how it is to be done within a community. It depends, in other words, not on conflict and competition for external goods for its existence, but on established practices in the cooperative pursuit of "internal goods." Enemies (*echthroi*) to the community may exist, be it a community of family, friends, or neighbors. But *philia* does not presuppose their existence any more than, say, parental love for children or love between good friends does. Significantly, in Aristotle's two detailed chapters on *philia* (Books VIII and IX of the *Nicomachean Ethics*) *echthroi* are hardly mentioned at all, for they play no role at all in defining it.

15. This is not to say that Aristotle's and Kant's ethics are mutually exclusive. Indeed Gadamer, as we will see subsequently, argues convincingly that they are actually complementary. See "On the Possibility of a Philosophical Ethics," KS I 189–91. It should also be noted here that from Gadamer's point of view Hegel's critique of Kant and rationalistic Morality turns out to be valid not so much in regard to Kant himself as in regard to twentieth-century "Kantians" and the "Kantian project" of Frankena, Dworkin, Gewirth, and others. For Kant, in fact, never denied that *Sittlichkeit* and *Sitten* were indispensable (see *Grundlegung einer Metaphysick der Sitten*). Rather, as Gadamer shows, his concern was precisely to secure these against the sophistic cajolery of our sensuous inclinations and our cravings for power. Hence being principled, as opposed to unprincipled, in Kant is not at all a matter of rationally contriving principles, rules, rights, or whatever *ex nihilo* but of steadfastness in holding to what is right, to what we ought to do—Aristotle's *to deon*.

16. This and the preceding quotations are taken from pp. 2ff.

17. As does the language of "speech acts," "performances," and so forth, to which, as we have seen, MacIntyre often reverts, the use of "agent" here predisposes his argument in a way which must eventually be called into question. Indeed, I would argue that it not only predisposes it but undercuts it. See Chapter 2 of this volume. At one point MacIntyre himself seems to call the use of "agent" into question (see the citation from AV 31–32 in note 25 below). However, compare, for instance, the account of the practical syllogism in *Whose Justice? Which Rationality?*: "In the initial premise or premises the *agent* affirms of a given type of action a predicate which has gerundive force. . . . In the secondary premise or premises the *agent* affirms that circumstances are such as to provide the opportunity and the occasion for doing what is to be done. In the conclusion the *agent* in acting affirms that this action *qua* such and such is to be done" (WJWR 139; emphasis added).

18. Gadamer points out that Aristotle in fact only uses the practical syllogism to illustrate the choice of means to an end, and hence "practical" here is closer to "technical" than to "ethical." To be sure, *phronēsis* or ethical reasonableness is concerned with the means to a good, but, as we will see, never just with the means. It always involves at least tacit knowledge of the good, that is, the "wants and goals" that MacIntyre says here are presupposed by, but not expressed in, the reasoning process.

19. The case of the wood dealer is an interesting one given the fact that, unlike most business transactions, buying wood still takes place somewhere in between Civil Society's system of need satisfaction and what remains of a realm of *Sittlichkeit*. Wood dealers, even within thirty-five miles of Boston, are mostly natives who speak the local dialect and with whom "trading," as they say, is not entirely a contractual exchange but in some part, at least, an ethical relationship bound by customs that even newcomers get on to after some years of living in the area. This is not to say that there are not plenty of unethical wood dealers. There are. But the very application of the word to them confirms the point: their dishonesty consists not so much in their failing to adhere to the legal terms of a contract as in their being "operators" beyond the pale of ethical decency, who do things that simply "aren't done."

In buying wood, it seems, the transactions remain much like those Aristotle considers in his analysis of distributive justice, which is to say that they remain prior to Legal Status. Needs are being satisfied here, but still within the community's *Sittlichkeit*, within the *politeia* where *to kalon* and *to aischron* remain determinant. Hegel is right when he foresees that business transactions in advanced Civil Society will become something radically distinct from trading among members of a community.

20. See *Essays on Aristotle's* ETHICS, ed. Amelie Oksenberg Rorty (Berkeley: University of California Press, 1980).

21. In drawing an analogy between the ethical choice and the translator's choice of the appropriate word. Hampshire distinguishes between those things that are in the "foreground of his awareness" and "a huge background of other contexts and associations determining his decision, but not now recalled" (MC 107). His point, like the one I am making, is that not everything, indeed not even most things, that ground the choice, can be raised to the level of consciousness. Rather, they remain at the level of "pre-conscious memories" (MC 108). We will take up this matter again when we consider the concomitance of *lēthē* and *anamnēsis* in Plato in the next chapter. I believe Hampshire is wrong in thinking that Plato expects complete explicitness in ethical reasoning (see MC 109) and would argue that Plato is closer to his own position than he recognizes.

22. The most immediate point in the systematic development of the Concept, the point at which to begin, is therefore the concept of Being, which is to say, Nothing or a total abstraction from anything determinate at all, complete indeterminacy. No one thing here is defined over against another in this pure abstraction that merely "is." The self-unfolding of the Concept will end in the Idea, which results as the fully mediated determinate synthesis of the entire series of concepts, each determined in relation to its contrary, thereby being negated and giving rise to a new concept. Thus by starting with a total privation of determinacy and ending with complete determinacy, the truth of the whole (Hegel: *das Ganze*) can be systematically explicated. At the beginning the concept stands in immediate unity with itself (Being). It passes over into its other (Nothing), the negation of itself, in order after the long travail of repetitions of this process finally to recover itself from all its self-externalizations. Essential to this process of mediation is that at its end we no longer have any form of what Hegel calls "bad infinity," which is to say, something determinate in relationship to something that remains indeterminate (L I 130ff.), but rather

the total elimination of indeterminacy and otherness. (See "The Idea of Hegel's Logic," HD 75–99.)

23. It will be necessary to note on several occasions that this book sets in abeyance any consideration of what Kierkegaard calls the teleological suspension of the ethical. It does not consider, that is, the transcendence of ethical obligation and ethical virtue founded on *philia* in "works of love" founded on *agapē* or charity. This much is clear: in surpassing the ethical, *agapē* would not include the ethical in the way Hegel's higher theses include and synthesize the positions they have transcended. Just as there is no synthesis possible of aesthetic and ethical existence, there is no synthesis possible of ethical and agapaic existence. That is why Kierkegaard speaks of a *suspension* of the ethical. Hence, charity cannot serve as an alternative to Hegel's "state," cannot serve, that is, as a synthesis that would resolve an apparent either/or into an and/also.

24. In his presidential address at the Eastern Meetings of the American Philosophical Association (New York, 1984), MacIntyre put great stress on the resolution of conflicts that arise when two or more ethical traditions come up against one another, for instance, the English and the Irish; and it is principally this kind of conflict, I presume, that he has in mind when he speaks here of "standing back" and developing appropriate "rational procedures" for its resolution—which is to say, for its *adjudication*. MacIntyre's neglect of *ius*, of right, haunts him here. Of course, the history of colonialism is replete with examples of missionary zeal, of one group's trying to force what it considers to be its superior way of life on another, and to this extent all struggles to assert or preserve one's customs and language are indeed ethical conflicts. Still "rational procedures" ascertaining which of the competing ways of life is "best" do not seem to be the way out here, but rather tolerance, co-existence, and eventual synthesis or "merging of horizons," as occurred between the French and the Anglo-Saxons after 1066. Viewed another way, however, such conflicts are not really ethical conflicts at all, but conflicts between *echthroi*, inimical strangers, in competition for the means of satisfying needs, with one side generally trying to maintain its privileges and to perpetuate the inequalities in this competition. Consequently, what is right here pertains mostly to *personae et res*. If it is not forced in war, a resolution here, i.e., the fair distribution of the means of need satisfaction, of the means of acquiring external goods and of these goods themselves, becomes a

civil matter much like the distribution of property between estranged partners of a marriage, save that here *philia* never existed to begin with. Where there never was *philia*, just as where it has ceased to exist—in short, wherever people are strangers—Legal Status and civility are the only alternative to force, violence, and war. That is something that Locke argues convincingly. And as he shows, if disputes here are to be resolved peacefully, the "standing back" of an impartial detached authority whose jurisdiction they are is indeed essential, an authority that holds to "rational procedures" in adjudicating the conflict and that has the power to enforce its decrees.

MacIntyre's own failure to distinguish between Civil Society, on the one hand, with its juridical reasoning, and *Sittlichkeit*, on the other, leaves him stranded somewhere between them, tending sometimes toward one and sometimes toward the other. Despite his emphasis on virtues that exist only for participants in communities, the moral reasoning he sometimes proposes is that of the bystander, the nonpartisan judge who looks for formal, universal standards transcending all particularity. His thinking, in other words, is often that of Legal Status, namely, Morality. Yet, paradoxically, he rejects the ideas of universal right and rights, which are essential to this sphere.

25. This is by no means to deny that MacIntyre has taken important steps in this direction. He himself calls into question the "modern self" and even its idea of the "moral agent": "It is in this capacity of the self to evade any necessary identification with any particular contingent state of affairs that some modern philosophers, both analytical and existentialist, have seen the essence of moral agency. To be a moral agent is, on this view, precisely to be able *to stand back* from any and every situation in which one is involved, from any and every characteristic that one may possess, and to pass judgment on it from a purely universal and abstract point of view that is totally detached from all social particularity" (AV 31–32; emphasis added). But in the very place where he raises the question of what authentic ethical reasoning might be—a question that would seem to demand the sort of distinctions that Aristotle and Gadamer following him make between *phronēsis*, *technē*, and *epistēmē*—MacIntyre himself proposes, as we have seen, that in regard to ethical issues the contending parties do indeed "stand back" in their search for the "appropriate rational procedures" (AV 260).

2

Language as the Medium of Understanding

IN THE LAST CHAPTER we saw that MacIntyre is indebted to Wittgenstein for his ideas of what makes a language, and specifically a moral language, "in order," namely, its coherent functioning within a life-world or form of life. And we also saw how effectively MacIntyre applies this Wittgensteinian criterion in showing that contemporary moral language is not in order. To this extent, it may be said that MacIntyre proceeds from a philosophy of language, derived in large part from the later Wittgenstein, to a moral philosophy. Gadamer, to be sure, nowhere explicitly takes this particular step. In his case a philosophy of language, largely Platonic in its origins, as we will see here, provides the foundations for his theory of interpretation and understanding of texts, but not for any express ethical theory. The thesis of this book, however, is that Gadamer's philosophy of language can provide just such a basis for ethics. The transition could have been made in Gadamer, as it was in MacIntyre, from a philosophy of language to an ethics. Indeed, we saw in the last chapter that according to Gadamer all forms of understanding, be they of what is true *or of what is good*, are reached in language. To know either the true or the good we must follow Plato's "flight into the *logoi*" (*Phaedo* 99E). It makes sense then, that in order to build an ethical theory on Gadamer's hermeneutics, we must first go back to the basis for it in Gadamer's philosophy of language, and that is what I propose to do here.

Gadamer begins the third and final part of his *Truth and Method* with these words from Schleiermacher: "*Alles Voraus-zusetzende in der Hermeneutik ist nur Sprache*,' " or, in approximate English, "Language is everything and the only thing that is to be presupposed in hermeneutics" (WM 361). The use of this quotation and the fact that the conclusion of Gadamer's major work on hermeneutics is devoted to an investigation of language give a clear indication that, at least as Gadamer conceives of it, hermeneutical theory is indeed philosophy of language and, to be more precise, philosophy of language as it is ordinarily spoken. For the *Rückverwandlung in Sprache*, the transformation back into language that he says is the task of hermeneutics, is meant specifically to be a transformation of written texts back into spoken dialogue or discussion, that is, *Gespräch*. Accordingly, at the heart of the theory of hermeneutics lies a philosophical account of discussion.

That fact offers a unique possibility for the "merging of horizons" (*Horizontverschmelzung*) that I am seeking, for a merging of a foreign frame of thinking, that is, with an important component in the tradition of modern English language philosophy. For however much Gadamer's hermeneutics might depend on Plato and Anglo-American language analysis on Wittgenstein, the concern of hermeneutical inquiry, on the one hand, and of language analysis, on the other, is in one respect the same: namely, getting clear about what we say, about meanings in language as it is spoken, about the meanings of ordinary language. Hence, a good part of what Gadamer is doing is translatable in terms of ordinary language philosophy.

In the course of this chapter I will first give a preliminary indication of the overlap of ordinary language philosophy with hermeneutics, the overlap on which a merging of horizons can be established. Second, having established the convergences, I will proceed to the divergences. This way we may come to understand better how MacIntyre and Gadamer, who in many ways come so close, ultimately part ways; to a great extent, it is what each takes and each leaves of a Wittgensteinian approach to language that separates them. Third, since the reasons for Gadamer's divergence from Anglo-American ordinary language philosophy are traceable to Plato, or at least to Gadamer's reading of him, we must elaborate Gadamer's discussion of Plato on language. Here we will take up once again—and now in some detail—the turn Plato takes in the *Phaedo* to *hoi logoi* and *ta legomena*, to assertions and arguments we make and to what we say. We will see that despite Plato's apparent intention to penetrate behind the disconcerting ambivalences and ambiguities of spoken language, he in fact depends on it. Finally, we will consider a passage from the *Gorgias* that will display how, following Plato's turn to the *logoi*, one might reach an ethical understanding in the medium of language, an understanding, in this case, of what is *kalos* (fair, noble, honorable) and what is *aischros* (ugly, despicable, shameful). Only by turning to Plato, upon whom Gadamer relies so extensively, can we fully grasp what divides Gadamer from Wittgenstein and the tradition that follows from him. And consequently and most importantly, only in further elaboration of Gadamer's reading of Plato can we open up new paths to ethical philosophy beyond those MacIntyre has already broken.

1. GADAMER'S HERMENEUTICS AND ORDINARY LANGUAGE PHILOSOPHY

Let us proceed directly to an example that will give the idea of a possible merging of the horizons of Gadamer's hermeneutics with those of ordinary language analysis some credibility. Perhaps the single most elegant application of Gadamer's hermeneutical theory is to be found in his essay on Hegel's *verkehrte Welt* (the reverse–perverse world) (HD 35–53). Those who have tried their hand at Hegel at some time or other will admit that the section of Hegel's *Phenomenology of Mind* dealing with the *verkehrte Welt* is one of the most inscrutable texts in a book no part of which is easily accessible. The text on the *verkehrte Welt*, then, would test the mettle of any interpretative technique. And how does Gadamer approach it? By attempting to clarify the ordinary use of *verkehrt* and the other words near it in the semantic field over which it ranges. Gadamer builds his interpretation on the double use of the word in German. On the one hand, *verkehrt* is used in a value-free sense that refers to the position of something and thus functions as does *umgekehrt* or inverted, i.e., reversed, backwards, inside out, and so forth. On the other hand, it has a range of uses relating to perverted, which imply at least some degree of evaluation. The example Gadamer cites is the common German expression, "*Das ist eine verkehrte Welt*," meaning, roughly, "That's a topsy-turvy world." Here the inversion is more than a change in position; in this use of *verkehrt* a twisting of things is also implied. Things are not in the order or relationship they ought to be in. Gadamer is led from this sense to the satirical, where what is *verkehrt*, slaves playing masters, masters playing slaves, etc., is presented that way deliberately in order to clarify *e contrario*, as he puts it, the perversity of *Verkehrtheit* of what we had thought ought to be the right relationship. All these uses of *verkehrt*, Gadamer contends, are at work in Hegel's presentation and understanding of the *verkehrte Welt*, and for us to understand the text, these uses are what we need to know.

Just how close Gadamer comes to ordinary language philosophy in this approach is made explicit in the following passage: "Ordinary German usage," he writes,

quite confidently distinguishes between *falsch* (false) and *verkehrt* (inverted or backwards). Of course, an answer that inverts things or gets them twisted is not correct, but the elements of truth are recognizable in it and only need to be put right. A false answer, on the other hand, contains no such possibility of making it right. Thus, for example, the information someone gives you can be called *falsch* if it is deliberately given with the intent of deceiving—but in such a case it could not be called *verkehrt*. For an answer which is *verkehrt* is always one that was meant to be correct and which turned out to be false [HD 52n13].

The principle here, one which extends to all Gadamer's interpretations of Hegel, and which in fact underlies his hermeneutics as a whole, is that native language as it is spoken is the root of all philosophy. Hence, in interpreting a philosophical text, one must put the dead ink on the page back into the context of live, spoken language. The vitality of Hegel's philosophy derives from his native tongue, German, and Schwabian German in particular. Thus, the value of his thought lies not in any artificial expressions that he invents—thesis, antithesis, synthesis might be said to come under this heading—but rather in his explication and application of the rich meanings contained in *Aufheben, an und für sich*, and, of course, *verkehrt*. Hegel's "speculative" philosophy, Gadamer argues, is valuable not because of some sort of correspondence to a supposed logical structure of a reality apart from ordinary language, but because of its subtlety and sensitivity in unfolding the significances of the language-constituted reality within which we "always already find ourselves under way."

What is the conception of language that underlies such a hermeneutical method as Gadamer's interpretations of Hegel employ? Again I quote from *Hegel's Dialectic*:

it was only after the new information theory had brought modern science to its perfection that the problem of the dependence (and relative independence) of our thought on (from) language came into full view. . . . Thought is dependent upon the ground of language insofar as language is not merely a system of signs for the purpose of communication and transmission of information. Where there is real language, the thing to be designated is not known prior to the act of designation. Rather within our language relationship to world, that which is spoken of is itself first articulated through language's constitutive structuring of our being in the world [HD 115].

This passage makes evident that for Gadamer there is no extra- or pre-linguistic reality that language could be said to picture. Language does not chart reality and give us information about it; it constitutes reality. Thus, information theory's idea of a logically perfected language freed from the inadequacies of ordinary speech is misconceived from the start. Perfect, exact could only mean adequate for the subject to signify objective reality precisely and "scientifically." However, if language does not work that way, if it does not signify a reality external to itself, the whole idea of a perfect language becomes meaningless. And in practice any attempt to find a more exact, rigorous terminology for "reality" would lead to the uprooting and withering of language.

What is striking about all this is its similarity to Wittgenstein's criticism of his early work and his own return to ordinary language. There is a difference in what specific object is criticized—logical atomism as opposed to Hegel's and Husserl's systematic science—and an important difference in the purpose of the criticism, which we shall come to subsequently. Nevertheless, in a number of respects Wittgenstein's self-criticism ends up being very similar to Gadamer's revision of Hegel and Husserl. For Wittgenstein too reached the conclusion that language usually does not chart or map a pre-given reality, though at the time he wrote the *Tractatus* it seemed to him that that was its primary function. In the *Tractatus* Wittgenstein had maintained that "the ultimate constituents of the world are a unique set of atomic facts whose combinations are pictured or mirrored in the relations among symbols in a logically perfect language," that the "world can be described completely by knowing all these atomic propositions," and that "there is one basic use of language: to convey information." As a consequence, "all language which conveys information is exact and determinate."[1] Obviously, in criticizing this view, as Wittgenstein does in his *Philosophical Investigations*, he is criticizing the very same thing that Gadamer's hermeneutical theory places in question: language as precise designation.

Gadamer, whose sense of history is far greater than Wittgenstein's, traces the informational concept of language to what he believes to be its origin in Plato's attempt to combat sophistic rhetoric by overcoming the *dynamis tōn onomatōn*, that power of names which the sophists so skillfully exploited to confuse and confound any belief and argument, no matter how sound. (Compare *Phaedo* 90B–C on *antilogikoi* or sophist counter-arguers and their ability to throw everything seemingly stable into Heraclitian flux, *anō kai katō*, up and down, or, as we would say, back and forth. The analogy is drawn here with the tidal straits of Euripus.) It seemed to Plato that words had an almost demonic potential for asserting themselves in the place of that which they name (see Gadamer's "Dialectic and Sophism in Plato's *Seventh Letter*," DD 93–123). Accordingly, he becomes the first in a tradition that seeks to get clear about the things in themselves—περὶ αὐτοῦ τοῦ καλοῦ, καὶ αὐτοῦ τοῦ ἀγαθοῦ καὶ δικαίου καὶ ὁσίου (about the noble [*kalon*] itself and the good and just and pious itself) (*Phaedo* 75C)—to get clear about them apart from the distortions and inaccuracies of language as it is spoken. This tradition developed from Plato through Liebniz' projected ideal of a universal notation to precisely the sort of endeavor to which Wittgenstein's *Tractatus* is committed.

Its task has always been a double one. First, there is the critical task of displaying the insufficiency of language as it is spoken ordinarily, the vagueness of its correspondence to what is, or, worse, its lack of correspondence to anything at all. (Metaphysical talk is the sophism at which Wittgenstein takes aim.) Second, there is the positive task of replacing ordinary language with an invented sign-system that will precisely correspond to the structure of what is. Beginning with Plato the paradigm for this project becomes the "language" of mathematics: "Thus the word like the number becomes the mere sign of a well-defined and, accordingly, pre-known reality" (WM 390).

Though Wittgenstein, unlike Gadamer, does not concern himself with the historical origins of it, it is precisely this theory of language that his own self-criticism leads him to reject. The change in Wittgenstein's position apparently resulted from the intrusion of certain "linguistic" phenomena that the tidy theory of the *Tractatus* was unable to account for. Gestures, curses, greetings, exclamations such as "Water!" "Ow!" "Help!"—all these must be counted as language, yet none can be accounted for in terms of a theory that tells us that language should be precise designation of some sort of reality "in itself." Thus it became evident that a false expectation was perhaps blocking the phenomenological investigation of the subject matter. Wittgenstein therefore calls for an unprejudiced examination of the phenomenon of language: "Don't say: 'There must' . . . , but look and see."

Significantly for our purposes, what he sees is what Gadamer sees: language as it is spoken, live language in the context of human activity or the life-world. That language is not a perfected, exact system of invented signs, but something quite different—ordinary language, inherited, traditional language: "Our language can be seen as an ancient city: a maze of little streets and squares, of old and new houses, of houses with additions from various periods and this surrounded by a multitude of new boroughs with straight regular streets and uniform houses" (PI § 18). The modern additions are the languages of the sciences. Wittgenstein's primary concern now, however, is with the irregular diversity of the inner city.

What is the language that is found there? It is language in the context of the human world, the world of buying things, building things, playing games, singing, joking. "The speaking of language is part of an activity, or a form of life" (PI § 23). It follows, then, just as it does in Gadamer's hermeneutical theory, that understanding something that has been said is possible only within the context within which it was said, i.e., within a world or a form of life.

And there are other implications of the insight Wittgenstein reaches here. First, it becomes clear that there is what Gadamer calls an inner unity between the word and the world. As a form of life, language forms life, shapes it, constitutes the world of the things we deal with. As Heidegger, and Gadamer following him, have also seen, we do not have atomic perceptions that we then proceed to signify; we do not hear sounds, but wind in the chimney, and "wind" and "chimney" exist for us only because language "lets" them be what they are, "brings them into the clear" as the things they are. Wittgenstein's way of putting this same thing is in terms of language frames. The world of things among which we live is seen as it is because it is framed in the language we speak. And our task is to "get clear" about what we say.

Second, and as a consequence, our relationship to language cannot be that of a reflective consciousness devising signs or termini for a world we wish to dispose over. It cannot be that of subject to object, for we do not so much invent language as find ourselves under way within it. We do not create language; we learn it. It is always already there like the city in which we were born and in which we live. To be sure, this implication is not fully comprehended by Wittgenstein, though it ought to be a conclusion drawn from the standpoint the *Philosophical Investigations* attains. In this respect Gadamer is more consistent and deeper. Ultimately, in fact, it is his hermeneutically oriented philosophy of human finitude that alone can provide the ontological and linguistic legitimization for any would-be ordinary language philosophy. But we are getting ahead of ourselves.

How Gadamer and Wittgenstein approximate each other here—and how they differ too, as we will see—can best be elucidated by reference to the model to which both of them advert continually: *das Spiel*, that is, game or play. In Wittgenstein the contextuality of language is to be shown in terms of *Sprachspiele* or language games. Whatever form of life I am involved in, building a house, buying apples, and so on, is an activity based on language, and therefore it could be said that it is "played" according to the rules of that particular language game. To act in the language-constituted world I must know the appropriate language games and that means knowing how they are "played" and under which circumstances. To use Wittgenstein's expressions, understanding means knowing the "rules" and thereby knowing "how to go on" when someone has said something to me. It means knowing what behavior, linguistic or otherwise, is called for in response to what has been said.

Further, it is essential to note that the game aspect of spoken language shows how it exceeds the limits of any informational sign-language. As part of life or activity, it does not purport to represent reality, and therefore its utterances are not properly spoken of as true or false, but, as Austin points out, as felicitous or infelicitous. That means they either fit the game or are out of place in it. The judge who begins the trial proceedings with "Batter up!" has said nothing true or false, though he or she has said something that could be meaningful in another context. Language, then, is to be understood in its proper application in the circumstances. Its meaning is not some thing it describes but its use within particular contexts, and this, the contextuality of language, is what the "game" metaphor is meant to indicate.

(MacIntyre, as we saw, finds moral utterances in our present, "emotivist" context to have the appearance of meaningfulness but to be in fact as out of place as "Batter up!" would be in a court proceeding. And in large part his project is the Wittgensteinian therapeutical one of showing that such use of them in a context in which they no longer make any sense is the source of the confusions or "interminable debates," as MacIntyre calls them, in which we needlessly ensnare ourselves. MacIntyre too is at least partially concerned to "let the fly out of the flybottle.")

Certainly there is a great deal here that corresponds to the theory of language underlying Gadamer's hermeneutics. For Gadamer, hermeneutics, taken in his sense of interpretation of written texts, implies, as we know, a transformation back into spoken language. This means that the dead letter is to be restored to life by converting it back into speech, into the spoken word. Only in this way can the task of hermeneutics be accomplished and the understanding of meaning (*Verstehen von Sinn*) brought about. And Gadamer too sees all *Verstehen* as part of a process, part of an activity, or, to use Wittgenstein's expression, part of a *Lebensform*. Gadamer's way of putting this same thing is to say that *Verstehen* is *Sichverständigen* or that understanding is reaching an understanding with someone else in a situation. All live language is dialogue, *Gespräch*. Thus the hermeneutical task of reviving what lies dead in the written text means restoring it to the context in which it was said to someone for some reason.

It means as well that if we are to understand, we must be enabled to stand in the position of the one who is spoken to by the text. For example, if we find it said in Plato's *Gorgias* that doing injustice is uglier (*aischion*) than suffering it and wish to understand what is meant, we must know how to go on in the life form or language game in which that is said. It is the task of hermeneutics to extend the part of the city of language in which we are active and with which we are familiar to that part in which the language of the text is spoken. This would hold as well if the text speaks of *die verkehrte Welt*; we must reach an understanding (*uns verständigen*) about its meaning within the "live meaning of words as they are spoken" and that, as Gadamer puts it, implies knowing how they are to be applied (WM 291). In understanding, he says, "there is always some sort of application of the text to be understood to the situation of the interpreter" (WM 291). Put in Wittgenstein's words, that means that the language games we play must be brought to overlap with the game played in the text, i.e., that the text speaks to us as the ones who are addressed and that we respond to it within contexts, ours and its, that have become continuous with each other. (This, incidentally, is the essence of the "merging of horizons" referred to at the outset of this chapter.)

The example Gadamer uses to make this very Wittgensteinian point is that of the command (WM 316). A command, as he says, can exist only where someone is there who should obey it, and "understanding a command means knowing how to apply it [follow it] in the situation in which it is given" (WM 316). Thus, Gadamer continues, if historians find a command in a text and wish to understand it, they must go through the same process as the one to whom it was originally addressed completed before the latter carried it out, which is to say that they must grasp how it applies in the given context or "game" (*Spiel*); they must see "how to go on." This example, like that of the curse, which Gadamer also uses (HD 95), makes clear that he, just as much as Wittgenstein, has gotten beyond the traditional conceptions of understanding and meaning that prevailed as long as philosophy had devoted itself exclusively to language as a statement, true or false, corresponding to and representing states of affairs.

Like Wittgenstein's theory of the "language game" or *Sprachspiel*, Gadamer's hermeneutics shows that the proposition or statement (*Satz*) is an abstraction if it is considered out of the context in which it is uttered. The full meaning of any statement can be understood only if the occasion for its being said is taken into account—who says it, to whom, when, and for what reason—along with whatever propositional value it might have. For Gadamer, as we shall see, that holds not only for curses and commands, but for the statements of speculative philosophy and ethics as well:

> the speculative statement is not a judgment restricted in the content of what it asserts any more than a single word without a context or a communicative utterance torn from its context is a self-contained unit of meaning. The words which someone utters are tied to the continuum in which people come to understand each other, the continuum which determines the word to such an extent that it can even be "taken back." Similarly, the speculative statement points to an entirety of truth, without being this entirety or stating it [HD 96].

Thus, when Hegel speaks of the *verkehrte Welt*, that too is addressed to somebody and can only be understood if I know when and why someone would say something like that. I have to know when and why such an idiom is ordinarily used. I have to know, in other words, how this particular "language game" or *Sprachspiel* is played.

This much, it could be argued, is quite in keeping with Wittgenstein insofar as both he and Gadamer, as we see, think of language (*Sprache*) in terms of its game (*Spiel*) characteristics. But though there is this close correspondence between Wittgenstein's reliance on the *Spiel* metaphor and Gadamer's, there is a point at which the two thinkers diverge even here, and that is precisely in regard to what the *Spiel* metaphor makes visible about the language event in which all understanding takes place. We must now take up the differences between these two philosophers of language, starting with their differences in regard to *das Spiel*.

2. GADAMER'S DIVERGENCE FROM THE CRITICAL INTENTION OF ORDINARY LANGUAGE PHILOSOPHY

What does Gadamer tell us of *Sprachspiele*? It might be said that in his case it is the "play" traits of the family whose resemblances make up *Spiel* that concern him and not the "game" traits. Why do we enjoy play? Because authentic playing, not competitive sport to be sure, but, say, playing the violin, playing a part in a play, or dancing, is selfless. Playing, if it comes off, releases us from the constrictions and inhibitions of self-consciousness. In play we are not aware of ourselves, and, conversely, it is the spoilsport's (*Spielverderbers*) insurmountable self-consciousness that makes him or her unable to "play along." As opposed to Wittgenstein, it is this feature of play that Gadamer seizes upon: "The subject of the play is not the players," he says; "rather the play can only be said to manifest itself through the players" (WM 98). Thus there is something one-sided about the grammar of "I play a game," as Gadamer, availing himself of Huizinga's analyses, goes on to point out (WM 99n). As other (German) expressions show us, it would be more adequate to say that the game plays itself out (*sich abspielt*), for it is not really I who do the playing but the game itself. "The most basic sense of *Spielen*," Gadamer tells us, "is that of the Greek middle. Thus we say that something is played out [*sich abspielt*] or that something is in play [*im Spiele*]" (WM 99). These expressions would indicate that *Spielen* cannot be understood primarily as a form of my doing something (WM 99), and precisely that is the point Gadamer carries over into his analysis of the *Sprachspiel*, the language game:

> Language games are that in which we as learners—and when do we cease to be that?—are raised to an understanding of world. Thus we can refer here once again to what we established about the nature of play: namely, that the relationship of the players to the play cannot be understood as a relationship of subjectivity [to its object], since, on the contrary, it is the play that plays in that it draws the players into itself and thus itself becomes the actual subject of the play [WM 464].

That brings to light something Wittgenstein did not see. To be sure, he maintains that language must be understood in reference to how it occurs in a context, but he does not grasp what that means in regard to the subject–object model of speaking; Wittgenstein sees only what is displayed in the transitive active "I play a game," and he extends that one-sidedness into his analysis of language games. For him the playing of a language game is still seen as something that we do and, consequently, as something that fits within a subject–object structure. For Gadamer the play character of language makes clear that we are not so much agents as participants. But that is missed by Wittgenstein, who places the human being at the center of the occurrence of language and who thus thinks of the action of speaking and thinking in a language as the *actus* originating in the *agens*, in the *agere* of the human agent.[2] In this he is followed by Austin and Searle, for whom speech acts become primary. And, as we have noted, MacIntyre too does not entirely succeed in getting free of this way of thinking.

From Gadamer's point of view Wittgenstein and those who

follow him are not quite radical enough. They do see that language is much more than propositions or statements (*Sätze*) invented by human beings to correspond to states of affairs; and it is that insight which leads them to abandon the program of perfecting ordinary, spoken language by replacing its ambiguities with exact signs precisely designating a supposed extralinguistic reality. But their critical intention remains with them as a framework that biases their vision of language and thus confounds the effort to which Wittgenstein devotes himself with such brilliance and intensity, the effort to avoid presuppositions and to see language as it is. Wittgenstein wishes to mark off where we use words properly from where we are misled by them. In the very same passage, in fact, in which he announces the phenomenological project—"we must do away with all explanation, and description alone must take its place"—he announces the critical project as well: "Philosophy is a battle against the bewitchment of our intelligence by means of language" (PI § 109). That last assertion puts Wittgenstein squarely within the tradition after Plato, the very tradition that Gadamer has told us we must get behind if we really are going to see the phenomenon of language. It will be recalled that Plato too was motivated by just such a critical desire to break the spell cast by language in sophistic misuse of it. That led him to distrust ordinary spoken language and to seek a kind of thought purified of the *dynamis tōn onomatōn*, a kind of thought that like mathematics would presumably reflect the logical structure of reality clearly and exactly and thus be immune to sophistically induced distortion and befuddlement. That mathematical ideal led later to the project of inventing a sign-language (*Zeichensprache*) that would "cure" the inexactitude of ordinary talk, a step, incidentally, that Plato himself never takes for good reasons that we will see subsequently. It is a step Wittgenstein ends up not taking either, but his reasons are very different.

The fact is that one cannot reverse this attack on spoken language completely if one does not abandon its therapeutic motive, abandon, that is, the critical intention behind it. That shows in Wittgenstein. His rejection of the informational sign-tool in the service of human objectification of the world is really only a qualification. Wittgenstein emphasizes that just to have assigned a label to a thing is not yet to have made a "move" in a language game; it is only preparatory to that. The sign wins life only when the game is played in which it serves, and the game implies many other kinds of words with other kinds of use. Each sign is a tool along with other sorts of tools, commands, requests, greetings, etc., in the "carpenter's box" of language. In this respect Wittgenstein goes beyond the semiotic theory of the *Tractatus*, which argued that the primary tool of language was the sign and the primary function of language, designation. Furthermore, he sees that the ideal of an invented perfect language is somehow misconceived and that language should be "in order" as it stands. Still, he wants human beings to prevail over language, to have it at their disposal, and that leads him to maintain the tool concept even if signs are now seen to be just one of many tools available. The tool aspect of language is focused upon to the exclusion of other aspects precisely because of the critical intention that Wittgenstein shares with the linguistic tradition extending from Plato onward. The idea is still to purify us of misuses of language, "idling" or "language on a holiday," so that we can use language properly.[3] Only in this way can it be ensured that we have power over language and not it over us. In short, Wittgenstein's vision of philosophy as therapeutic critique prevents his escape from the subject–object conception of language; the human being remains for him the speaking subject, with words of all kinds there for him or her to employ.

It is this critical intention, perhaps, that keeps Wittgenstein, and those who followed him in the tradition of language analysis, from hearing the double sense of the German *Sprachgebrauch* or language usage. To them it sounds so reasonable that language usage is how we employ, use, words. But once the word *Gebrauch* is thought of as use, a dimension of it is shut off. *Gebrauch* means use, but it also means custom, and that it has this meaning too puts language usage or *Sprachgebrauch* in an entirely different light. Insofar as language is customary, we do not invent it but find ourselves "always already under way" within it. And making use of language would not be so much employing it, "doing something with words," as availing ourselves of it in conforming to it. Proper usage is not invented by individuals except in the extreme case of artificial languages, the regularized suburbs of the city of language. Proper usage is customary in ordinary language, and that means that we play according to its rules, not ours. Here, as opposed to what Wittgenstein suggests (PI § 83), we cannot "make up the rules as we go along."

Gadamer, whose intentions are hermeneutical rather than critical, is able to see what eludes Wittgenstein: our embeddedness in language or what he calls the *Umschlossensein unser selbst durch die Sprache*, our being surrounded by language. It is not as though there were a world of things and opposite that a self that knew them before formulating and communicating its knowledge in language. For seen this way language is there to begin with as that which makes knower and world possible in the first place, as "*die Mitte in der sich Ich und Welt zusammenschliessen*," the medium in which I and world come together with each other (WM 449). Thus the speaking of a language is not picking up a tool when we need it, for we do not find ourselves first in a languageless condition in which we then reach for a word to communicate something we knew all along: "Learning to speak does not mean being introduced to the use of an instrument already there for the designation of the world we know and are familiar with; rather it means acquiring familiarity and knowledge of the world itself as we encounter it. We grow up, we learn to know the world, to know people and ultimately ourselves, in that we learn to speak" (KS I 96).

Consequently, Gadamer does not seek to free us from, but to free us for, the power of language. In this enterprise he is, of course, greatly indebted to Heidegger. *Die Sprache spricht*—"It is quite literally more correct to say that language speaks us than that we speak it" (WM 439)—and the hermeneutical task is to *hear* what it says. The whole emphasis in hermeneutics is thus not on getting or having something at our disposal (Heidegger: *verfügen über*) but on yielding and fitting in (Heidegger: *sich fügen*). The language event "is not our doing something to the thing [language], but the doing of the thing itself" (WM 439). Consequently, in order to reach any understanding we must overcome any self-centered obstinacy; we must often give in. All understanding takes place within the universal medium of language, Gadamer tells us. That means that no *Vorstellen*, no re-presentation of language is possible, or, literally, no "putting it in front" of us at our disposal. As long as we cling to the critical intention, however, we strive to remain in the position of a self-conscious subject over against a language that we do expect to get control of after all—a tendency that prevails in MacIntyre, for instance. But un–self-conscious participation in the event of language is thereby closed off to us, and in refusing to yield to what transcends us, we become, as it were, the *Spielverderber des Sprachspieles*, the spoilsports of the language game.

This decisive difference between wanting to have language at our disposal and being willing to remain under way within it shows up most sharply in Wittgenstein's and Gadamer's contrasting treatment of vagueness. In turning to ordinary language both, of course, acknowledge vagueness. Wittgenstein accepts it because on most occasions vague or inexact statements work quite as well as they need to, better, in fact, than the purified propositions of scientific language. "Stand over there!" is usually a better tool than "Stand 2.57 meters from points X and Y!" Gadamer too acknowledges vagueness in customary spoken language, but this language's usefulness as such is not the issue. What is at issue is the violation of natural language that takes place in the attempt to produce exact scientific designation: "In comparison to the live meaning of the words of spoken language, to which, as Alexander von Humboldt correctly points out, a certain breadth of oscillation is essential, the term is a petrified word and the terminological use of the act, an act of violence perpetuated on language" (WM 392). It very often happens that in creating a term for precise designation a "word already in use is cut out of the fullness and breadth of its semantical relationships and pinned down to a determinate sense" (WM 392).

To develop terminology in this way is to move in a direction precisely opposite to that taken by hermeneutics. For Gadamer's hermeneutics, in seeking to bring the dead word back to its life in spoken language, would open the word up into the unlimited richness of meaning that issues from it. The hermeneutical experience, Gadamer says, is an experience of the "open-endedness of the meaning event, which cannot be closed off" (WM 448). Vagueness, ambiguity, then, is significant as an indication of the actual relationship that we have to language as speakers of it. We are under way within the event of language, which continually transcends us. We go from place to place within the city of language in which we dwell, all the while never being able to see the end or beginning of any of the innumerable streets that lead to and from any point where we happen to be. Vagueness, accordingly, is a manifestation of the infinitude of language as a whole in relationship to the finitude of human speaking; it is evidence of the boundless, indeterminate reality that exceeds whatever can be said at any time, and thus it makes apparent why we find ourselves following the streets of language, so to speak, without a map, and why, as Gadamer asserts, "speaking in no way means putting something at one's disposal and making it predictable" (WM 429).

On occasion, when he is not pursuing his "therapeutic," critical objectives, Wittgenstein himself bears witness to the ultimacy of the hermeneutical experience of finite awareness. For all his emphasis on the "tool" aspect of language, Wittgenstein is not at all insensitive to the fact that we are under way within language. The "Preface" to his *Philosophical Investigations* gives a clear demonstration that he too found himself within the medium of language without any overview of the whole. As a result, his insights could never be put together as a system; they could only be formulated as inconclusive "observations" (*Bemerkungen*) made from any number of points of view *within* the subject matter:

> my thoughts were soon crippled if I tried to force them on in any *single* direction against their natural inclination.— And this was, of course, connected with the very nature of the investigation. For this compels us to travel over a wide field of thought crisscross in every direction.— The philosophical remarks [*Bemerkungen*] in this book are, as it were, a number of sketches of landscapes which were made in the course of these long and involved journeyings [PI ix].

Here, at least, there is no *verfügen über* but only *sich fügen*, no disposing over language but only submitting to it, only following wherever the *Gespräch* or discussion in his "thinking aloud" might lead him. And here, at least, he belongs (*gehört*) to what he experiences and listens to (*hört*) and he obeys (*gehorscht*) what it tells him.

All this is of the greatest significance for the program of ordinary language analysis as it has been defined by Austin, Searle, and others who followed Wittgenstein, including MacIntyre. For one thing, if Gadamer's hermeneutical conception of language is correct, ordinary language philosophy could be given a justification for itself that, as its positivist critics have rightly perceived, it currently lacks; and, for another, and most important for us, it would acquire speculative and ethical content in place of the sometimes inconsequential matters with which it has concerned itself.

As regards the first point, there is a patent circularity in the undertakings of Austin and others when they try to solve philosophical "problems" by recourse to the authority of ordinary usage, all the while maintaining that language is something we invent and use for our purposes. If we invent language for our use, why should we make a fetish of it? Why should we ever submit to its authority? That would mean becoming the tool of

our tools—something which hardly seems defensible.[4] But recourse to ordinary language would be justified if Wittgenstein's
and Gadamer's insight into the structure of our relationship to
language as a city within which we are "at home" were made
the foundation. Then, obviously, to learn the truth of things we
would have every reason to turn to the center of language in
which the truths of our world display themselves. But that would
mean a decided shift in emphasis, for instead of asking the
critical question "How do we do things with words," as Wittgenstein or at least those who follow him do, we would pursue
the hermeneutical endeavor of coming to understand how words
do things with us.

The result of this shift in emphasis would be a renewal of
concern with what Heidegger has called apophantic language.
In *Being and Time* we find the following account of *apophansis*,
or showing-forth, as this occurs in language:

> In contrast [to making a judgment, *Urteil*], *logos* as speaking
> amounts to *dēloun*, i.e., making open and plain that which is
> being spoken of in "the speaking" of it. Aristotle explained this
> function of speaking more precisely as *apophainesthai*. The *logos*
> lets something be seen (*phainesthai*), namely, what is being
> spoken about, and that, *for* the one speaking—hence the Greek
> middle—or for the ones speaking with each other. Speaking "lets
> be seen," *apo* . . . , i.e., coming from that itself which is being
> spoken of. In speaking (*apophansis*), to the extent that it is
> genuine, *what* is said should be drawn *out of* [*apo* . . .] that being
> spoken of, so that in what it says the spoken communication
> makes what it is speaking of clear and accessible to the other
> person. That is the structure of *logos* as *apophansis*. Not all
> "speaking" has *this* property of making open in the sense of
> pointing out and letting be seen. Pleading (*euchē*), for example,
> makes clear too, but in a different way [SZ § 7, B].

Significantly, Heidegger makes a distinction here among three
modes of *logos* or speaking: speaking that reveals, speaking that
makes a judgment, and speaking that has some function, or, as

Austin was later to specify it, performative speaking in which the illocutionary and perlocutionary forces predominate, for example, pleading. What is of particular interest is the order set up here within what Austin simply calls the constative aspect of language: we do make judgments about states of affairs, Heidegger tells us, but that does not come first and is not what speaking does originally: "*Logos* in any case does not mean judgment [*Urteil*] primarily . . ." (SZ § 7, B). For a state of affairs to be established (*konstatiert, constaté*) in a judgment, things must already be in the open, and it is apophantic speaking as bringing-into-the-open, letting shine forth, *apophainesthai*, therefore, that makes uttering a judgment possible in the first place. Further, it should be underscored that *apophainesthai*, not *apophainein*, is the basis of *apophansis* as Heidegger understands it, i.e., the middle and not the active form. Establishing a judgment (*konstatieren, constater*) may be called a speech act, perhaps, but the letting show forth (*phainesthai*) of *apophainesthai* certainly cannot be. The latter starts from (*apo*) what is displaying itself, not from the subject-agent. That is what Gadamer also is getting at when he says that the *Spiel* of the *Sprachspiel* must be understood in the sense of the Greek middle (see WM 99). In these two respects, then, that of being distinct from and prior to constative speaking and that of being "medial," language in Gadamer's hermeneutical understanding of it may be said to be apophantic.

To be sure, he himself does not use the word in this sense. Indeed, it will be recalled that Wittgenstein and Gadamer too emphasize precisely the non-apophantic modes of discourse, pleas, commands, curses, and so forth, in order to display, first, the limitations of a theory of propositions (*logoi apophantikoi*) (see WM 316ff.) that says that language pictures a world apart from itself and, second, the contextuality of language. Ordinary language philosophy has followed Wittgenstein in this by stressing the performative over the constative aspect of language, and in ethics that, as MacIntyre has shown convincingly, only lands us in emotivism. But what if it is recognized that language is not primarily a tool that performs functions, does things? One would be led back behind constative language to language that displays truths, that lets things be, apophantic language.

Gadamer's hermeneutics is a significant new step precisely because it makes this return to the apophantic possible without reversion to a picture theory of language. The hermeneutical return to apophantic language obviously restores a principal concern of the *Tractatus*, specifically, the concern with the world as it is displayed in language. However, the fatal weakness of the *Tractatus*, its picture theory of language, would not be found in Gadamer's language idealism, in which both self and world are seen to originate in the matrix of language. Never in Gadamer would it be said, "Wir machen uns ein Bild der Tatsachen" (we make ourselves a picture of the facts).[5] For apophantic language, it is now clear, does not re-present what is; it presents it: "In der Sprache stellt sich die Welt selbst da" (in language the world presents itself) (WM 426).

Now, Gadamer would argue that this understanding of language as the "place" where reality "presents itself" is, despite his odd way of putting things, not some invention of Heidegger's, but a rediscovery of an ancient Platonic-Aristotelian tradition that was lost in the philosophy of the schools that followed Aristotle (see IGPAP 3–4). Indeed Plato and Aristotle are alike in basing their thought on what language displays to us. For instance, Aristotle's examination in the *Categories* of the various ways in which we *say* a thing "is," *pōs legetai*, is in fact to be understood as an extension of the *logos* philosophy that Plato's Socrates announces in the *Phaedo*. Proposing the "hypothesis" of the *eidos* or form, Socrates tell us in a passage whose ethical significance I have alluded to before that he found it fruitless to go on with the previous accounts of reality given in terms of physical substances and their interaction, and thus he was driven to look for the truth of what is in a "second best" place, in the *logoi*, in the words we say and arguments we make (*Phaedo* 96Aff.). The "form," which is to be established in order to head off sophistically induced confusions, will be found in how we speak. It is easy to overlook the irony in this "second best" and, as a consequence, easy to miss this essential turn in Plato's thought. As "Socrates' " rejection of any naturalistic revision of mythogical explanations, and his passion for discourses (*hoi logoi*) make clear in the *Phaedrus* (229c, 228c), and as the critique of the "materialists" makes clear in the *Sophist* (246Aff.), Plato is convinced that the *logoi* are not at all the "second best" place for philosophy to look for what is real; they are the first place. Of that Gadamer is also firmly convinced, and in the next section we will investigate the consequences of this conviction for his reading of Plato and, beyond that, for our attempt to develop a hermeneutical ethics.

Gadamer's renewed emphasis on what I have called the apophantic dimension of language does not mean in the least that he loses sight of the contextuality of language, and accordingly, he does not fall behind the advances that Wittgenstein (and he) had made in pointing out the relevance of the circumstances or situation for the meaning of what is said. As regards any *logos*, the issue remains what occasioned it, except that the concern with apophantic language is not so much a matter of what purpose the assertion was meant to perform as what truth it displays and, consequently, what question the *logos* answers in presenting a truth in the way it does (see WM 344ff. on the "Hermeneutic Priority of the Question"). In regard to apophantic language the contextuality of understanding (*Verstehen*) is maintained, and the foundation of dialogical, spoken language preserved, by insistence on who says what to whom *in response* to what. As Gadamer shows us, nothing is said out of the blue. Furthermore, what is said is not only a response but in turn a new question. At the same time as it answers a previous question, it addresses another question to yet someone else, who must know how to "go on" in the unending process of *Sichverständigen* or our reaching an understanding with one another.

Accordingly, there would be nothing lost in the return to apophantic language that hermeneutics makes possible. On the contrary, much would be gained. For instead of worrying about men eating poppies in a field or red-headed goldfinches that might be woodpeckers, and the like, instead of making minute "distinctions" or spelling out all the "rules" for when I can say "Open the door!" we might come to see the reality of the *verkehrte Welt* or what it means to say that "*die Wahrheit des Seins ist das Wesen*" (Hegel, L II 1), or in ethics, for example, ". . . αἴσχιον εἶναι τὸ ἀδικεῖν τοῦ ἀδικεῖσθαι" (Plato, *Gorgias* 475D).[6] I have taken examples from Hegel and Plato here, for Gadamer shows us how such a "speculative" philosophy as theirs can be rehabilitated, namely, as a phenomenological exposition of the reality constituted or "framed," as Wittgenstein would say, in language as we speak it.

To emphasize apophantic language is not at all to deny the existence and importance of either performative or constative language in which, respectively, an agent-subject either gets something done or passes judgment on a state of affairs. For the latter to occur, the original unity of self and world in the apophantic event has to have split into a subject on the one side and "facts" on the other, and apophantic language has to have petrified into word-tools for use by an agent-speaker. This *is* our situation much of the time, and thus it would be quite wrong to say that we never use words to represent states of affairs and that language is never communication of true or false information. Gadamer does not deny this; his aim is only to show that although words can be tools an agent uses, they are not that originally, and that although there can be communication of information and of misinformation, there is behind these things the more fundamental discussion in which communication means entering the community of the shared world constituted in the language we speak.

For our purposes here—to develop a theory of ethical understanding—this distinction is crucial. It is one thing, for instance, to treat Plato's characterization of doing injustice (*adikein*) as a true or false statement by means of which an agent either represents or misrepresents a state of affairs, to treat it, that is, as constative language. It is quite another to ask what it itself makes clear (and obscures) about the Greek world and our own insofar as we continue to be capable of participating in the tradition of that Greek world, capable of translating it, as it were, into our own. When MacIntyre takes the example of "X is a good sea captain" and argues that in a navigational context it is true or false, he is treating it as a constative statement that someone makes. But that is a distortion of how ethical utterances or sayings originally come down to us. "Originally" (Heidegger: *ursprünglich*) Plato's characterization of doing injustice either displays or fails to display a segment of a world involving what is *kalon* and *aischron*, worthy and despicable. MacIntyre is concerned only to move ethical utterances back from the emotive realm, where their function is performative, into the constative realm. But if Heidegger and Gadamer are right that would not be enough.

The issue of the appropriateness of the word "agent" arises once again when the truths being said are apophantic. On the level of both performative and constative language we do have speech acts and to that extent the word agent does apply here; lying, certainly, is something that someone, an agent, does. But getting things wrong (*verkehrt*) or getting them right, which is what occurs in our experience of apophantic language, is something that happens to us. Properly speaking, we do not do it. Indeed, the process of submitting to apophantic language, of getting things right in dialogue and seeing what is right (*dikaios*) in deliberating (*bouleuesthai*), is precisely a process of overcoming insistence on one's own agency and of letting oneself be shown something.

In this regard too Plato is instructive. To be sure, in Gadamer's view Plato is the beginning of the end, insofar as he wishes to replace vulnerable and indeterminate ordinary language with something less likely to be thrown by sophistical wrestlers' tricks. But he is also the end of the beginning, for in his work the paradigm of mathematical knowledge, of science as *epistēmē*, has not yet suppressed the discursive character of language at all; rather he continues to rely to the latter. In Plato's dialogues each participant begins with his particular interests. Yet in the course of the conversation each is liberated from those interests so that he can follow the movement of the subject matter beyond his personal preconceptions, expectations, and opinions (*doxai*); each is freed to learn, to see the truth of the matter that displays itself in language, or, as Gadamer puts it, in *was zur Sprache kommt* (what comes to be spoken of). Clearly there is a difference between dialogue of this sort and an argument between competing interests. Competing interests win, one over the other, and which wins is a function of power. In the case of an argument between interests, the power involved is the persuasive power of words, the *dynamis tōn onomatōn*. Are we always sophists though? Is there not some justification for Plato's differentiation between the rhetorical *makros logos* (grand speech) and a philosophical discussion? For one thing, everyone knows that a good discussion (*dialogos, Gespräch*) is not "won" by anybody. Consider too in this regard Plato's distinction between having learned (*memathekenai*) and having been persuaded (*pepeisthai*) (*Gorgias* 454cff.) and the parallel distinction we have made between the *Spiel* of *Sprachspiel* and competition. We have an indication here that for Plato spoken language is not always, and in fact not even primarily, a tool that can be misused and that needs to be overcome. And we have an indication too why the very same Plato, who would transcend the confusions introduced by ordinary language, could also be taken as a paradigm for someone who, like Gadamer, would make ordinary language the center (*Mitte*) of the process of reaching an understanding of something.

3. The *Logoi* as the Place or Locus Where Truth Is to be Sought

We need to go back. It will be recalled that Gadamer found in Plato the beginnings of a tradition quite different from any *logos* philosophy, a tradition, namely, that proceeded through Leibniz to modern logical analysis in Russell and the early Wittgenstein.

This tradition, far from trusting what we say, sought to over-come the weakness (Plato: *astheneia*) of words and names by getting behind these to the things themselves, *para auta*, and ultimately, though Plato himself did not take this step, to de-velop a system of designation that would represent these things without the distortions inherent in ordinary ways of speaking. In Plato, Gadamer argued, there begins the tendency that Gada-mer himself would reverse, not the reliance on ordinary language but the discrediting of it.

To develop that line of thought, in Part III of *Truth and Method* Gadamer takes up Heidegger's argument that Plato somehow shifts the place (*Ort*) of our original experience of truth and focuses that argument on the problem of language in Plato, something that Heidegger, though he certainly acknowledges the primacy of language in any experience of the world, largely omits from his discussion of the allegory of the "cave" and the transcendence of the cave in the "sunlight" or realm of the ideas.[7] By concentrating on the problem of language Gadamer succeeds in making clear what the motive is for Plato's turn to the ideas: the cause here is not some ineluctable destiny (Hei-degger: *Geschick*), but something rather more straightforward, namely, Plato's insight into the perversion that results from the obvious misuse of the power of words, the *dynamis tōn onoma-tōn*, in sophistic rhetoric. Indeed, the sophists may be accused of "bewitching our intelligence," to use Wittgenstein's phrase. And, as we have seen, in essence the "critical" thrust of modern analytical philosophy, even among its proponents of ordinary language, is in response to precisely this same phenomenon. Before the advent of sophism the Greeks "dwelt," as Heidegger would put it, trustingly and quite un–self-consciously within their language. They were at home in it.

But with the introduction of sophistic rhetorical "tricks" that reduce language to a tool to be used for misrepresentation and persuasion by mere emotion, language seemed obviously to sever itself from the reality being spoken of. Thus Plato and his contemporaries found themselves in the circumstances where language ceases to be apophantic and acquires what we, following Austin, might now call its constative and performative functions: on the one side, so it appears, is a self with language at its disposal and, on the other, a world to be spoken of and of things to do with words. Once that split occurs, a distinction between the word and what it is used to designate becomes unavoidable. And it is precisely this distinction that appears to be essential to Plato's understanding of language and to give rise to an abstraction from what Heidegger calls "original thinking," thinking, that is, in which things display themselves (*apophainontai*) as what they are in the language that we speak to others and to ourselves.

Gadamer makes the *Cratylus* his point of departure in elaborating this reading of Plato (WM 383ff.) and shows that the juxtaposition Plato makes there between the word-name (*onoma*) as a conventional sign agreed upon to designate an object and the word-name as some kind of image—e.g., onomatopoetic—of what it names in fact reveals that an abstraction from the original language that displays truths to us has already taken place. For that abstraction is presupposed by either one of these possible explanations of language. They both begin "too far along" (WM 384), for they leave unsaid that it is language itself in which the thing to be designated either unconventionally or onomatopoetically first displays itself as what it is, or, as Heidegger would put it, "presences": "*Kein Ding sei wo das Wort gebricht*" (There could be no thing where the word breaks down), Heidegger reminds us. Hence to start with, word and thing are indissociable; "originally" we find ourselves under way within language, which, far from being a tool at our disposal, is the medium (*Mitte*) within which our world becomes known to us. But given the sophist *mis*use of language, it is inevitable that one would be forced beyond this original experience of language and come to see language as something that is indeed used by some agent—used either correctly or incorrectly. That, Gadamer tells us, is exactly what seems to happen to Plato.

The point of Plato's discussion of contemporary theories of language is to display that in language, with its claim to speak correctly (its claim of the *orthotēs tōn onomatōn* [correctness of word-names]), no real truth of the thing itself [*alētheia tōn ontōn*] is in fact attainable, and that one must know without words [*aneu tōn onomatōn*], purely, starting from the real thing itself [*auta ex heauton*] (*Cratylus* 388c). That amounts to a radical shifting of the problem to a new level. The dialectic designed to effect this shift claims to put thinking on its own and to reveal the true objects of thought, the ideas, in such a way that the power of words [*dynamis tōn onomatōn*] and the demonic technique of using that power perfected by the sophists are overcome [WM 384].

As Heidegger had pointed out, truth now becomes correctness (*orthotēs*), but Gadamer extends this idea by specifically tying this transformation of truth into language: in original apophantic language—dialogue, discussion, speaking—the true is what is disclosed, what comes to be clear out of surrounding and persisting obscurity. But once the "radical shifting" to a new level has occurred (compare Heidegger on the transferral of the place [*Ort*] of truth), true language becomes language that would correctly state the being of what is, and the correctness of language is to be assessed using the standard of pure knowledge of the thing itself, knowledge purified of the obscurity and ambiguity that accompanies all ordinary speaking of things. Consequently, as Heidegger had also pointed out, but again not specifically in regard to language, we have the beginnings of the subjectification of truth here: the word and its truths become something, not in which human beings "dwell," but over which they dispose and that they, as agents, use correctly or incorrectly. The problem, as Plato sees it, is that in sophistic misuse words cease to direct us to the realities they mean and captivate us instead; we no longer get beyond them. Given this circumstance, he argues, it would be best to overcome words altogether, to think the realities (the forms) without them.

The model here is mathematics and specifically the number as a paradigm of pure intelligibility (WM 390), the sign used to designate a well-defined and previously identified reality, and the meaning of which can be precisely set by the human subject. No longer could it be said in mathematics that "There could be no thing where the word breaks down." On the contrary, in the case of mathematical entities, the thing, the circle, for example, is there first. The task, consequently, is to know it without words (*aneu onomatōn*) and then to find significations for it that are as little susceptible to sophistic misuse as possible, as little susceptible to making the circle, for instance, appear to be something it is not, namely, a continuum of very small straight segments.

We are led here to the "term," which quite literally terminates the oscillation of meaning, the indeterminacy, that inheres in any word in original, spoken language. The "term" thereby "overcomes" the original concomitance of clarity and confusion, *alētheia* and *lēthē*, truth and oblivion, that persists in spoken language, which both discloses and conceals the matter under discussion (WM 392). In that way the term precludes sophistic misrepresentation. But in this way of thinking Gadamer finds a "fundamental covering up" of the nature of language (WM 385).

And on the face of it, at least, it would seem that Plato no longer considers the fact that our thinking and knowing are inextricably bound to language and that we cannot get out of language, so to speak, in order to get it around in front of us and to dispose over it as we see fit—as his project presupposes we can. However, this Plato of the *Cratylus* who paves the way for language analysis as we know it in the twentieth century is not the whole of Plato by any means, and that Gadamer will also make clear. For in Plato perhaps more than anyone else in the tradition except perhaps Aristotle, a sense of original language and truth is in fact preserved. There is, of course, the critical Plato of the *Cratylus*, but there is also and above all the dialogical, hermeneutical Plato, and we must now pursue Gadamer's understanding of the latter.

It is not hard to understand that in a situation in which words (*onomata*) are "spinning free" of their context in valid traditional usage, when they are used merely to sway the emotions, one might seek the truth of things without (*aneu*) them. Nor is it hard to see that the model for an insight without words would be mathematics. Mathematics provides insights that are invulnerable to the sophistic word games, the proponents of which claim to be able to refute any position that someone might take, able to confound any insight. And as Gadamer points out, it was precisely that kind of invulnerable insight into *the good and the just* that Socrates seemed to have in an era when others were shifting from one unsteady opinion to another. Socrates apparently saw the good with the same clarity as a mathematician sees his truths, and no argument could dissuade him from his unerring adherence to it any more than a mathematician could be dissuaded from the insight that the circumference of a circle is equidistant at all points from its center (DD 201). Thus Socrates seemed to provide the secure and certain foundation upon which one might rebuild ethics in much the same way as geometricians build from point to line to plane to solid, untouched as they are in each of their sciences by the sophistic misuse of the power of words to bewitch our intelligence. In an age of crisis Plato (like Husserl) turns to the invariable and incontestable, seemingly with the hope that the ethical too might become a matter of strict science, a matter of *epistēmē* rather than *doxa*.

Gadamer points out, however, that although Plato takes mathematics as his paradigm, he fully recognizes that in these matters of the good and the just, which is to say ethical matters, things are actually quite different from the mathematical realm. For better or for worse, there is no proceeding *more geometrico* in regard to ethical truths, and consequently there is no possibility of adducing cogent demonstrations of the truth that would convince someone who is not disposed to accept that truth. The justification that one must give for one's ethical stance, in an age such as Plato's where innocent adherence to traditional customs has become impossible, always remains contestable. Unlike those in mathematical demonstration, the conclusions one comes to in one's deliberations about what is right remain uncertain and insecure. They remain inconclusive. Plato fully acknowledges this, and insofar as he does, he remains true to the original experience of apophantic language after all.

The problem with the just, right, and good, which Gadamer will show is essentially the problem of human finitude and discursivity, is taken up in the essay "Dialectic and Sophism in Plato's *Seventh Letter*" (DD 93–123). There Gadamer points out that our ethical deliberation, however much we might wish to end its dependency upon language and to transcend the inherent ambiguity of the latter, takes place in language, spoken language. Hence, it is inevitably afflicted by the "weakness" of the *logoi*, of discursive statements, of speaking. If one examines the symbolic "means" with which we, as discursive human beings, get clear about something—and just such an examination is what Plato undertakes in the excursus of the *Seventh Letter*—a common trait emerges in all of them: they all convey the truth, but they all obscure it as well. For they all tend to assert themselves as means instead of displaying the truth. Thus they disclose and conceal "equifundamentally," as Heidegger would put it, and in them the truth that they make available to us may be said to "presence" "originally" as a concomitance of *alētheia* and *lēthē*, that is, of what discloses itself and of what at the same time closes itself off from view.

The "means" that Plato lists are word or name, definition or conceptual determination, example or illustration, and our insight itself. Now, as Gadamer has indicated in his discussion of the *Cratylus*, given the sophistic misuse of words, there is no intrinsic guarantee that the word or name and what it means correspond, and even precisely defined conventional signs, since they are interchangeable and have no essential connection with what they designate, can assert themselves instead of what they mean. The weakness of the second "means," the conceptual determination, is not as precisely elaborated here in this propaedeutic text, but as the *Sophist* and *Statesman* (and Aristotle) will point out, there is always indeterminacy here in what genus one chooses to divide and what species it is divided into, and again there is no guarantee that the definition arrived at will not divert us from the truth as much as it might lead us to it. The illustration fares no better: anyone can see that a circle drawn in the sand is not the real circle, and as attempts to square the circle demonstrate, the appearance which the drawn circle gives of being a sum of minute chords can divert one from the circle itself (DD 106).

But what of the fourth "means," our insight itself? When I see what a circle is, intuit it directly, can I not be sure? Do I not have indisputable evidentness? And does that not also hold for insight into the good? The problem here, Gadamer argues—a problem far more acute in ethical matters than in the mathematical case of the circle that Plato takes as his example—is that it is I, not a god, who has this insight, and thus it is caught up after all in a discursive, verbal process: it "comes to me," "I get it" in the experience Plato calls *nous* or intellectual intuition, but it "escapes me" as well and often I "get it wrong." Any human insight, even a mathematical one, is temporal. It is a partial insight now that then recedes into oblivion (*lēthē*), whence it might or might not re-emerge. That is what Heidegger meant when he argued that the truth "presents itself" (*anwest*) in our insights but "absents itself" (*abwest*) as well.

The self-assertion of this fourth "means" in place of the thing itself becomes evident in my clinging to my view contentiously, as we all do, instead of attending to the thing itself that I have in view. Thus precisely because it is "mine," my very insight can become an impediment to seeing the truth. It conceals as well as reveals. Here again Plato shows his awareness of the inescapable linking of clarity and obscurity in any truth that might become accessible to us in discussion (DD 111). And the place (*Ort*) of all ethical truth, after all, is discussion, language and discourse—either with others or the "discussion of the soul with itself."

It is significant here that Plato lists our insight itself among the "means" of knowing, for that he does gives a clear indication that in the end he too acknowledges the insurmountability of human discursivity. And this, perhaps, is the reason why it never occurs to him to substitute any term for the ordinary Greek words *agathon, kalon, hosion, dikaion* (good, beautiful or noble, holy, just or right) and so forth, even when he means them as *eidē* or forms. And thus it is wrong to translate *auto to kalon*, for example, as "absolute beauty." For that gives it the appearance of terminological determinacy that "beautiful itself" would not. Though the argument of the excursus would seem once again to point to the necessity of a knowing without words, concepts, illustrations—to a knowing of a truth beyond all these—Plato makes it evident that precisely such a direct knowing is not given to human beings: their very knowing itself is a medium in which the truth shows up but conceals itself as well. Their knowing, accordingly, is inconclusive and conditioned by the indeterminacy inhering in the language in which it proceeds. It is an unending movement that even in the most successful discussion reaches only partial clarification of what is meant and sought, never full comprehension of it (DD 121ff.). Human, discursive knowing has the structure of remembering (*anamnē- sis*), where some aspects of a thing come to mind, but others inevitably remain forgotten or lapse into oblivion (*lēthē*).

Thus, as Gadamer shows, in the *Seventh Letter* a quite different Plato emerges alongside the critical Plato of the *Cratylus*. In the *Seventh Letter* we see a dialogical Plato who knows that *our* insights remain contingent, language-bound, and that *our* truths are therefore not to be arrived at with methodical security and certainty. Indeed, human thinking arrives at no final answers and must persist in the questionable. Certainly there is no move here beyond the "cave" of spoken language, as Heidegger had argued, but rather a persistent and faithful "being under way within" it.

Of particular interest in this regard is the *Phaedo*, for it is here that Plato is generally thought to announce his doctrine of the ideas and here, accordingly, where we might expect to find the critical and not the dialogical Plato. Surprisingly, however, what we actually find is not at all a critical attempt to transcend spoken language, but rather an immersion in it. Importantly, what is said of the ideas (*eidē*) and of the *hypothesis* of them comes within the context of Socrates' flight not from, but into, the *logoi*, a flight, that is, not from, but into, what we say.

To understand the significance of Socrates' so-called "flight into the *logoi*" (*Phaedo* 99E) we need to know its place in the argument Socrates has been developing when he comes to speak of it in the *Phaedo*. Simmias and Cebes have raised questions that, if Phaedo's and Echechrates' off-stage response is any measure (*Phaedo* 88cff.), threatened to overthrow Socrates' previous purely analogical arguments that the soul is immortal. True, the soul is more *like* what is divine and rules than what is moral and obeys. And true, the soul may be most *like* what is divine, undying, noetic, uniform, indissoluble, and what always keeps itself in the same state (*Phaedo* 80A–B). However, such an analogy provides only the appearance, and no convincing demonstration, that the soul does not cease to exist or dissipates when the body dies. Indeed Socrates himself admits that, like people we once naïvely trusted, these arguments can end up deceiving us, and that because of their deceptiveness, we might come to mistrust any argument (*logos*) at all and become "misologists" just as one becomes misanthropic when one has been disappointed by people one has relied on. As a matter of fact, Phaedo relates to Echecrates that this general mistrust of all arguments had been precisely the reaction of those present upon hearing Simmias' and Cebes's objections: "We had been firmly convinced by the preceding argument, but they [Simmias and Cebes] appeared to unsettle us and plunge us again into disbelief and mistrust not only of the assertions and arguments [*logoi*] made before, but also of those yet to be stated . . ." (*Phaedo* 88c). In the background here is the threat of those sophistic word-tricks that unsettle (*anatarattein*) whatever seems stable and credible and thereby induce skepticism and mistrust. Here, to be sure, there is no "Eleatic Palamedes"—Zeno renamed after the great wrestler—trying to throw us with his rhetorical prowess, merely two young men of good will who have provoked such consternation. But if this happens even with them, how much more vulnerable are we to those who would deliberately confound us for no other motive than contentiousness. It is to this threat that Socrates must now respond: he must find a form of argument that is invulnerable, a firm stance from which one cannot be "taken down." Hence we hear at 100D–E, in regard to the hypothesis or supposition of the *eidos*, "For this, in answer to myself or another, seems to me least susceptible of being thrown down [*asphalestaton*], and once having firm hold [*echomenos*] of it, I consider myself incapable of ever coming to a fall [*pesein*]." The image and language here is taken from wrestling.

In answer to Cebes's objection, and after considerable deliberation, Socrates takes up the question of the cause (*aitia*) of coming-into-being and passing away (*genesis kai phthora*) (*Phaedo* 95Eff.), for the issue now is whether or not the soul *is* the sort of thing that passes away, and no longer whether or not it is merely *like* what is mortal and changing. An answer to this question of the cause will not be forthcoming, Socrates maintains, if one stays on the level of physical antecedent causes or what after Aristotle were to be called "material" and "efficient" causes. Optimally it ought to be forthcoming, he continues, if one seeks an explanation for what comes into being and passes away in terms of what divine intelligence (*nous*) finds *best*, and here one sees an adumbration of Aristotle's *hou heneka* (that for the sake of which) or the "final" cause. What happens in the physical world, that is, ought to be explainable in the same way as Socrates' remaining in jail is to be explained: namely, not as the consequence of the action of unintelligent matter—in this case, his bones and muscles—but of intelligent choice of what is right and best. Significantly, we have already made the transition here to ethical and not just physical justification or giving an account of something (*logon didonai*); indeed, physical accounts of things are to be put on the basis of the ethical accounts one gives for one's choices and actions.[8] There was a promise of such explanation in Anaxagoras, but as is well known, a disappointed promise, says Socrates. And in the end he finds neither himself nor anyone else capable of providing this sort of explanation of coming-into-being and passing away.

At just this point, namely, in the absence of an account in terms of what is good and best, Socrates undertakes his "second-best voyage" (*deuteron ploun*) (99D)—second best, as Gadamer points out, in that in the absence of favorable winds, one must make what headway one can by strenuous rowing. That was the actual navigational sense of this expression. It is clear that one should turn away from straight material accounts of coming-into-being and passing away and that if one could, one should turn to teleological ones. Given the seeming unavailability of the latter, Socrates finds it necessary "... εἰς τοὺς λόγους καταφυγόντα ἐν ἐκείνοις σκοπεῖν τῶν ὄντων τὴν ἀλήθειαν" (99E): having fled to the *logoi*, to look in them for the truth of the things that are.

Logoi here has been the bane of Plato translators. Does he mean "arguments," "speeches," "conceptions," "theories," "statements," "assertions," or, even, "propositions"? He means all of these, unfortunately, and no one of them by itself. But above all he means things we say, in whatever form. *Logoi* must be seen in conjunction with *ta legomena* or what has been said. They mean the same thing except that in the latter there is a determination of tense. In sum, Socrates has "fled" to what is spoken (*legetai*) or to ordinary language, and the truth (*aletheia*) he seeks to look at (*skopein*) is now to be found not outside the things we say, but *in* them (*en ekeinois*)! The truth seen in the *logoi* is to be taken precisely not as a reflection or image referring to something more real outside the *logoi*: "οὐ γὰρ πάνυ συγχωρῶ τὸν ἐν τοῖς λόγοις σκοπούμενον τὰ ὄντα ἐν εἰκόσι μᾶλλον σκοπεῖν ἢ τὸν ἐν τοῖς ἔργοις" (For I do not concede at all that someone viewing in the *logoi* the things that are sees them in likenesses rather than in the facts) (*Phaedo* 100A). A careful reading of this passage shows that for us humans, at least, no transcendence of what we say, no overcoming of our discursivity, however unreliable and vulnerable to sophistic distortions it may be, is intended.

There has already been important confirmation of this point at 85c–d when Simmias distinguishes between human arguments (*hoi anthrōpinoi logoi*) and a divine argument (*logos theios ti*). In such difficult and weighty subjects as the immortality of the soul, he says, one could hope to learn definitively how the matter stands, but if that is impossible, one must "seize upon the best of human arguments and, borne upon this as if on a raft, navigate [*diapleusai*] one's way through life, risking its dangers, unless, that is, one could be carried with firmer purchase and safety on some steadier divine argument and could make one's way through on that" (85D). One can scarcely overlook the prefiguration here in what Simmias says of Socrates' *deuteron ploun* or second-best voyage in the absence of a (divine?) argument that would definitively account for coming-into-being and passing away in terms of what is best, and of Socrates' resorting to the *logoi*. And even at 107A–B, after Socrates' exposition of the hypothesis of the *eidē* or forms of soul and of life and death, this same Simmias, while allowing that this argumentation has been more trustworthy, says, "Given the magnitude of the subject that the arguments [*logoi*] have treated, and having a poor estimation of human weakness [*hē anthrōpinē astheneia*], I, for my part, am still compelled to mistrust the things said." To which Socrates responds, "And not only that but also our principal hypotheses [*kai tas hypotheseis tas prō-tas*], even if you trust these, should be scrutinized more clearly" (107B). We see here that we humans, even in positing the forms of things, never leave the level of our human discourse, *hoi anthrōpinoi logoi*. The truth for us is *in* what we say of it, though the truth for a god might transcend this, and hence the stability we humans can attain, we need to attain, to keep from being thrown by sophism, is never ultimate and no argument is ever completely secure at its beginnings (*hai hypotheseis hai prōtai*) or conclusive at its end.

A closer examination of the *Phaedo* thus reveals that one must be cautious about equating the *eidē* as they are spoken of here with those otherworldly ideas in the myths and metaphors of the *Phaedrus* and the *Republic*, ideas separate (*chōriston*) from the world of appearances and pure (*katharon*) of the deceptiveness of our world. As Gadamer's *The Idea of the Good in Platonic-Aristotelian Philosophy* argues convincingly, we must be careful not to take Plato's allegorical talk literally and not to confuse it with the logical argumentation in his dialogues. In the *Phaedo* too there is a large amount of myth and metaphor about the afterlife and the "pure" knowledge we might hope to attain there. But in the logical exposition of Socrates' turn to the *logoi* and of the method of hypothesizing the forms it is never said that our knowledge of the forms would be free of the contingencies of all human knowing and that they would accordingly set us free from the finitude the discursivity of our knowing imposes on us. To be sure, the task of the *Phaedo* is to stabilize the meaning of what we say, and the hypothesis of the form or *eidos* that Socrates proposes is designed to achieve just this stabilization. But it is never said that we can wholly transcend the oscillations of meaning and even the interference of contrary meanings in what we say. It is never said, in other words, that we can attain to absolute knowing. The hypothesis of the form occurs *within* the turn to the *logoi* and does not posit something beyond it.

Just what is the problem that it addresses? Why is stabilization needed? And what sort of stabilization? Once again the concern is sophistic refutation which makes something seem to be opposite of what it is and thus confounds any assertion we might have made about it. We might naturally assert, for example, that one man is taller than another by a head, but a "head" is short, so how could a man be taller by a short thing? Or two might come into being by adding one thing to another or by dividing the same thing. But how could opposites such as separating halves of a thing and combining something with it produce the same results? (Compare *Phaedo* 96D–97B.) Such paradoxical reasoning moves within the framework of the contemporary physical explanation of coming-into-being and passing away by combination and separation of material. What is the way around these puzzles? We must abandon talk in reference to physical things and processes and distinguish *within our logoi* among levels in what we say. We must not run the levels together; rather, we must keep them separate (*chōriston*). On the one hand, there are things (*ta onta*) we speak of as being tall or as being two—not things "out there," it must be noted, but things present within our speaking of them. On the other hand, we speak of tall itself and two itself. Similarly, we speak of a beautiful thing (*kalon ti*), a color or shape and so forth, and of the beautiful itself, *auto to kalon*. To translate the latter as absolute beauty is misleading precisely because it then appears that our speaking does refer beyond itself, and in two directions: to some fluctuating thing outside our speaking in the illusory physical world and to some otherworldly eternal reality, outside our speaking and absolved from its indeterminacy, in the "heavens." But in fact, here, at least, Socrates is only distinguishing among and within the things we say, the *logoi* themselves. Thus we may distinguish, for instance, among what we say to be number, say to be duality, or say to be two things (or four, or six, and so forth). Or we may distinguish among what we say to be number, say to be unity, or say to be one thing (or three things, or five, and so forth). Each thing we say is a part of, and takes part in (*metechei*), what precedes it in these sequences. Contrary to the way Aristotle portrays it, *metexis* or participation is—if one leaves the myths aside—not the participation of ontologically different things in each other, that is, of physical reality in distinct (*chōrismos*) eternal reality, but the participation of lower levels of our speaking in higher levels: *metexis* implies nothing more than the former's being a part of the latter (see IGPAP 11). Sophists do two things: they conflate these levels of our speaking indiscriminately when these ought to be kept separate (*chōriston*), and they import things into the sequence at lower levels that the higher levels exclude, for instance, addition (combination) and division (separation) into the sequence of number, even, duality, two. It is just this sleight of hand that the hypothesis of the *eidos* is meant to head off:

> Well then, if one is added to one, would you not take care to avoid saying that the cause of two is the addition, or if one is divided, that the cause of two is division? Would you not loudly protest that you know no other way a given thing has come into being than by taking part in the being proper to each thing in which it takes part? Would you not protest that in these instances you admit no other cause of two coming into being than its taking part in duality and that what is to become two must take part in duality and what is to become one, in unity? Would you not pass up divisions and additions and other such refinements, leaving them to those wiser than you [*tois seautou sophoterois*]? And if anyone should lay hold of your hypothesis itself, would you not let that pass and not reply until you had looked at the things that issue from your hypothesis to see for yourself whether they are concordant with each other or discordant? And when you were obliged to give a reason [*didonai logon*] in support of the hypothesis itself, you would give it in this way, positing in turn another hypothesis—whichever appears to be the best of the higher ones—until you come to one that suffices. And if you wished to find any of the things that are, you would not mix things up by speaking simultaneously of the starting point [*archē*] and what issues from it, as do the controversialists [*antilogikoi*] [*Phaedo* 101Bff.].

At stake is what sort of reason (*logos*) we can give (*didonai*) to account for something's being what it is, for example, one or two, fire or snow, dying or undying (*athanatos*), and, ultimately, for something's being good or bad, noble (*kalos*) or despicable (*aischros*). Sophists (*hoi seautou sophoteroi*) are able to make things *appear to be* the opposite of themselves, but we can defend against their sleight of hand if we account for a thing's being what it is by establishing what it is a part of, that is to say, by hypothesizing its *eidos*. Two cannot be passed off as one if we establish it to be part of duality, which is not consonant with unity; nor can the soul be passed off as mortal (*thanatē*) if we establish it to be part of life, which is not consonant with death (*ho thanatos*). And if someone should "lay hold" of our hypothesis, for example, duality, we would account for it in turn by yet a higher hypothesis, for instance, even, or still higher, number.

When it is said that controversialists mix things up by conflating the higher with the lower, what is meant is evidently that in order to confound us, they might say something like "Warblers are songbirds; warblers are not sparrows; therefore, sparrows are not songbirds," which, of course, they are. To head off this trick, one must insist on the fact that the *eidos* or form, songbirds, is not on the same level as the lower *eidē* (forms) that are part of it, namely, warbler, sparrow, thrush, and so forth. These are inconsonant with each other—a sparrow cannot be a warbler—but the higher "songbird" is consonant with all of them. Of course, it is trivial and transparent when someone tries to make a sparrow appear not to be a songbird. But it is neither trivial nor transparent when someone tries to make what is bad appear to be good (*Phaedrus* 260D) or, to take the example to which we will turn in the next section, when someone tries to make doing injustice (*adikein*) appear to be noble (*kalon*) and good (*agathon*) when it is really the opposite of these, *aischron* (ugly) and *kakon* (bad). To counter this, one needs to establish in just which *eidē* or forms *adikein* does take part and with which, on the other hand, it is inconsonant. That will require careful examination of what we say, our *logoi*.

Though relying heavily on Gadamer's reading of the *Phaedo* (see IGPAP, DD), I have extended it here well beyond what he says. Still, I have not violated the sense and spirit of his interpretation. Gadamer is led to his insights into the dialogical nature of Plato's thought and the importance of the "flight into the *logoi*" as a consequence of his concern with hermeneutics. As we know, one, if not the major, task of hermeneutical philosophy as Gadamer conceives of it, is to reach an understanding of the dead written word by transforming it back into spoken language. The written word has an aura of finality about it; it is apparently a conclusion, a definitive answer arrived at finally. But to understand it, he tells us, we must not be deceived by this appearance. We must see any assertion as a response to a question raised within a specific context, and once it is seen that way, it becomes evident that the answer the written text seemed to give is anything but final. Rather, it in turn raises questions for those who respond to it in their efforts to understand it, to reach an understanding of what is said. Every text, then, derives its significance from its place in an unfinished and inconclusive *Wirkungsgeschichte*, which is to say, a continuing history of effects and effecting, of promptings and responses that in turn prompt new responses. Obviously the model here is dialogue, spoken language, which is an unending play of questions, answers, and new questions. And where else but in Plato would one look for exemplification of that unending play?

Even in *Truth and Method*, where, as we have seen, Plato is portrayed as the first to have abstracted from the original experience of language, Plato is also singled out as precisely the philosopher who preserves the play-game (*Spiel*) character of spoken language and the priority of the question over any final answer. For Plato does not write treatises, but inconclusive dialogues (see WM 344ff. on the "Hermeneutic Priority of the Question"). Plato seen in this context is a very different Plato from the Plato of the *Cratylus*. For the emphasis at this point in Gadamer's development of his hermeneutic theory in *Truth and Method* is not on the critical Plato's attempt to overcome the *dynamis tōn onomatōn*, but on the dialogical Plato's willingness to enter into, to submit to, the *pathos tōn logōn*, the experience, or, quite literally, the suffering, of language, suffering, that is, of what it does to us. Rather than trying to rise above language to an insight without words, the Plato we see here would allow language to have its way with us. And here such submission to language, Gadamer points out, is by no means said to lead to some sophistical "bewitchment" of our intelligence. Gadamer uses Wittgenstein's exact word, *Verhexung*, in making this point (WM 107). On the contrary, only in submitting to the back-and-forth of the play of language can we glimpse the truth of what is under discussion, the truth as it is given to finite human beings and accompanied, as it inevitably is, by obscurity and oblivion.

The critical Plato of the *Cratylus* seeks to transcend the level of language in order to ensure that it is used correctly. He would, so it seemed, found spoken language on the ideas, i.e., on a reality unclouded by the medium of words. And using the pure ideas as a standard, he would then assess the correctness (*orthotēs*) of spoken language. But the dialogical Plato who now comes to the fore and who sees that even insight itself is a "means" that obscures as well as reveals recognizes that such a transcendence of the *logoi* is not possible, that we are under way within discourse and therefore cannot get it around in front of us to evaluate it. Language for the dialogical Plato is play and a game (*Spiel*), in the sense that the participants in it do not have hold of it; rather, it has hold of them. Just as the individual players become subordinate to the game itself when they get caught up in it, so the speakers become subordinate to the movement of a discussion when they yield to it (cf. WM 97ff.). And in the later dialogues Plato is careful to select interlocutors in whom there is a minimum of spoilsport contentiousness and a maximum of willingness to follow where the discussion may take them, "tractable" youths, as Gadamer refers to them. Thus here one cannot begin at all with the speech acts of the individual speakers, as the critic of language, who sees it being used correctly or incorrectly, might do. Rather, one must begin with the effect of language itself on those who are involved in speaking it.

Those critically disposed toward language must view all of this negatively, for they put their efforts into surmounting ambiguities in ordinary language usage. As we have seen, even the later Wittgenstein, who accepts ordinary language, remains critically disposed too, in the sense that rather than submit to language, he would clarify the rules that ensure its proper (correct) use, ensure that it is "in order." And here, I think, MacIntyre also shows critical intentions concerning our ethical language. But the hermeneutical insight of the dialogical Plato is that the inconclusiveness of discourse experienced in the *pathos tōn logōn* is far from something negative to be surmounted. As Gadamer points out, in Plato all *aporia* is the beginning of *euporia*, all confusion and perplexity the beginning of the way out to a glimpse of the truth (DD 238). The Socratic *elenchos* (refutation) leading to knowledge that one does not know is no mere pedagogical device; it is an exemplification in discussion of the ancient Greek principle of *pathei mathos*, "by suffering learned" (WM 339).[9] In the *pathos tōn logōn* the truth begins to display itself against the background of our being confused and unclear. Thus despite the ever-present danger of sophistic distortion it is indeed better to yield to the *Spiel* of language than to be a *Spielverderber* (spoilsport) who stands critically on the sidelines of the language event wishing to control the course it takes.

The genius of the dialogical Plato is that though his dialogues are indeed written, they are so structured that the reader becomes a listener as well as a reader, and ultimately a "player" (*Spieler*) in a live discussion. The literary form of the dialogue thus overcomes the appearance of finality and conclusiveness in written texts: it restores "the original [*ursprüngliche*] movement of discussion" (WM 351). Hence, far from being the first "metaphysical" thinker (Heidegger), Plato, in understanding the original nature of language, the experience of its spokenness, is the philosopher who has found perhaps the best means to preserve what Heidegger calls the "earlier," pre-"metaphysical" experience of truth—the play of "equifundamental" *alētheia* and *lēthē*, of what is included and occluded in question and answer, of *euporia* and *aporia*, of insight and confusion.

4. The *Logoi* as the Place or Locus of Ethical Truth

Gadamer is especially successful in bringing this dialogical, "original" Plato to the fore, the Plato of spoken language, in his study "*Logos* and *Ergon* in Plato's *Lysis*" (DD 1–20). To see why, we must first make the distinction clear between his hermeneutical approach to this text and an analytical logical approach. For the latter, mathematical argumentation is the model, and it is assumed that as in mathematics an understanding of the truth of what is stated can be reached without considering the context in which that truth is stated. To see that the square of the hypotenuse equals the sum of the squares of the other two sides of a right triangle one does not need to concern oneself with who is presenting the demonstration of this theorem, what occasioned the presentation, to whom, when, or in response to what question. In short, one can overlook all these contingencies that constitute the spokenness of the event. What one does need to concern oneself with, on this view, is the logic of the argument, its validity and internal consistency. Of course, if one proceeds in this way, one puts oneself in the stance of Hegel's "external reflection," which is, after all, the stance of analytical philosophy as a whole. And many, in fact most, interpreters of Plato within the English-speaking world, Cornford, Crombie, Vlastos, Hackforth, to name a few, have taken precisely this approach in their interpretation of Plato. The principal issue they raise is in regard to the logic of the argument made in the dialogues. They look for a methodical demonstration in which each point is expected to follow from the previous one and the appropriate conclusion drawn. Their tacit assumption is that the spokenness of what is said can be stripped away baring the essential logic of the argument, an assumption that might be valid indeed if Plato were consistently the critic of natural language he appears to be in the *Cratylus*— but he is not, and that is exactly Gadamer's point. What they usually discover is that either Plato's logic or his method is faulty, or both; for viewed this way, the arguments that his Socrates presents are full of fallacies and the demonstrations elliptical at best and sophistic at worst. Generally their response is to fill in the gaps in Socrates' logic, rather than to declare him a sophist, but even such a masterful effort as Cornford's to uncover the logic of the incredibly dialectical arguments in the

Parmenides, for instance,[10] leaves one wondering if such an approach really makes Plato accessible. Can it be that his thought, unbeknown to him, was so muddled and in need of logical restructuring?

Gadamer proceeds on a quite different set of assumptions: namely, that Plato is a most skillful writer who knows precisely what he is doing, and that he is not following a logical method of demonstration, but the hermeneutical logic of what displays itself in live discussion, spoken language. The English and American interpreters, holding to the opinion that there is often a concealed logic behind Plato's garbled ways of putting things, expect to make the dialogues clear, where possible, by displaying the logical structure underlying the propositions of the dialogue. And where that is not possible they seek to display logical confusions. In other words, they treat Plato as Plato of the *Cratylus*, it seems, would treat the sophists: one should get behind the often misleading surface of his particular language, they tell us, to the abstract logical structure that underlies it. We have seen that developments even within Wittgensteinian philosophy, insofar as it proceeds from the purely constative to the performative function of language, cast some doubt on the appropriateness of such an approach for any instance of ordinary language like Plato's dialogues. If we add to these developments the further step of Gadamer's return to apophantic language, it becomes clearer still that Plato ought to be read in a quite different way from the way the majority of contemporary English-speaking commentators read him. He should be read hermeneutically, for any dialogue, Plato's included, is a process of reaching an understanding of something within spoken language as that something, the subject matter (*Sache*), shows up (*apophainetai*) and obscures itself in an often apparently erratic back-and-forth through the "means" of speaking.

Though it might seem that as "means" the words spoken serve to establish (*constater*) a reality, a state of affairs, apart from the words, and that consequently we have three tiers—the subject matter to which the spoken words refer, the spoken language itself which Plato uses, and the formal essential structure or logic of the spoken language—this is actually not the case. Discussion, dialogue, is not at all the establishing of a pre-existent state of affairs, but rather a disclosure of something, a bringing something to light, a letting the subject matter show forth (*apophainesthai*), *in* the medium of the *logoi* or things said. The content or subject matter is immanent in the speaking of it,[11] not something else besides. Moreover, there is a kind of logic in the movement of the discussion in Plato, not the formal logic of a purified language apart from its content, but the substantive logic of things displayed in any speaking of them. There is a logic, in other words, insofar as one thing leads to another in the experience of running up against *aporiai* or dead ends and then finding ways through, *euporiai*, to a more felicitous result. That logic, however, is not necessarily sequential and consequential on the propositional level. Indeed, as analytic interpreters have made clear, it seldom is. As apophantic, the discussion often shifts abruptly from aspect to aspect of the thing, bringing one side of it to light while losing sight of another.

Yet a further distinction between the mathematical and the hermeneutical approach follows from this first point: if we would understand the movement of a dialogue—and it is the task of hermeneutics to do this—we cannot treat it as we would some mathematical object, from which the impartial knower can maintain theoretical distance. Rather, we must be drawn out of "external reflection," the critical, analytical stance, into the activity of speaking ourselves, so that the subject matter is linguistically reconstituted in us: "Like all knowing, philosophical knowing is identification of something as what it is and has the structure of recognition or 'knowing again.' But the object of philosophy is not given in the same way as the object of the empirical sciences. Rather, it is always constituted anew, and that occurs only when one tries to think it through for oneself" (DD 128). Our own horizons of discourse must therefore fuse with those of the interlocutors in the dialogue, and like them we must be drawn into the movement of the discussion. That means that the crucial distinction in any analytical approach between what is clear to us, who, from the outside, have established the supposed logic of what is said, and what is clear for the consciousness on the level of the discussion itself and caught up in its play cannot be maintained. We cannot transcend the "cave" of the discussion any more than the interlocutors can. Like them we must understand while remaining under way within spoken language.

The *Lysis*, Gadamer points out, is one of those dialogues that logical analysts are most likely to seize upon as displaying fallacious reasoning, for many of its arguments are seemingly sophistic. How are we to take this work? Is it more than a dramatic portrayal of an especially captious Socrates? Gadamer argues that it is indeed more. It is, in fact, the propaedeutic discussion of the same subject matter (*Sache*) thematized in the great dialogues on love, the *Symposium* and the *Phaedrus*, and in Aristotle's chapters on *philia* or friendship (EN VIII, IX). But how that subject matter is developed can be understood only if, first, one considers to whom it is that Socrates addresses his questions and responses, namely, two young and inexperienced boys. As Gadamer points out, Socrates says explicitly that the argument would evolve very differently if he could find more mature men to question (DD 8). And one can understand the development of the subject matter only if, second, one pays attention to the circumstances under which the discussion takes place: specifically, one of the boys is being pursued by an older admirer whom he shuns. Thus the situational contingencies, the "scenic" background or setting for this discussion, are indispensable for determining the significance of what is said. And if one keeps this in view, one can see that there is a "logic" in what Socrates says after all—not the deductive logic of a mathematical demonstration, to be sure, but the pedagogical logic of articulating something in language, allowing it to display itself, given the character, perspective, and motives of those involved in the discussion. Consequently, it serves no purpose to leave the "performative" background out of the account. The *logos* or what is said is not to be divorced from the world of behavior and deed (*ergon*) in which it is said: "our task can only be to activate the context of meaning in which the discussion takes place even if we find fault with the logic of that discussion" (DD 53).

Again, this conclusion ought to have been drawn from the later Wittgenstein's or Austin's ordinary language philosophy. Language, we learn from them too, can be understood only in the circumstances, in the *Sprachspiel* or language game in which it is used. But the differences displayed in Wittgenstein's and Gadamer's understanding of *Spiel* are plainly reflected here as well, and we should not overlook them. The "activation" Gadamer has in mind implies that we enter into the situation of the discussion, that we become participants in it and give ourselves over to the *pathos tōn logōn*, the experience of what comes to be spoken of. Though we, like Socrates, may be ahead of these youths in our insights, neither they nor we maintain a perspective of reflection external to the discussion, from which we ourselves might ascertain a logical structure inaccessible to those caught up in the movement of the discussion. And this fact implies in turn that no clear starting point for a deductive argument nor any clear conclusion is to be expected, but instead an inconclusive wavering between *aporia* and *euporia*, between impenetrable puzzlement and successful penetration into the subject matter. And precisely such an inconclusive wavering is what occurs here in this provisional exploration of the nature of *philia*, friendship, and *philos*, what is dear.

In an argument geared to both the circumstances and the interlocutors, Socrates traces two of the possible meanings contained in "dear." He traces, that is to say, the thing or subject matter as it displays itself, *apophainetai*, in the double sense of the word "dear," loving and lovable. In the process all the discussants are led from "dear" to *to oikeion*, that which in belonging to house and household (*oikos*) pertains to individuals and makes them "dear" to one another in a way that transcends what is "dear" only as long as one's need for it has not been satisfied. Thus the argument moves entirely within the reality constituted by the "means" of words, words that lead us through confusion to *euporiai*, to a view of the thing meant, but often mislead us into dead ends (*aporiai*) as well. Significantly, the level of the *logoi*, what is spoken in words with all their ambiguities, is not transcended here. Put another way: we remain on the level of apophantic truth and falsity, evidentness and obscurity. No attempt is made to achieve indubitable certainty by overcoming the ambiguity and obscurity inherent in ordinary language, and no attempt to get behind what is spoken to either a logical structure or the things themselves to which spoken words might be thought to refer. The intention here is quite different. For far from seeking to suppress the *dynamis tōn onomatōn*, Socrates draws upon it: he submits to the spoken word, yields to the course of the discussion, and follows it where it takes him. The *Lysis*, accordingly, reveals the dialogical Plato who emphasizes the *pathos tōn logōn*.

As a consequence, no ultimate conclusion is achieved, yet aspects of the phenomenon of love as it is displayed in the words *philos* and *oikeion* do come into the open insofar as that is possible given the circumstances. And clearly a youth who shuns an overly forward admirer can be brought only so far in coming to see what love and friendship are. Thus it is fitting that the dialogue ends in puzzlement with the question left open. That is the point of Socrates' *elenchos* (refutation). It is not meant as a rhetorical trick to stifle an opponent and end the discussion, but as a protreptic inducement to persist in the direction of what is sought but never attained (DD 247).

There are many instances, of course, where Plato's dialogues proceed and end in just this way. Does the *Meno* ever make definitively clear in what sense *aretē* belongs to the kind of things that can be taught? Does the *Sophist* ever make definitively clear what kind of thing a sophist is? Or the *Phaedrus*, what kind of thing love is? In the last, for example, the first hypothesis of an *eidos*, irrational desire, displays the "left" or sinister (*skaios*) aspect of love. But Socrates posits a second *eidos*, divine madness, to show that the first, while bringing one side of love to mind, had kept another in oblivion (*lēthē*). Since our concern is with what comes to light in ethical language, let us, following Gadamer's approach, examine another passage in Plato that specifically treats crucial expressions in the ethical realm of discourse, namely, Socrates' dispute with Polus concerning the relationships between what is *dikaion* and what is *adikon* (right and wrong, just and unjust), what is *agathon* and what is *kakon* (good and bad), and what is *kalon* and what is *aischron* (fair and ugly, worthy and shameful) (*Gorgias* 461B–481B).

First, in regard to the "scenic" background here, Plato gives us very precise indications of which we must take careful note, for it is essential, if we are to take the hermeneutical rather than the mathematical approach to this passage, that we grasp who is saying what to whom, when, and why he is saying it. It is essential, in other words, that we grasp the *occasion* for what is said if we are to follow the *apophantic* logic in Socrates' argumentation here. For as we have seen, the process of getting clear about what particular words and sentences (*logoi*) display to us can be followed out only within the context in which they are said.

Analogically, we could say that we must approach our subject matter in the manner not of geometricians but of surveyors who have a specific terrain of which they must take the measure. Geometry, of course, meant earth measurement and had its origins there. But precisely as mathematics, it (plane geometry, at least) abstracts from particular surfaces that are to be measured to a consideration of the universal forms that are applied in *any* measuring of area. In this it is much like formal logic, which abstracts from the specific occasion of an argument (*logos*) and the specific things said (*logoi*, *legomena*) to a consideration of the universal forms of inference that are applied in any argumentation. If Gadamer is correct, however, precisely that abstraction must be reversed if we are to understand anything said to us—a point, incidentally, MacIntyre also establishes, using the wry example of a total stranger who says to me at a bus stop, "The name of the common wild duck is *Histrionicus histrionicus histrionicus*" (AV 210). Though I might know the universal meaning of the words used, I can still make no sense of what he is saying unless I can reconstruct the particular context in which he is saying it, unless, in other words, I know the occasion for his saying something like that. And that holds for understanding what Plato has his characters say, which is astonishing, perhaps, if one considers that it is Plato himself who, as the critic of ordinary language, stresses precisely such geometrical abstraction in the training of his "guardians" (see *Republic* VI).

Now, we know from other sources that Polus is a student of Gorgias' and an enthusiast for the new rhetorical art who produced a handbook himself on turning phrases (see *Phaedrus* 267c), and, indeed, these are things that Plato could assume any of his readers would know and that he could therefore leave unsaid. (Is the reference to Polus' treatise [*syngramma*] at 462c a reference to this handbook, and is the example of Polus' style at 448c excerpted from it?) That he was young and that he had come to Athens from elsewhere was, certainly, also common knowledge, but Plato finds it necessary to underscore these facts explicitly at 461c and 461e. For in regard to the first, we must note that Polus, precisely as a young man, will not be constrained to keep up the gentlemanly air of his teacher, Gorgias, who, he feels, was undercut in the argument with Socrates by his sense of decorum. Precisely as a young man, that is (see also 463e: "Πῶλος δὲ ὅδε νέος ἐστὶ καὶ ὀξύς" [But this Polus, the colt, is young and hot-blooded]), he is free to breach etiquette and to state brashly and even shamelessly what his master could not bring himself to say straight out: that considerations of things noble and good (*ta kala* and *ta agatha*) as well as of things just (*ta dikaia*) are to be set aside completely when practicing rhetoric (461b–c); for the concern is but one: namely—as emerges shortly thereafter at 466c—the power to dispose, without restraint and as we see fit, over the life and death of others.[12] It is to exactly this bluntness and uninhibited ardor of youth that

Plato refers when he has Socrates respond to Polus by saying at 461c, with the usual touch of irony, that the young are needed in their words and deeds (*en ergois kai en logois*) to set the lives of the older ones straight. Plainly it is important to Plato that we see what Polus says, his *logoi*, against the background of who he is and how he behaves, against the background, that is, of his *ergoi* (deeds). And that holds for Plato's Socrates as well—a point to which we must return, for *logos* and *ergon,* word and deed, are indissociable in him too (see IGPAP 96–97 and "*Logos* and *Ergon* in Plato's *Lysis*," DD 1–20).

That Polus is a newcomer to Athens (*Athenaze aphikomenos*) is also important insofar as it further specifies just what sort of a person, in word and deed, Socrates must respond to here: as a sort of cosmopolitan forensic artist and amoralist, he stands outside the customs of any particular place and can be expected to abjure them as mere conventional restraints to which, he feels, no one owes more than lip service. Again, he thinks that power is the sole concern, and like his youth, his being an outsider sustains him in the conviction that it is. Still, he speaks Attic Greek, if somewhat affectedly (see 467c), and it will turn out that consequently he is not so far removed from customary thinking as he might imagine himself to be. It remains for Socrates to show him that he is not.

The very beginning of the exchange between Polus and Socrates gives us a further indication of Polus' character and displays again the inseparability of what someone says and who someone is. Polus essays to be the questioner here, a task at which he proves wholly inadequate (see IGPAP 59). For his manner of proceeding is that of legal advocacy, of making claims and adducing grounds in the form of testimony either to support his claims or to refute those of his adversaries. Hence his "questions," when they are questions at all, tend to have the form of interrogation rather than inquiry. And very often they are not questions at all but declamation—"'Ερώτημα τοῦτ' ἐρωτᾷς ἢ λόγου τινὸς ἀρχὴν λέγεις;" (Are you asking a question or beginning a speech?) (466b)—and even accusation: Μὴ κατηγόρει, ὦ λῷστε Πῶλε . . ." (Leave off the accusing, my dear Polus . . .) (467c).

What is needed, of course, is the very different art of guiding a discussion to an insight by asking questions that bring the truth of the matter to the fore. That only Socrates can do. Like a lawyer trying to extract a "yes" or "no" answer from a witness, Polus keeps forcing the question whether Socrates considers rhetoric *kalon* or *aischron*, to which Socrates finally responds, "*aischron*," because he calls all things *aischron* that are bad (*kakon*) (463D). But he adds immediately that to say this now is to get far in advance of the exposition of the subject matter up to this point, and he then proceeds to provide the needed clarification of what has admittedly not yet been made clear. But he proceeds to provide it, we should note, not to the impetuous (*oxus*) Polus, but to the much more tractable and leisurely Gorgias. Only after Socrates has shown rhetoric to be a sort of flattery does Polus join in again, and still in the fashion of forensic interrogation: "What are you saying? That you believe rhetoric to be flattery" (466A)?

There now comes a series of "yes" or "no" questions, some of which Socrates parries and some of which he answers. The gist of the dispute is the following:

> "Are rhetoricians considered worthless then?"
> "They aren't considered to be anything."
> "But don't they have power?"
> "No."
> "But can't they do anything they think fit?"
> "Are you stating your opinion or asking a question?"
> "Asking a question."
> "They do nothing they wish to do, only what they think best."
> "Is that not power?"
> "No."
> "If they do what they think best, don't they do what they wish?"
> "No."

Omitted in this summary is Socrates' clever maneuvering of Polus, several times along the way, into being the one who answers, for example, at 466E–467A. And at 467E Polus gives up altogether and declares himself ready to let Socrates ask the questions.

With that the discussion assumes a very different character. For Socrates now begins his famous midwifing of right beliefs. In bringing forth assertions (*logoi*) and putting them to the test (*elenchos*), he disabuses his interlocutor of obstructive misconceptions so that he might finally give birth, as it were, to the truth of the matter. In the course of the inquiry, it emerges that we do not say that one does what one "wishes" (*bouletai*) in regard to actions that are means to a good, but only in regard to the good itself. When one chooses to walk, for instance, we do not, properly speaking, say he "wishes" to walk, but rather that he "wishes" the good health to which walking is a means. The latter, as Wittgenstein's and Gadamer's German puts it, is the *Sprachgebrauch*, the customary usage. Very artfully, Socrates has led up to the considerations of things that it would have been premature to consider before, considerations, namely, of what we say as good and bad, helpful and harmful, and, ultimately, right and wrong, just and unjust. Discussion of these would have been foreign in the context of Polus' forensic argumentation, and he had hoped to have obviated it anyway by treating power, not as a means, but as an end in itself.

Even here (468E) Polus is not yet ready to take this step. He falls back on his initial position: Would not everyone, Socrates included, choose, if he could, the freedom to do whatever he thinks fit and would he not envy those who are in fact free to kill, or banish anyone they felt like, or take away his property? These, of course, are powers the rhetorician may acquire through the courts, and it is Polus' aim to acquire them. Whether they are used justly or unjustly is of no concern to him, or at least he thinks that it is not. But Socrates, in a new run at it, will show Polus that that is not what he is actually saying. We have now come to the second juncture in their interchange: Socrates asks, "Δικαίως λέγεις ἢ ἀδίκως;" (Are you saying justly or unjustly?) (468E).

Polus believes this question to be irrelevant: "οὐκ ἀμφοτέρως ζηλωτόν ἐστιν;" "Is this [freedom and power] not to be envied and strived for either way?" he asks (469A). Given who Polus is, Socrates must now cast his response within certain horizons, the horizons, that is, which are those of Polus' prudentialism and which are set by the semantic range of *chrēia* (need), *chrēsimon* (useful in fulfilling a need), and, above all, the determining words in sophistic vocabulary, *ōpheleia* and its opposite, *blabē*, which is to say, advantage, benefit, profit, interest, utility, aid, and help, on the one side, and harm, injury, or damage to one's interests, on the other. Other words that have an aspect within these horizons yet at the same time have aspects that exceed them, words like *dikaios* and *adikos* (right and wrong), *agathos* and *kakos* (good and bad), *kalos* and *aischros* (fair and ugly)—all these will have to be introduced at first within the range of Polus' understanding of them if, in fact, the horizons of his thinking are ever to be widened and merged or fused with those of Socrates. For at first Polus understands these words only within the limited range of their meaning which they display within his sophistical thinking. The task will be to widen his understanding beyond its initial limits, and these other words, which extend from within his horizons to beyond them, will provide the means of doing that. He will come to see that what he has said is more than he had at first understood. He will, in other words, undergo the *pathos tōn logōn*, the experience of the words he uses.

Once again, here evidently to lure Polus out into the open in word and deed, Socrates departs from his questions and interjects his own answers—well ahead of time, we might say, for what he says can only seem a nonsensical enormity to Polus at this point: he who does wrong is to be pitied, not emulated, for doing wrong is the greatest of evils, greater even than suffering it and a greater evil still if one is not punished for it. Polus, producing "witnesses" and gruesome counter-evidence, heatedly attacks these suggestions in his accustomed forensic manner of refutation (*elenchein*) (470Dff.). That provides the occasion for Socrates to distinguish his own method of refutation from Polus', or from "what those in the law courts [*en tois dikasteriois*] consider refutation" (471E). Socrates will not advance "many" witnesses; instead he will test (*elenchein*) the words and statements (*logoi*) of the one witness he is asking questions of. (See also 474B.) In the end he will show Polus that Polus himself is saying the very same things that now seem so monstrous to him: "I will in fact attempt to get you too, my good companion [*hetairos*], to say [*legein*] the same things as I, for after all, I do consider you a friend [*philos*]" (473A). It is important to note that though Polus is an outsider to Athens and though there is more than a trace of irony in this statement, he and Socrates are bound in friendship in some degree, at least, by the community of the Greek language they share. (See Chapter 1, Part 3, above on *philia* or friendship and *philos*, which is to say "dear," or the quality that endears someone as a friend.)

At this point (474C) Socrates resumes his questioning. To be sure, what follows could be interpreted as a sequence not of questions but of propositions and inferences, in which case Polus is to be dismissed as a passive listener to whom something is to be demonstrated *more geometrico*. Looked at this way, what we have is approximately as follows: anything *kalos*, here meaning fair in the sense of beautiful, is fair or beautiful by virtue of either the pleasure it provides or its utility. Hence, by negation, what is not beautiful, which is to say, ugly, is so by virtue of either one or both of the opposites of pleasure and utility, namely, the pain it causes or its being bad for you. Doing injustice is ugly. So either it is a source of pain or it is bad for you. Doing injustice is certainly not painful. So it must be bad for you. And if we wish to abstract further from who is saying what to whom here and why, we could formalize the argument:

$$X \supset Y \vee Z$$
$$\sim X \supset \sim Y \vee \sim Z$$

$$S \supset \sim X$$
$$S \supset \sim Y \vee \sim Z$$

$$\sim (S \supset \sim Y)$$
$$\therefore \quad S \supset \sim Z$$

But clearly, whether valid or fallacious, this formal analysis is useless and irrelevant for reaching an ethical understanding. For it tells us nothing about the just or unjust, the good or bad, as these are displayed here. To make sense of the argument one must put it back into its dialogical context of the actual words exchanged between the two particular people who say them. Only in this way can we ourselves reach an understanding of what is shown or, better, of what shows itself or shows up, *apophainetai*, in their speaking of it.[13]

Let us, then, come back to the particular exchange, the words themselves and the context in which they are actually said. What is shown when Polus says initially that suffering injustice (*adikeisthai*) is worse (*kakion*) than doing injustice, but doing injustice is uglier (*aischion*) than suffering it? What does it mean when he says that the *kalon*, here meaning fair in the sense of decent or worthy, is not the same as the *agathon* (good), and that the *aischron* or ugly—but "ugly" here in the sense of mean and shameful—is not the same as the *kakon* (bad)? It is clear that the dimension of good and bad that he perceives is only that of advantage and disadvantage relative to self-interest. Good and bad for Polus apply to what is good for somebody or bad for him as an individual. Since Polus, itinerant that he is, has no sense of loyalty to a particular community, the communal and familial dimension of these words, where good and evil or good and wicked, would be the appropriate translations of them, remains hidden to him. He is oblivious to the *kakon* in disloyalty to a friend, for instance, or to anyone to whom one might be obligated by bonds of *philia*. That one should do what is right (*dikaion*) by someone makes no sense to him either. For what is right by another and just has no correlation with what is good or bad for the individual doing it unless a penalty (*dikē*) for not doing it coincidentally establishes one.

And yet he is not without some sense of community after all, for he allows that doing what is unjust, what is "wrong," is somehow *aischron*, somehow an ugly thing. Certainly the sense of ugly as despicable, contemptible, is not quite what he has in mind yet, and Socrates knows that. Nevertheless, that the word has that dimension, as Callicles' assessment of what happens to Polus here will make clear later, is somehow in the back of Polus' mind. And this range of its meaning could be brought to mind. Just such a recollection (*anamnēsis*) of what lingers on the edge of oblivion (*lēthē*) is what Socrates sets out to induce here, or, better said, what Plato sets out to induce in the reader; for Polus himself never gets beyond the propaedeutic "shock" of Socrates' scorpion-like sting.

When we say that this dimension of *aischron* remains hidden to Polus, the Greek for "remains hidden" would be *lanthanei*, upon which Plato builds when he juxtaposes *lēthē* with *anamnēsis*, for example at *Phaedrus* 248c, "τινι συντυχίᾳ χρησαμένη λήθης τε καὶ κακίας πλησθεῖσα βαρυνθῇ" (having suffered a turn of fortune, and filled with obliviousness [*lēthē*] and evil, it [the soul] is weighed down), versus 249c, "τοῦτο δ᾽ ἐστὶν ἀνάμνησις ἐκείνων, ἅ ποτ᾽ εἶδεν ἡμῶν ἡ ψυχή" (this is a recollection [*anamnēsis*] of those things our soul once saw). To the end of bringing to mind what remains hidden to Polus, Socrates begins with the dimensions of *aischron* that are in the foreground of awareness and present to one such as he whose framework is self-interest, namely, that *aischron* implies pain as opposed to pleasure, harm as opposed to benefit. It should be noted, of course, that already at this point, Socrates artfully substitutes *kakon*, or what is bad, for the opposite of benefit. Though Polus is being led in directions he does not foresee, he raises no objection. After all, for him what is bad means what is bad for someone, what is harmful or *blaberon*. Thinking in these terms,

Polus comes to see that if doing injustice is uglier, as he acknowl-edges, it is somehow bad too, or at least it "appears so" (*phainetai*) to him (475E). Of course, he is more perplexed than anything else by what he is saying, for it runs completely counter to his beliefs about self-interest, of which Socrates is trying to "purify" him (see *Sophist* 230B–D). Socrates has him on the verge of seeing that injustice is (takes part in, *metechei*) ugly and bad in the social sense of despicable and evil. Still, that it is remains the unsaid—and uncomprehended—implication. What follows, with increasingly provocative absurdity, continues to take *kakon* as what is bad for someone: if injustice is bad, then it would be good to rid oneself of it by paying the penalty (*dikēn didonai*). Suffering just (*dikaios*) punishment is good for us. And since we, out of self-interest, wish our enemies ill, we must see to it that, while we seek out the quickest punishment for our-selves, they are never punished for their injustices. For if they were, that would be good for them. Plato knows quite well how to keep us aware of what is really going on here. Off-stage, as it were, he has Callicles ask Chaerephon: "Is Socrates serious or is he only playing around?" (481B).

These "scenic" clues cannot be overlooked if we are to understand what is said here. Socrates' *eirōneia*, his ironical not saying what he is really saying, is something that only a herme-neutical logic can pick up. Only when one sees how something is said in a particular situation can one grasp what is meant. Socrates does not mean what he states here, and what he states means something else. If someone says "That's just dandy!" only the particular context will make clear what is meant. A formal propositional logic of statements, "There is an X and X is dandy," will tell us nothing. Socrates "states" that it is in one's interest to let one's enemies get off scot-free for their injustices. That is so absurd, however, that it can only call the linking of self-interest with good and bad, fair and ugly, just and unjust into question. And that, in fact, is how what he says is meant.

Socrates' argument, then, is a reductio ad absurdum put

ironically (compare 489E; Callicles: "Εἰρωνεύῃ, ὦ Σώκρατες"
[You are being sarcastic, Socrates]). In its setting, and only
there, we can see that the sense of what he is saying is the
opposite of what he states: if one starts from the position of
antisocial self-referentiality, and if at the same time one says
that it is *aischron* (uglier), and then *kakion* (worse), to do
injustice rather than to suffer it, one lands in an absurdity. Either
the premise of antisocial self-referentiality or the linking of
aischron with *adikein* must be abandoned. That this dilemma is
the actual result is made clear by the wholly fictitious character
Plato invents to radicalize the argument, that is to say, "Callicles," who is Plato's reductio ad absurdum *ergōi* and *logōi*, in
what he does and what he says, of sophism itself: "You [Calli-
cles] say clearly what the others think, to be sure, but are not
willing to say" (492D). This "Callicles" rejects the second
premise, the linking of *aischron* and *adikein*, and then proceeds
to run the premise of self-referentiality out to its extreme,
making clear *negatively* by his very extremity that it is in fact
this first premise that is to be rejected and that the *eidē* or forms
of *adikein* and *aischron*, to use the language of the *Phaedo*, "are
consonant" (*symphonousin*). In Callicles we have Plato's own
eirōneia, his own not saying what he really means. What is
stated by this character, whom Plato's readers would know to
be fictional, is the opposite of what Plato means by it, and hence
here again a logical analysis would be beside the point. It
remains now for the readers to get clear about what is shown
here and to perceive for themselves the incredibility of
"Callicles'" radicality, *ergōi* and *logōi*, in attacking the philosophical choice of life. It is really the readers who are addressed
when Socrates would persuade the incorrigible "Callicles" "to
choose [*hēlesthai*] the life of order and of satisfaction with what
suffices for it at any time, instead of the life of insatiability and
wantonness" (*Gorgias* 493C–D; see also 487A, 492D, and 500C).[14]

This "Callicles" develops the shadings in *aischros* that link it
to *aischynesthai*, namely, feeling ashamed of oneself. Seen in
this light, the *aischron* is what is shameful, and someone who is

called *aischros* is, by inversion, someone characterized by *anaischyntia* or shamelessness; having no sense of shame, he does what is shameless. In an argument astonishingly reminiscent of Nietzsche's, Callicles maintains that these words are all part of the device that the mass of inferior people use to inhibit the superior individual: the latter is to be made to feel ashamed of himself for breaking the rules that the inferior lay down to keep him at their level, which is to say, for his doing "injustice." Polus, says Callicles, fell victim to just this trick of the mass of people when he felt ashamed to say that doing injustice was *kalion*—here in the sense of "more admirable," not "more fair"—than suffering it, and said instead that injustice was *aischron*, in other words, unfair and shameful.[15] Socrates, weakling and mass-man that his "philosophy" has made him, simply played upon Polus' sense of shame, says Callicles, but the task should have been to free him from it. To that end a distinction must be made between *aischron* in the sense of being bad at something, being impotent, incapable, inferior, and *aischron* as shameful. (Or, as Nietzsche would put it, a distinction must be made between what is by nature *schlecht* [bad] and what the herd calls *böse* [evil].) The latter represents only the conventions or *nomoi* of the mass of people, their written codes (*grammata* [484A]; Nietzsche: *Talfeln*) and snares, tricks, and devices (*magganeumata*). *Nomoi*, in short, are nothing but τὰ παρὰ φύσιν συνθήματα ἀνθρώπων (492c), all too "human contrivances against nature." Exemplary in this regard is the popularly proclaimed and universally decried ultimate "vice" of *pleonexia*, or wanting to have more than one's "fair share." By nature (*physis*) every thing wills to have more than the others (see 483c: τὸ πλέον τῶν ἄλλων ζητεῖν ἔχειν). To do so is natural, to do so is *kalon*, to do so is *agathon*, and to do so is, of course, to do what the mass of people repudiate as "unfair" and "unjust." To suppress such nature and to keep the superior even (*isoi*) with the inferior, or, better said, to get even with them, social convention, *nomos*, inverts and perverts the natural values: no one should will more. *Pleonexia*, everyone says, is *kakon* (evil).

Callicles' line of argument is never really refuted by any counter-argument, and he is never convicted of being wrong or convinced by Socrates that he is. More than anything he is simply provoked. And as a matter of fact, Socrates' responses are mostly captious. But that is precisely the point: someone who has chosen the sophistical way of life in deed (*ergōi*) cannot be made to understand by words alone that he or she is wrong (see "Dialectic and Sophism in Plato's *Seventh Letter*," DD 93–123). The words Callicles draws upon display a different meaning only for those who can hear it, to those whose souls are not suffused with *lēthē* and who are capable of *anamnēsis*.

Indisputably, the *aischron* is shameful, and from the standpoint of self-referentiality shame is simply the experience of objectification by others. It undercuts self-referentiality insofar as in the experience of shame one ceases being for oneself and becomes something for others. That Sartre has shown clearly in his analysis of shame (*l'honte*).[16] But understood in another way not accessible to a "Callicles," shame, as the awareness that one has done something despicable and shameful (*aischron*), initiates the positive experience of coming to see oneself as a participant in communal values. It introduces the transition from self-centeredness to *synesis* and *gnōmē*, to understanding for others and considerateness. As a matter of fact, it is likely that the *synesis* that Aristotle says first enables children to sense *philia* for their parents is closely tied to the experience of shame and perhaps even dependent on it (see Chapter 1 above on *synesis*.) For someone with no sense of what is shameful, someone who is insolent or shameless, could scarcely see things from his or her parents' point of view and, for that matter, scarcely from the point of view of anyone else at all in the community. Shamelessness and self-referentiality presuppose each other, as "Callicles" shows in word and deed. Put in later terms: we might say that shame introduces the transition from Descartes' *ego cogito* (I think) to *cogitamus* (we think), from subjectivity to community; and that is a transition that the Sartre of *Being and Nothingness*, at least, was quite unready to make.

Furthermore, we may say that shame first spiritualizes what would have remained an animal existence without it. In shame one recognizes that copulation, birth, drinking, eating, dying—all these *natural* functions—are redefined by communal *nomoi* and thereby lose their sheerly animal quality. The animal in us is thereby made social; we become the *zōion politikon*, and animal insatiability and wantonness (*akolasia*) are tempered. That too is made clear by Callicles: "You [Callicles] are now speaking of a life of a plover . . ." (494B).

Aristotle sheds considerable light on this phenomenon of spiritualization in his discussion of *aidos* and *aichynesthai*, modesty and feeling ashamed, in the *Nicomachean Ethics* (EN 1128B 10ff.). Properly speaking, he says, these cannot be called a virtue (*aretē*) insofar as they are a feeling (*pathos*) and not the reasonable disposition (*hexis*) toward a feeling in which any virtue consists. In part, at least, they are even an immediate physical response, namely blushing, which is the same sort of thing as blanching in immediate physical response to what is frightening. Shame is like fear, in other words, and not like the virtue of courage, which consists in a reasonable disposition toward fear. Still *aidos* and *aischynesthai* do befit the young, who have not yet attained reasonable dispositions toward their feelings, for it restrains (*koluei*) the feelings in the absence of virtue. *Anaischyntia*, not feeling shame, is thus bad, for it would be wrong not to feel shame, he says, at doing *ta aischra*, or things that are shameful. But this does not mean that in an adult feeling shame for base acts is good, for if adults feel shame, they have done something shameful (*aischron*) that they ought not to have done in the first place. Consequently in regard to a good man, we may speak only counter-factually (*ex hypotheseōs*): if a good man were to do shameful things (*ta aischra*), says Aristotle, he would feel shame. Seen this way, Callicles emerges as irredeemable: insofar as he lives on the immediate animal level of puerile *anaischynthia*, of feeling no shame at shameful things, he has neither a rational disposition nor the chance of acquiring one. He is completely unrestrained, whereas Polus is at least restrained by the shame he feels, much as children are restrained by shame before they have acquired virtue and self-restraint. "Such a one," says Socrates—who given Callicles' deaf intransigence now finds himself expatiating monologically—"can be befriended [*prosphilēs*] with neither another human being nor a god. He is incapable of communing [*koinō-nein*], and where there is no communion [*koinōnia*] there is no friendship [*philia*]" (507E).

It remains for Plato's readers, not this "Callicles" foil for Plato's Socrates, to hear what Callicles cannot and to find corroboration of what they hear in the character of Socrates. It remains for the readers, that is, to reach an understanding of what is displayed in the words *aischron, aischynton, anaischynton, ainaischyntia*, and in the particular man, Socrates, who speaks of them and their opposites. For Callicles is most of all a spoilsport who himself withdraws from the play of language, the *pathos tōn logōn*, in which Plato would involve his readers. And with that he withdraws, as he actually does in this dialogue,[17] from the medium in which our ethical understanding is reached and from the community of those *philoi* who can have understanding of, and show understanding for, each other.

NOTES

1. I quote here several of a list of assumptions that Barry Gross finds basic to the *Tractatus*. See his *Analytic Philosophy* (New York: Pegasus, 1970), p. 143.

2. David Pears, quite properly, I think, speaks of Wittgenstein's "extreme anthropocentrism" (*Ludwig Wittgenstein* [New York: Viking, 1971], p. 179).

3. Pears (ibid.) points out that the critical concern is what unifies the whole of Wittgenstein's philosophy. Like Kant in his *Critique of Pure Reason*, Wittgenstein undertakes a sort of "policing action." In Wittgenstein's case this is to establish the limits of the proper use of language and thereby to expose the invalidity of language that proposes to operate beyond these limits. That holds for both the *Tractatus* and

the *Philosophical Investigations*. It is this Kantian sense of critique I have in mind when I speak of Wittgenstein's critical intention.

4. Austin meets this criticism with an argument reminiscent of Edmund Burke's defense of tradition against the French Revolution; it is the argument of English conservative empiricism: ". . . our common stock of words embodies all the distinctions men have found worth drawing, and the connections they have found worth making, in the lifetimes of many generations: these surely are likely to be more numerous, more sound, since they have stood up to the long test of the survival of the fittest, and more subtle, at least in all ordinary and reasonably practical matters than any you or I are likely to think up in our armchairs of an afternoon" ("A Plea for Excuses," in *Ordinary Language*, ed. V. C. Chappell [Englewood Cliffs, N.J.: Prentice-Hall, 1964), p. 46). For my part, if this were the only argument in support of traditional language, I would join the "revolutionaries" in saying "Away with it!" For it is not so sure at all that the people of the past would have invented the best tools for their own circumstances, to say nothing of ours. It would in fact be reasonable to assume that the past is much more a legacy of perpetuated misuses and inaccuracies than a fund of useful language. If language were a tool, then we should be radically pragmatic about it. Not the traditional, but that with cash value (James) now is what we should consider worthy. And this, as I have attempted to show in Chapter 1, is precisely the attitude that MacIntyre ultimately takes in regard to our ethical language and practices. Expediency is the measure of tools. If a tool does not work, we throw it out and replace it with the best one available, or, as MacIntyre puts it, the best one "to date." The tool itself deserves no respect, has no authority. But if language is not a tool, both this argument and Austin's are seriously skewed.

5. Ludwig Wittgenstein, *Tractatus logico-philosophicus*, trans. D. F. Pears and B. F. McGuinness (New York: Humanities, 1961), 2.1.

6. The expected translations might be "The truth of being is essence" and "Doing injustice is, you would say, uglier than suffering it." But the point here is that the meaning is contained *in* the German and Greek as such and that translations are thus necessarily inadequate. The problem is that there are no single words in English that coincide with the semantic field of the German and Greek words and that, accordingly, would render all the nuances of meaning in them. Consequently, for *kakion*, to take an example, we will need a number

of English words to translate the various and shifting senses of it that emerge in Plato's exposition of what the word contains and displays, among them, more ugly as more ignoble or unworthy, but also as more despicable, contemptible, and unfair. The latter senses, as we will see, provide Plato with the link between what *kakion* is and what *adikein* is, which is to say doing what is unjust in regard to the distribution of wealth and power, but also doing what is ethically wrong. (It must be kept in mind that Plato precedes the division between Civil Society and Legal Status with its justice [*ius, iustitia*], on the one side, and *Sittlichkeit* with its right or wrong, on the other. Hence, to choose either "unjust" or "wrong" to translate his *adikos* is to abridge the meaning of it.)

7. Although we are learning a great deal more about Heidegger's understanding of Plato as the publication of Heidegger's collected works proceeds, for our purposes the clearest and most succinct formulation of what we need to know of Heidegger's critique of Plato is still to be found in his *Platons Lehre von der Wahrheit* [*Plato's Doctrine of Truth*] (Bern: Francke, 1954). The central argument there is that in Plato the experience and understanding of truth shifts radically: a change in the "place" (*Ort*) of truth occurs. This argument, one well known by now in the English-speaking world, is based upon an interpretation of the allegory of the "cave" in Book VII of the *Republic*. Though some of Heidegger's language in characterizing the existence of the inhabitants of the "cave" is ambiguous and has an apparently negative tinge to it—*zunächst und zumeist* (to begin with and for the most part) and *alltäglich* (everyday) are used here, which remind one of inauthenticity and forgetfulness in Heidegger's *Being and Time*—other words, *verlässlich* (reliable), for example, make it clear that from the later Heidegger's point of view, this existence in-the-world, this "dwelling" of the inhabitants of the "cave," is indeed closer to the original, earlier truth of things. The inhabitants of the "cave" live trustingly within a world as it first presents itself. They do not seek to penetrate to a ground behind what appears to be true to them, a seeking, so it is argued, which is basic to Plato's *philosophia*, and which, were they to pursue it, would remove them from their original and natural embeddedness in the world that surrounds them.

But Plato is not so trusting: for him their world is a world of mere shadows, a "cave." Thus in Plato the transition is made to a realm beyond the "cave"; the "mind's eye" is redirected to a "real" reality behind the shadow reality originally experienced. Consciousness is transferred to a place or locus in which what really is, *to ontōs on*, is said to present itself purely, uncontaminated by any non-being. Hence, the truth of the reality now experienced loses all traces of the "equi-fundamentality" (*Gleichursprünglichkeit*) of showing forth and con-cealment essential to the original experience of truth as *alētheia*.

A-*lētheia* means dis-concealment and implies a showing-forth that is wrested from, and sustained within, surrounding obscurity (*lēthē*). But the privative *a* of *alētheia* is lost sight of when, like Plato, one seeks to rise to an assumed higher reality where "true being" can be viewed purely as that which is, with no obscurity of hiddenness attaching to it. In Plato, Heidegger maintains, the emphasis is on light and visibility, light which makes the showing-forth of the thing as pure self-display, as *eidos*, as idea or form, visible. The "true" here is the idea in its luminosity, freed of contamination by darkness. Thus, properly speak-ing, it can no longer be said to show forth, *apophainesthai*, for true-being here is (*estin*) in steady presence and does not come into being (*gignetai*). Whereas the original truth of *alētheia* was a temporal showing, a coming-into-presence that then fades into absence, the truth of this higher reality is like the truths of a mathematician: it is steadily, without past or future: ". . . all these are parts of time, and 'was' and 'shall be' are forms of time that have come to be; we are wrong to transfer them unthinkingly to eternal being. We say that it was and is and shall be; but 'is' alone really belongs to it and describes it truly; 'was' and 'shall be' are properly used of becoming which proceeds in time, for they are motions" (*Timaeus* 37E—38A). The truth is like the geometrician's circle which always is what it is unvaryingly.

Heidegger sees a most important consequence of this purification of truth: in Plato truth becomes a function of knowing; truth is correct knowledge of real reality as viewed by the properly re-educated mind, a mind, the "eye" of which has been trained away from original "presencing" (*Anwesen*) of things in the "cave" and turned toward the ever-present that it finds within itself. Truth is now correctness (*orthotēs*) of insight, which is to be attained at the end of Plato's curriculum of *paideia* or education from the mere belief of the "cave" (*doxa*) to right knowledge (*epistēmē*) of what is truly or really (*to ontōs on*). And, Heidegger writes, "with this change a change in the place [*Ort*] of truth occurs simultaneously. As original disconcealment in the cave truth is a basic trait of existent things, but as the correctness of viewing, it becomes an attribute of the knower's relationship to what exists'' (PLW 42). From here the path is clearly discernible leading to the even more radical shifting of the place of truth to acts of human subjectivity that was to come in the modern period and that found its consummation in Nietzsche's claim that all truth is fabrication (*Lügen*), merely an invention of the human subject.

8. One of the principal themes in Gadamer's *The Idea of the Good in Platonic-Aristotelian Philosophy* is that despite Aristotle's attack on Plato's idea of the good as irrelevant to any account in either ethics or physics, Plato and Aristotle are in fact alike in seeking to make ethical justification, that is, justification in terms of what is good and best, paradigmatic for any account of nature.

9. For Gadamer this principle of the tragic experience in Aeschylus becomes the principle of human finitude in general: we learn in encountering the limits of our knowledge and in yielding to that which transcends us (cf. WM 339).

10. Francis Cornford, *Plato and Parmenides* (New York: Liberal Arts, 1957).

11. Heidegger likes to point out the ambivalence in the "of" here, for though it appears to render a *genitivus objectivus* and provide the object of the act of speaking, it is also, even primarily, a *genitivus subjectivus* indicating that to which the speaking belongs. The speaking, in other words, is "its," the subject matter's, and we must start from there, not from the agent who is saying something.

Building upon Aquinas' idea of the inner word (*verbum interius, verbum mentis*), Gadamer extends Heidegger's thought here: "The intrinsic unity of thinking and saying something to oneself . . . implies that the inner word of the mind is not formulated by a reflexive act. He who thinks something, that is, says something to himself, means that which he is thinking. Hence, he is not directed back to his own thinking when he formulates a word. . . . In truth there is no reflection active in the formulation of a word, for the word does not express the mind at all, but rather the thing that is meant. The starting point for the formulation of the word is the subject matter itself (the *species*) that fulfills the mind" (WM 403). Gadamer explains the fulfillment here as follows: "The word is not formulated only then when the cognition is completed or, spoken scholastically, only after the information of the mind by the *species* has been concluded. Rather it is the execution itself of the cognition" (WM 401). Put another way, and as we have seen, we do not first have a thought and then look for the word to express it as a carpenter might look for a tool in his box to implement a task he had already completely planned out.

12. See Werner Jaeger, *Paideia* II (Berlin: De Gruyter, 1959), p. 196.

13. As Gadamer's frequent adversions to the "scenic" might have made evident, there is surely a great deal to be learned from the world of theater in regard to the inadequacies of any "geometrical" analysis of a speech (*logos*). For any understanding and interpretation of what is displayed in speaking requires a re-enactment by us of what the character is saying in his or her setting; it requires a *mise en scène*. As we have emphasized, the *logoi* in any of Plato's dramas are, unlike geometrical proofs, indissociable from the *ergoi* or actions of the people who are saying them. And as we have emphasized too, the *logoi*, again unlike geometrical proofs, are also indissociable from the context or occasion in which they are put forth. The point here, though self-evident and elementary for any actor of however meager ability, was neverless given sublime demonstration by Ian McClellan in his virtuosic one-man show "Acting Shakespeare." On one occasion he took Macbeth's "Tomorrow and tomorrow and tomorrow . . ." as his example and succeeded, as any less gifted actor surely could not have, in making clear what it means to change the dead written word back into spoken reality, elaborating for his audience all the nuances in delivery—intonation, timing, emphasis, phrasing, and so forth—that an actor must consider in interpreting this speech and, for that matter, a musician in interpreting a piece. (Compare above on the hermeneutic task of *Rückverwandlung in Sprache*.) At the same time he displayed another Heideggerian-Gadamerian theme regarding the inadequacy of taking anything said to be a statement or proposition, the theme, namely, of what is said precisely by being *not* stated, to which we will return in treating Socrates' *eirōneia*. In re-enacting these lines from *Macbeth* (V.v.24–28),

> Life's but a walking shadow, a poor player
> That struts and frets his hour upon the stage,
> And then is heard no more; it is a tale
> Told by an idiot, full of sound and fury,
> Signifying nothing

he showed how the last line breaks off into emptiness; there is *nothing* said in the missing last half of it. Against Derrida I would argue that this is evident in looking at the written text, to be sure, but only retroactively. One has to have *heard* the text re-enacted for the sense of that line to be brought home.

Silent reading is, as we noted before, a peculiarly modern distortion and perhaps a function of the impoverishment of language insofar as language comes to be thought of as a transmitter of information about states of affairs, as "news," so to speak. Any Greek or Latin writer could count on his text being read outloud, spoken, if only to the reader. In his lectures over the years in Heidelberg Gadamer referred several times to an instance where Rilke read aloud to a small group one of his impenetrably opaque *Duino Elegies*. And, Gadamer relates, everyone present understood it then. Only then.

14. Gadamer points out that for Aristotle too the difference between philosophers and sophists consists not so much in what they say as in what they do, which is to say, in their respective *prohairesis tou biou*, the life they choose to lead (IGPAP 100).

15. Callicles does not think of what is *kalon* as fair, for he has precisely no sense of fairness at all. The English "fair" and "unfair" give us a nice way of getting at the ethical dimension of *kalos* and *aischros*, and of establishing the connection between what is beautiful or fair aesthetically and noble or fair ethically. They also make the connection clear between the *kalon* and the *dikaion*, or, we might say, between what is fair and what is right and just. Fairness is a crucial word in Anglo-American thought, most notably in John Rawls, and is closely tied to doing what is just and to justice as such. We tend to think of it primarily, though, as we do of justice, namely, in relationship to Civil Society and its laws governing the distribution of wealth, opportunity, power, and so forth. Hence, fairness has come to mean abiding by the rules of the game, as it were, or being law-abiding. MacIntyre, for one, however, correctly discerns that there is an abstraction in treating the virtue of fairness or justice this way. And the fact is that we can and do still think of what is fair as the opposite of what is ugly and hence unfair in an ethical and not merely juridical sense. The "sense of fairness" upon which Rawls builds so extensively is, as closer scrutiny reveals, a sense of decency (Gadamer: *Anständigkeit*) displayed in our relationships to others; and its opposite is something that runs much deeper than just breaking contractual rules.

The unfair is shabby, contemptible, unconscionable. (All these meanings are contained in the Greek *aischros*.) In emphasizing our "sense of fairness," Rawls points up the difficulty of keeping exclusively to the contractual level of Civil Society with its abstract right. (See Chapter 3, note 7 below.) Fairness is clearly an idea he imports from what Hegel calls *Sittlichkeit*, the realm of the ethical based on loyalty and filiality (Plato: *philia*).

Here, incidentally, is the crux of the differences between Rawls and Nozick. Nozick succeeds in working out his contractual theory without any reliance on the ethical realm whatsoever. As a consequence he is considerably more coherent than Rawls, who, try as he might, can never really justify someone's relinquishing his or her property to others on grounds of sheer prudentialism and self-interest alone. But precisely this discrepancy in Rawls (and Locke) makes his work far more fruitful than the barren tracts that Nozick covers in *Anarchy, State, and Utopia* (New York: Basic Books, 1974).

16. Jean-Paul Sartre, *L'Etre et le néant* (Paris: Gallimard, 1943), pp. 349ff.

17. Another sophist advocate of the unbridled pursuit of pleasure, Philebus, also withdraws from the discussion in the dialogue of the same name. As Gadamer points out, someone who says what Philebus says, but, more importantly, does what he does, could not be expected to engage in rational argument since he abjures reason altogether for the sake of gratification (IGPAP 106).

3

The Ethical Implications of Gadamer's Theory of Interpretation

All single individuals who are raising themselves from their physical nature find in the language, customs, and institutions of their people a pre-given substance, which, as in learning language, it is their task to make their own. Thus single individuals are always already under way in shaping themselves and becoming cultured. always already in the process of canceling their physical aspect insofar as the world into which they are growing is a human world shaped by language and custom [WM 11].

IN THIS QUOTATION FROM *Truth and Method* we find two key words for any ethical theory we might hope to develop from Gadamer's hermeneutics: language and custom. The latter, in German, *Sitten*, returns us to our earlier considerations of *Sittlichkeit* and to the idea of an ethics grounded in *Sitten* or, for want of a better English word, in what is customary. Such an ethics will again be our concern in this chapter. It should be noted right at the start, however, that the German word *Sitte* has many implications and connotations that the English "custom" does not. Above all, its semantic field more obviously extends into the ethical realm. *Gesittet*, for example, means cultured, well-mannered, gracious, to be sure, but behind these aspects of the word is its fundamental sense of having *Sitten* (Latin: *mores*) or temperate, reasonable ways of behaving. Similarly, *unsittlich* and *ungesittet* refer to actions that are vulgar and insolent, to be sure, but, more fundamentally, indecent or perverse, and even barbaric or bestial. *Unsittlich* and *ungesittet* are, in fact, largely coincident with a crucial word in Platonic-Aristotelian ethics, *aischros*, the shameful and shameless, ugly and detestable. Seen this way the connection is evident between what is *sittlich* and what is right (Greek: *dikaios*), or the right thing to do (Greek: *to deon;* Gadamer: *das Tunliche*).

What is "customary" in the English sense, on the other hand, does not carry this ethical weight; rather, it refers more to what is *merely* customary, to mere conventions and etiquette as opposed to what is right or wrong in any moral or ethical sense. The difference here will involve us in considerable difficulties, for there is no word in English that will allow us to get at what *Sittlichkeit*, *Sitte*, and *gesittet* display. Morality will not do, for as many English words have, it has acquired a quality of abstraction that disengages it from its Latin root, *mos, moris*—hence Hegel's perspicacious *juxtaposition* of Morality with *Sittlichkeit*. And because of the problems with the English "customs," something like "customary ethics," quite aside from its clumsiness, is also inadequate.

In this part of our study we will focus specifically on the ethical dimensions of Gadamer's hermeneutical philosophy, and we will see that insofar as he approaches what we would call an ethical theory, he draws extensively on a range of words like *Sitte*, words that most Anglo-American thinkers, if they treated them at all, would tend to relegate to the merely customary. For example, in addition to *Sitte* Gadamer relies on *anständig* and *unanständig*, which, as we will see, have to do primarily with decency and propriety. Generally in philosophy, at least, we have set aside consideration of these things because in the English-speaking world it goes pretty much without saying that ethics and moral philosophy must transcend what is customary. In the main our own efforts are devoted to giving moral theory a foundation in critical reason, a foundation in which obligation would be based precisely not on uncritical adherence to what is customary, proper, and the like, but on insight into rational principles. For the most part the customary, it seems, has to do with morally insignificant things such as which hand one uses to hold one's fork. And where it begins to go beyond these—for example, calling a servant by the first name—it becomes a vehicle of inequality and privilege from which any rational individual would seek to be liberated. Precisely in order to rid ourselves of the encumbrance of custom we have turned to utilitarianism or to universal human rights. Mill, for one, shows this clearly.

To be sure, Mill has been an easy target for those in search of muddled reasoning, and many a beginner's course in logical analysis has set students to work uncovering the contradictions in his *Utilitarianism* and in his attempt to give a utilitarian justification for the priority of human liberty in his *On Liberty*. Nevertheless Mill's doctrines themselves on individual auton- omy, whatever the difficulties analytical thinkers might find in his justification of them, have become and remained axiomatic for those arguing from the political right, the political left, and anywhere in between—so much so that they seem entirely above the firing line in most debate. It is taken for granted that nothing should suppress individual energies, originality, and creativity, and from this it follows, again without much if any question, that custom is just onerous dead weight:

> . . . to conform to custom merely *as* custom does not educate or develop in him [the individual] any of the qualities which are the distinctive endowment of a human being. The human faculties of perception, judgment, discriminative feeling, mental activity, and even moral preference are exercised only in making a choice. He who does anything because it is the custom makes no choice. He gains no practice either in discerning or in desiring what is best. . . . He who lets the world, or his own portion of it, choose his plan of life for him has no need of any other faculty than the ape- like one of imitation.[1]

In the end, of course, this argument from Mill's *On Liberty* is indeed based not on utility but on rights: whatever the benefits for all, each individual has the *right* to shape his or her own life spontaneously and in liberty from the interference of others. This is the rational principle that is to be applied critically to the practices of any society. And few, it seems, Durkheim being the most notable exception, would call this right to moral autonomy into question. Rawls argues for it with his "lexical" ordering; Nozick, in justification of the minimal state; and Marcuse, in defiance of oppression. Still, the possibility exists, one that we will entertain here, that arguing from this principle of moral autonomy in this way prejudices and skews any inquiry into the nature of ethical understanding.

Though we now sense a certain dubiousness in Locke's and Jefferson's claims to ascertain "self-evident" truths about "inalienable rights"—any such "intuitionalism" has become suspect for us—a significant part of the contemporary Anglo-American discussion of ethics continues to turn on the matter of an individual's rights as a starting point for critical, rational moral theory, either in advocating them as somehow self-justifying or in seeking other, utilitarian or post-utilitarian ways of justifying them, contractualism, for example. But if Gadamer is correct, we cannot begin any consideration of *ethics* with the issue of rights, at least not universal abstract rights as opposed to customary rights. For the former would have to be known in the way Plato wants to know mathematical verities, and in ethical matters, Gadamer would argue, we are not dealing with this kind of truth—as Plato himself recognized (see Chapter 2). This is not to say, of course, that abstract rights do not have a place in some areas of legal reasoning, namely, those that deal with individuals as equal "persons." As noted in Chapter 1, they unquestionably do. But it is not our task here to elaborate the kind of reasoning pertaining to adjudication of those disputes in Civil Society that are to be considered from the perspective of Legal Status. Our concern is with the ethical, with *Sittlichkeit* and *sittliches Verstehen* or ethical understanding.

Now, if Gadamer is right, ethical truth is given to us in the language we speak. Consequently, we do not uncover ethical principles in acts of autonomous critical reasoning; rather we learn them just as we learn the rest of the world that our language conveys to us. We come to participate in ethical truths as a cultural tradition of customs transmitted, like language usages (*Sprachgebräuche*)—*Gebräuche* is another German word for customs—in what we say, *logoi*, on the one hand, and in what we do, our deeds and practices, *ergoi*, on the other. These enable us to live in community with each other and to escape the "war of all against all" in which, as Hobbes so brutally puts it, life is "nasty, brutish and short."

And in truth Gadamer's emphasis on *Sitten* and *Sittlichkeit* is not at all a retreat from ethical concerns into blind and dumb conformity to what is merely customary. *Sittlichkeit*, being *gesittet*, is the opposite of brutishness. It is precisely that "canceling [of] their [the individuals'] physical aspect insofar as the world into which they are growing is a human world shaped by language and custom" to which Gadamer refers, a process, namely, that builds intellect (*Geist*), but, since it presupposes language *and* custom, *logos* and *ergon*, a process that will depend on the very imitation (Aristotle: *mimēsis*, *Poetics* 1448B 5ff.) that Mill rejects out of hand. It will not depend on *mimēsis* alone, of course, for, as we know, deliberation (*bouleuesthai*) and reasonableness (*phronēsis*) are also essential. But these are very different things from autonomous reason insofar as they are sustained by custom and habituation, which is to say, *mimēsis*, and not to be uprooted from it. Insofar as we are *sittlich* we belong to the community and are accustomed to its traditions. Insofar as we are not, we remain bestial.

This argument is of the greatest *ethical* importance, and Aristotle is better than Mill here and, to take another prominent figure in the tradition of English individualism, better than Hobbes. For, while recognizing as Hobbes does that the individual apart from the community (*polis*) is a mere animal (*zōion*) or inhuman brute, Aristotle also sees that within the community the individual's animality is transformed: he is the *zōion politi-kon*, the communal animal, who by ethical reasonableness (*phronēsis*) can indeed govern the animal appetition and fear that Hobbes maintains must always dominate him. And as Aristotle also makes clear, the rational preference and choice (*prohairesis*) for which Mill would liberate us are always possible only for one already accustomed and disposed by the community to transcend bestial impulse, that is to say, for one habituated by custom. Whoever would "choose" on the basis of undisciplined impulse cannot be said to make any rational choice at all.[2]

As Gadamer sees it, we live in an age where, much as in the age of sophism in which Plato and Aristotle found themselves, we are threatened by a diminishment of *Sittlichkeit* and a reversion to animal self-centeredness. An appeal to abstract rights will not help us here. For one thing, as we have learned from Hegel, though abstract rights do have their function in Civil Society and its Condition or Right, it is doubtful that abstract rights could ever be a substitute for "the ethical lost." And for another, even if they could, mere knowledge of them would not suffice to get anyone to abide by them. They lack the restraining force of customs to which we have been accustomed, their *vis constrictiva*, as we will learn from Aquinas later on this chapter. And as Aristotle's discussion of *akratia* or powerlessness over oneself makes clear (EN VII), reasoning correctly to what one believes one ought to do is a far cry from actually being disposed to do it. Choice of a course of action, *prohairesis*, is entirely distinct from belief (*doxa*) or even wish (*boulēsis*) (EN 1111B 20 – 1112A 14). A disposition (Aristotle: *hexis*) is prerequisite for any ethical choice, and intellectual insights alone, supposing that they are real in the first place, will not provide this. Long-standing customs, *Sitten,* are also needed.

Hence, those who in sensing gross inequity and the deterioration of the ethical order would replace it with a new order founded solely on presumed rational principles in fact only hasten the collapse of culture and a reversion to brutality. At first his collapse is greeted, often euphorically, as the emancipation of the individual from oppressive customs. And from the point of view of what we, following Hegel, have called the Condition of Right or Legal Status, it often is indeed emancipation and to this extent is to be celebrated. But as the revolution consumes its children, its idealism becomes disillusionment and *anomie* (Durkheim). Liberated individuals with nothing accustomed on which to rely find themselves thrown back on themselves and unable to replace their vanished community. In the end they are returned to Hobbes's bestial and infinite desire of "power after power that endeth only in death."

In essence this argument is characteristic of authentic conservative thought: practical reason, it is maintained, is never fully commensurate with the human historical social reality. Here more than anywhere we find ourselves under way within, and dependent upon, what always exceeds our comprehension. Autonomous intellection by itself will thus be insufficient and what Edmund Burke calls the "wisdom of the species," traditional culture and the inculcation of it, indispensable.[3]

Surprisingly, perhaps, it is not in someone like Burke that Gadamer finds support for his conservative convictions but in the supposedly rationalistic utopianism of Plato, who, as we have seen by now, is actually much more aware of the limits of practical reason than his critics—above all Popper, but Hampshire too, for example—have recognized. To make his point, Gadamer adverts to the miscalculation of the marriage number in Book IX of the *Republic*, which eventually brings the ideal state to ruin:

> The mystifying, yet ingenious, thing about this invention of Plato's, it seems to me, lies in the fact that this comical shortcoming of a comical institution symbolically displays why no system of human social order, however wisely planned or thought out, can endure. What can only be brought about by an artfully contrived institution will in the end be done in by its own artificiality. This is the insight Plato gives us here. . . . Because

we are human beings, not because we planned mistakenly, even an ideal self-sustaining organization in full accord with the plan for it will nevertheless go under in the rolling seas of historical life [IGPAP 73].[4]

This does not mean at all that reason is out of place in human affairs; Gadamer is not denying "the task of reason to shape action reasonably." "The disorder of human things is never complete chaos," he says. "Ultimately this disorder represents the periphery of a sensibly ordered universe that under any circumstances would have its periphery." And human reason is "fully capable of expanding into the historical world of vague regularities" (IGPAP 73). But in this capacity it must be reason of a very different sort from abstract reason and its understanding, very different from the understanding of timeless mathematical verities. Reason here exemplifies the insight expressed in Plato's theory of the One and the indeterminate Two, the *peras* and the *apeiron*, the definite and the indefinite: whatever this reason knows definitely, it uncovers within a temporal continuum of what exceeds its understanding. The order of what it comprehends has at its "periphery" disorder, indeterminacy. Hence, reason in human affairs is of necessity finite, and where that fact is not acknowledged, where *phronēsis* would be replaced with an "autonomous reason" that has excerpted itself from its historical setting, that limited reasonableness of which we *are* capable in our practice, will have been squandered.

In this final chapter I want, first of all, to turn specifically to Gadamer's theory of interpretation, the "hermeneutics" for which he is best known. At we know, ethics as such is not thematized specifically in Gadamer's project of elaborating a theory of interpretation (see above Chapter 1, Part 4). Ethical theory is referred to only insofar as it provides a model for a general theory of interpretation, in particular of texts and artworks—see WM 295ff. on "The Hermeneutical Relevance of Aristotle," for example. Nevertheless it is striking, and indeed no coincidence, that Gadamer's earliest "hermeneutical" or interpretive study is entitled *Plato's Dialectical Ethics* and that his other early Plato studies raise essentially ethical and political questions. And it is striking too that one of the more recent publications we have from Gadamer is *The Idea of the Good in Platonic-Aristotelian Philosophy*. I intend to show that Gadamer's interpretation theory originates in, and points to, ethical concerns and that his findings are indeed relevant for ethics, and to that end I will spell out in some detail the principles of his theory of interpretation, taking the interpretation of artworks as an example. My task here will be to show how these same principles of interpretation can be carried over into a theory of understanding and application of ethical principles. Second, I will take up what one might call the meta-ethical problem of the nature of justification in ethics, the problem, that is, of giving a reason (Plato: *logon didonai*) to oneself and to others in justification of one's ethical choices. At issue here will be the special nature of ethical reasoning as such, whose peculiarity, as I will argue, has received insufficient attention from Anglo-American moral theorists. Third, relying upon Plato and Aristotle and Gadamer's reading of them, I will consider the underlying excellence of the soul (*psychē*) that makes right (*orthos*) and just (*dikaios*) reasoning in ethical matters possible, consider, that is, what Aristotle calls the *sympasa aretē* or comprehensive virtue. Our concern here will be with the special nature of the human, as opposed to the divine, soul, and with the condition in which it must be in order to choose well. I will argue here that MacIntyre, in focusing on specific historical virtues, overlooks the basis of them all, or what Plato and Aristotle call *dikaiosynē*. (MacIntyre does treat justice as a primary virtue but justice in his sense is not what Plato and Aristotle have in mind.) Fourth, I will again take up the link in ethical reasoning of reason and character, word and deed, *logos* and *ergon*, but this time in particular reference to character formation by habituation, *ēthos* by *ethos*.[5] My point will be that we cannot *reason* well in ethics unless we *are* good—such is the nature of *phronēsis* or ethical understanding. Our being good depends on the state of our soul, its excellence or *aretē*, as will have been made clear in Part 3. But here the issue will be how we acquire that excellence. It will emerge that being good is not only a function of what we think but also of what Aquinas calls a *habitus* and *consuetudo*. With these words he is rendering Aristotle's *hexis*, or disposition, and *ethos*, which we might translate as custom or habit. The best translation of it, however, would be the German *Sitte*.

1. Interpretation and Application in Ethical Reasoning

Any theory of interpretation hinges in part on the conception one has of the thing one would interpret, for example, the artwork. Hence, as a first move in developing his theory of interpretation of artworks Gadamer wishes to counter the prevailing view of art that takes it to be a stimulus for some sort of subjective reaction. The assumption here, which in Gadamer's opinion can be traced to Kant and more specifically to Schiller, is that art does not tell or show us something of the world; rather it elicits a response, a sense of satisfaction (Kant: *Wohlgefallen*) or feeling in the reader, viewer, or listener. Consequently, the content of a work of art is no longer thought to have anything to do with its value as art. The "intrinsic bond of the artwork with its world is dissolved" (WM 80), and the "aesthetic differentiation," as Gadamer calls it, that is, the abstraction of art from any secular or religious meaning it might have in the culture that produced it, thereby completed. What Schiller calls "quality" now becomes the measure, and "quality" for him is entirely a function of the experiencing consciousness; in Schiller, Gadamer concludes, "aesthetic consciousness becomes the center of the experience [*Erlebnis*] in relationship to which any artwork is to be evaluated" (WM 80). Accordingly, in Schiller's radicalization of Kantian aesthetics, what had been a triadic structure, an encounter between self and artwork within a world from which they both derive, now becomes entirely self-referential: the work of art induces a worldless play of the self with itself. To use Hegel's forced German expression (see Chapter 1, Part 4), we might say that the self *erinnert*, interiorizes, the artwork to the extent that it no longer relates to the work as a thing in itself, as a thing that consists in itself, as Gadamer puts it (*besteht in sich*), but to the self's own reaction to the work. What we have here is the aesthetic dimension of thought that thinks itself thinking, of Descartes' *cogito me cogitare* and Hegel's *Denken, das sich selber denkt*.

More recently, Gadamer points out, we find Lukács saying that the artwork is an empty form, merely a node in which various possible aesthetic experiences are intertwined. And in Valéry we even find the artwork compared to a chemical catalyst that precipitates a subjective reaction. Schiller's aesthetic theory, it turns out, is only a preface to what has come about in the twentieth century. For us, Gadamer says, Schiller's doctrine of aesthetic consciousness has fulfilled itself in absolute "discontinuity," that is, in the collapse of the unitary aesthetic object into a multiplicity of private, subjective experiences (*Erlebnisse*) (WM 80).

But clearly, Gadamer maintains, this reduction of the artwork to a stimulus is mistaken. The artwork, he contends, says some *thing*, displays something. Thus contrary to what modern aesthetic consciousness might make of it, it has its validity in the thing it says or shows and not in our subjective reaction to it. "The pantheon of art," Gadamer writes,

is not an a-temporal presence given to pure aesthetic consciousness; rather, it is a collected historical spirit that gathers itself together. Aesthetic *Erfahrung* as a form of self-understanding thus comes about in relationship to an other that is *understood*. Hence, self-understanding presupposes acknowledgment of the integrity and self-identity of this other. When we encounter an artwork in our world and a world in the particular artwork, the artwork is no alien universe into which we are magically transported at the time and for the moment. On the contrary, we come to understand ourselves in the artwork. That implies that we

integrate the discontinuous point of each *Erlebnis* into the continuity of our existence [WM 92].

To fully comprehend Gadamer's critique of aesthetic consciousness we must be clear about the distinction he makes here
between experience in the sense of an *Erlebnis* and experience
in the sense of *Erfahrung*. The *Erlebnis* is the essential experience of aesthetic consciousness, in which the latter retreats into
itself and revels in the worlds of its own fantasy into which it
transports itself. Accordingly what is experienced as an *Erlebnis*
is entirely enclosed within itself and "removed from any relationships of things to each other in the real world" (WM 66).
The *Erlebnis* consists in private moments of exhilaration in
which the subject, aesthetic consciousness, literally enjoys itself, enjoys, that is to say, not something other than itself, but
its own consciousness of what has stimulated it. (We had a good
deal to say about this reversal of referentiality in the discussion
of *anamnēsis*, *Erinnerung*, and self-consciousness in Chapter 1).

Experience as *Erfahrung*, on the other hand, is, as Gadamer
emphasizes, an experience of an other and not an experience
that I have of myself. For just this reason the word *Erfahrung*
carries with it negative connotations that place it quite close to
suffering: an *Erfahrung* is at first an experience of my own limits
with respect to an other that asserts itself in all its otherness.
Seen this way *Erfahrung* is the sometimes painful experience of
the unforeseen and unknown. It is in this context that Gadamer
adverts to Aeschylus' *pathei mathos*, "by suffering learned,"
namely, to bring out this negative side of *Erfahrung* (WM 338).
However, as Aeschylus' saying also makes clear, the negative
side of *Erfahrung* is ultimately transcended. For my initial
suffering (*pathos*, *paschein*) in my experience of the other
results in understanding, not only understanding (*Verstehen*) as
understanding of my own limitations, but understanding as openness to, understanding for, the other (*Verständnis*, *synesis*).
Whoever is experienced (*erfahren*) has been released from the
confines of merely private opinions. Like Socrates he now

knows that he does not know, and only then is he open to what is new: "The truth of *Erfahrung* is always tied into further new *Erfahrung*. Hence, a person is called experienced who not only has become experienced through experience, but who is also open to new experience" (WM 338). As opposed to an *Erlebnis*, then, an *Erfahrung* is not self-referential at all; rather, it has the structure of dialogical interplay with an other within a world: I "encounter the artwork in a world and a world in the individual artwork." Not the self but the world as the *Mitte* or medium between the artwork and the self is the center of the event. In the interplay between the self and the artwork this third thing, world, comes to the fore.

Gadamer exemplifies this triadic structure of *Erfahrung* with *das Spiel*, that is, the game and play. Just as the players in a game are subordinate to the game being played (compare Chapter 2, Part 2), so too self and artwork are subordinate to the world that "presences" in their encounter. And if we take theater as an instance of both art and play, it becomes clear immediately that in the interpretation of the script some *thing* is brought out, some segment of world. And not just here but in all interplay of self and artwork, in all interpretation, this presentation of world has priority.

Consequently, Gadamer opposes an aesthetic "non-differentiation" (WM 112) to Schiller's "aesthetic differentiation," which in reducing the artwork to a stimulus of an *Erlebnis* in the aesthetic consciousness severed the artwork from any context in a world. Gadamer's point is that artist, work, and audience are all to be tied back into the world as it displays itself in the interpretive event, in the aesthetic *Erfahrung*.

Furthermore, the *Erlebnis* cultivated by aesthetic consciousness is characteristically discontinuous in time. Since there is no consistent thing in reference to which the *Erlebnis* occurs, since all occurrences are merely contingent stimulants for aesthetic consciousness and are quickly left behind, each *Erlebnis*, once had, is over and done with. It was, as Kierkegaard puts it, a "great moment" and hence just that: momentary. In contrast, experience as *Erfahrung*, the experience upon which Gadamer wishes to base our understanding of the artwork, is ongoing and therefore continuous with past and future experience. It is historical insofar as it builds upon the past while remaining open to the future. For this reason, Aristotle points out, the young are not capable of *Erfahrung* (Aristotle: *empeiria*), for though they feel events intensely, they are not yet able to integrate the individual events in their lives into a continuum of experience. Their impressions remain discrete, and they do not learn from them. Consequently, they are not yet ready for the ethical life (see EN 1095A on the susceptibility of youth to the *pathē* [feelings]).

Obviously it makes an enormous difference for any theory of interpretation whether one holds that art stimulates a subjective *Erlebnis* or maintains with Gadamer that our *Erfahrung* with the artwork brings an historical world into view. Indeed, if the former view is maintained, the word interpretation becomes severely restricted in its applicability. For interpretation (*hermeneuein*) generally presupposes some *content* that gets interpreted, usually by someone for someone. Hermes brings a message from the gods to mortals. That at least is how Gadamer understands it. Operating on the assumption that art is what Gadamer says it is and not in fact a mere stimulus for aesthetic consciousness, let us now proceed to a more precise delineation of what its interpretation involves.

For Gadamer, interpretation has, we might say, a receptive and an active dimension which correspond to the "effected" and "effective" in *wirkungsgeschichtlich*. In the first place interpretation implies that we open ourselves to the past from which the artwork comes, that we let that past obtain in ways that may be counter to our expectations and preconceptions. That much has become clear in our discussion of *Erfahrung*. But beyond that, interpretation implies that we project the past of the artwork within our present toward the future, that we "apply" it, as Gadamer puts it, taking, as his paradigm, the judicial application of a law in any interpretation of that law.

We can now see more precisely what Gadamer has in mind when he says in the passage cited above that in interpretation we "integrate the discontinuous point of each *Erlebnis* into the continuity of our existence": the task is to raise my merely private and momentary experience of the artwork into the historical continuum of understanding, thereby linking "my" present with "our" past. It turns out that the two dimensions of interpretation—of opening ourselves to the past and of projecting the past within the present into the future—are in fact indissociable. In opening ourselves to the past and establishing continuity between it and our own experience, we must at the very same time be bringing the past to bear now. Thus it is plain that while interpretation is something that happens to us, so to speak, it is also something that we must "do." While listening to what the work says, we must lay out what it says within the field of the present world. To interpret something is to carry it on or, literally, to trans-late it from a past world over into the world within which we are now under way.

Put another way: the task of the interpreter is to bring to life in the present what is given in a petrified form as a mere relic from the past, for instance, written texts, scripts of dramas, musical scores, and so forth. As Gadamer points out, the work to be interpreted is in many ways like a festival that has its actuality, not in a fixed set of historically prescribed rituals, but in being celebrated anew each time, in prescribed rituals, but in being celebrated anew each time, in being made present again. For the artwork to exist it must be interpreted, just as the festival must be celebrated: interpretation is a bringing to life now (WM 117). It is in this regard that Gadamer speaks of a *Rückverwandlung* or a transforming-back into the present—of dead texts into what is spoken, of dead scores into music, of dead scripts into drama. The task of the interpreter is to apply what the work displays to his or her own world and in so doing extend that world to the world of the work. (Compare WM 289ff. on *Horizontverschmelzung* or the "merging of horizons.")

It is important to note, given our interest in the ethical

implications of Gadamer's theory, that no timeless ideal exists which the interpreter may be said to approximate in the application. There is no paradigmatic Mozart's "Haffner" Symphony to be interpreted any more than there is one perfect Thanksgiving that one should seek to celebrate as closely as possible. (Nor would there be an immutable essence of an ethical principle.) Each application is right (or wrong) precisely for the given occasion. Hence an interpretation cannot be faulted for making concessions that compromise some assumed standard. There is no paradigm of which the interpretation could be said to be a more or less accurate copy; rather, the "Haffner," for example, is what it is, comes into its own, in each performance for a particular situation (see WM 137ff. on the "occasionality" of the artwork). Consequently, as opposed to those who see any interpretation inevitably falling short of the ideal, Gadamer argues that the artwork cannot be said at all to lose actuality in the performance or interpretation. On the contrary, it achieves its actuality each time it is performed or interpreted. Each performance, each interpretation, is a *Zuwachs an Sein*, an accretion in its reality. For we are dealing here, not with an eternal reality that shows up only distortedly in the temporal world, but with an historical reality that becomes what it is in each successive interpretation. Interpretation is the artwork's self-presentation (*Selbstdarstellung*), its being "there" (*da*). It has no other being apart from this. And so too, as we will see, the ethical principle exists only as the tradition of its applications to given occasions.

Gadamer's point here can be illustrated nicely by showing how it bears on the dispute in musicology regarding "authentic" performances on original instruments. If Gadamer is correct, the attempt to approximate some fixed standard of what a piece should sound like is misguided. For one thing such an historically researched paradigm, even if discoverable, remains nothing but the dead relic severed from its life in the tradition of its interpretations. And, for another, adherence to it, far from ensuring a "true" interpretation, leads to an interpretation that is often inappropriate for the present occasion. (I am reminded of one musicologist's quip that we might re-create eighteenth-century sound, but not eighteenth-century ears.)

On the other hand, in rejecting such attempts at objectivity in interpretation Gadamer is by no means opening the door to the romantic excesses of subjectivity to which those who emphasize strictly "authentic" performance are evidently reacting. Gadamer successfully evades the dilemma of the modern interpreter, who seems forced to choose between the stiff academism of supposedly objective interpretation and the idiosyncracy of many modern conductors and performers. Or, put in terms of ethics, Gadamer succeeds in finding an alternative to both inflexible rule deontologism, on the one hand, and situation or act ethics, on the other.

And again, given our concern with ethics, it is significant for us that Gadamer has taken as his paradigm the application the judge makes of the law (see WM 301 on Aristotle's *dikastē phronēsis*).[6] In interpreting the law, judges apply it to the situation and thereby concretize it. That by no means implies that they make concessions that compromise the law, for the law does not exist as a fixed ideal apart from its concretions, but only as the tradition of these concretions. Thus judges fulfill the law each time they interpret it. In bringing it to bear on the occasion, they give the law its actual existence. There is something to be said for Gadamer's argument here, for obviously one form of misinterpretation of the law consists precisely in the failure to apply it sensitively to the circumstances, which is to say, in adhering inflexibly to the dead letter of the law as if it were a fixed ideal: *summum ius – summa iniuria*. Hence, also in regard to a law—and an ethical principle—particular interpretations cannot be said to diminish what is interpreted. On the contrary, they augment it. What is right and true here is constantly forming and extending itself by virtue of the "productivity of the individual case" (WM 35).

It would be mistaken, accordingly, to try to rectify the capricious interpretive excesses of aesthetic consciousness by turning to scientific exactitude. As we saw in Part 4 of Chapter 1, the interpretive application differs from application in any applied science insofar as the latter objectifies the reality with which it has to deal, which is to say that the "subject" removes itself from the situation in which it initially encountered the things to which it now applies its scientific insights, and is no longer under way among them. From a vantage point above, it maps the patterns, the essences, the laws of what appears in the historical world, patterns, essences, laws that provide the basis for its undertakings. Interpreters, in contrast, remain under way within the historical tradition of interpretations, the tradition that shapes their own interpretation. They do not look for some "essence" of the artwork behind its appearances in the tradition of interpretations of it, an essence to be ascertained by removing themselves from the level of appearances.[7] On the contrary, their task as participants in the tradition is to carry that tradition further, to apply it to the occasion now. Unlike the Enlightenment's "man of reason" who was said to think independently of historical influences, interpreters remain a part of what they interpret. In this regard Gadamer speaks of their *Zugehörigkeit* or belonging to the tradition. In drawing upon the tradition to which they belong, interpreters extend that tradition, thereby perpetuating an historical continuum of being effected by the past and effecting the future. In opposition to the Enlightenment's consciousness, which would sever itself from its context in history, hermeneutical, interpretive consciousness remains historically effected and effective; it is *wirkungsgeschichtlich* (see WM 283ff.).[8]

That fact implies that in the interpretive application there can be no stripping away of the traditional inheritance of prejudgments and presumptions built into our interpretations. In short, here we cannot replace authority with critical, autonomous thought as the Enlightenment set out to do. On this point Gadamer affronts our modern sensibilities, perhaps, for as Mill has exemplified for us, it has been widely assumed in the English-speaking tradition that each individual's reasoning, of whatever sort, always can, and always should, be liberated from the biases of past authority and dogma. But Gadamer, who sees things from a very different vantage point, argues convincingly that aesthetic interpretation, at least, cannot operate in this way. (Compare WM 261ff. on the rehabilitation of authority.) Interpreters of art do exercise reasonable discretion whenever they bring the past to bear on the particular situation. They deliberate and arrive at reasonable choices and decisions concerning the way a work is to be understood and interpreted, but they do this within the horizons established by the tradition. Thus in their reasoning there is no break with the past; rather, their interpretive discretion builds upon the past, thereby presupposing it. Interpretation necessarily relies on tacitly accepted precedent as a foundation for its judgments. And this, it is evident, also holds for ethical interpretations.

When the Enlightenment's pure reason presumes to replace historically effected consciousness in matters of interpretation, interpretive discretion is undercut, and the result is idiosyncrasy more or less well camouflaged. Pure reason may give us insight into eternal realities such as those with which the mathematician deals and even the universal legal rights of the "person" with which the critical thinker is concerned, but as we have seen, for the interpreter of an artwork and, I would now add, of customary ethical principles, there are no such realities. Hence Gadamer argues that in interpretation only *Zugehörigkeit*, belonging to the tradition, ensures that there is no discontinuous series of one interpretation after another each as gratuitous as the next.[9] Does this argument not indeed apply to the interpretation of the principles of ethics also? Here too, Gadamer would say, history has taught us that in the end a reasonableness grounded in the tradition and not autonomous reason is the best protection from whim and excess (WM 251). (But we are getting ahead of ourselves.)

To say that interpretation remains embedded in the tradition and that it builds upon and presupposes it is by no means to say that interpretation is wholly determined by the past. We are dealing here with what Gadamer calls "the dialectic of the established and the fluid" (HL). Within the established tradition there remains a degree of indeterminacy, for the tradition is never over, the possibilities of interpretation, never exhausted. In this regard Gadamer speaks of the *Unabschliessbarkeit* or inconclusive unendingness of the interpretive tradition. Any interpretation takes over what is partially but never finally defined. A free play is given—the free play, for instance, that a judge has in interpreting the law on a particular occasion or, correspondingly, that a performer has in interpreting a traditional work.

This fluidity might seem to imply that we are back where we started, that is, that the interpretation is at least partially subjective if not entirely so, and that any talk of a true or false, right or wrong interpretation is misplaced. We would then find ourselves returned to subjectivity of aesthetic consciousness, or, put another way, returned to what MacIntyre has called "emotivism." Certainly one of the usual criteria of truth and objectivity and correctness (*orthotēs*), namely, the correspondence to a fixed paradigm (*eidos*), is inapplicable here, for the interpreter, as we have seen, has no fixed paradigm to adhere to. Thus the question arises what criteria could be used to establish whether the interpreter has been true to the work in his or her interpretation of it, or, for that matter, the interpreter of an ethical principle, to this principle. Indeed with regard to interpretation what justification is there for speaking of true and false or right and wrong at all? Perhaps it really was more accurate to speak instead of a subjective response rather than an interpretation; for the latter implies some claim of validity, and just this claim, it seems, cannot be made here. Indeed, it might appear that Gadamer has in fact led us to nothing more than the aesthetic equivalent of a situation or "act" ethics.

If we are to penetrate this semblance, we must not lose sight of the key role played by the critique of aesthetic consciousness in Gadamer's development of his theory of interpretation. Without this critique his invalidation of objectivity in interpretation would in fact have led only to radical subjectivity—in aesthetics as well as ethics. But, as we have seen, Gadamer's critique of aesthetic consciousness has secured him against this result. Gadamer did show that the truth of the artwork is not objective, but that by no means implies that interpretation of it is subjective. It will be recalled that the model of authentic aesthetic experience, *Erfahrung* as opposed to an *Erlebnis*, is the dialogical interplay of interpreter and work in which a "third" comes to the fore, namely, the world of the work, which in the interpretive application becomes continuous with the world of the interpreter. The subjectivity of the interpreter is not central here. As translators, so to speak, interpreters do bring the world of the work to bear on the present occasion, but that does not mean at all that they are free to make of it anything they wish. The work comes down to us as interpreters in a tradition of applications that we ourselves are to continue in our application now. We are not free to break with this tradition. The work, as it is passed on to us in the history of its interpretations, is encountered as an other to which we are obligated to *listen* faithfully. The model here is the I–thou relationship, which, if it is not to be subverted, demands a willingness on my part not to objectify you, the other, but to hear what you have to say (WM 340ff.).[10]

We are beginning to see the outlines of a criterion of truth and falsity in interpretation, truth and falsity that transcend anything merely subjective. At the very least, a prerequisite for any true interpretation has now emerged: precisely this willingness to listen to what the "other," the work, has to say. This willingness alone does not ensure the truth of an interpretation, but one who would interpret without it most assuredly interprets falsely. With that we are brought back to the interpreter's *Zugehörigkeit* to the tradition, his or her belonging to it. At this point in our discussion a particular element of the German word comes into focus, namely, the *Hören* or listening. Beyond embeddedness in the tradition, *Zugehörigkeit* implies just this willingness to listen, to yield, to follow the course of the dialogue with the past without spoiling it by insisting petulantly on one's own point of view. In contrast, self-assertion and not listening impede the emergence of the truth. Gadamer speaks in this regard of a necessary *Sich-Hineinhören-in*, or, literally, "listening-oneself-into a thing," in which one gives oneself over to what is said (HL). This presupposes a readiness to be disabused of one's private opinions. We have seen that no understanding is possible without preconceptions, but valid interpretation requires that one does not inflexibly insist on those that in the course of the dialogue with the work prove to be merely idiosyncratic. We saw that it lies in the nature of *Erfahrung* that one yields, that one relinquishes what is merely one's own. Only this readiness to yield ensures that the interpreter does not in fact kill off the thing that the interpretation was supposed to bring to life, the world shared between the interpreter and the work.

Still, up to this point we have only the prerequisite of a true interpretation and not the criterion we are looking for. Gadamer finds this criterion of truth in interpretation to be what he calls appropriateness or propriety (*Anständigkeit*) (HL). Significantly, since we are ultimately interested in the ethical implications of Gadamer's hermeneutics, this word is taken from the sphere of human practice and has to do initially with considerations of taste, decorum, tact, but, most fundamentally, decency. The *Unanständig*, or inappropriate, is at least obtrusive; it is often tactless, and at its extreme it is even indecent. *Unanständig* thus refers to a range of misbehavior extending from the innocuous—one often speaks of an *unanständiges Kind*, a misbehaved child—to much more serious violations of what is acceptable. Gadamer's point here is that just as the actions of someone one who is well-behaved (*anständig*) are unobtrusive, so an interpretation that is true has a certain unobtrusive "of-course-ness" (*Selbstverständlichkeit*) about it, which is to say that it is both suited to the occasion and in accordance with what the tradition leads us to expect (HL).

The opposite, obtrusiveness, is made clear by what we call over-interpretation. In an over-interpretation the interpretation asserts itself as an interpretation, and thereby the interpreter, him- or herself in the place of what was to be interpreted. An appropriate (*anständige*) interpretation goes almost unnoticed as an interpretation, so completely does the presence of what is said in it predominate over the act of saying it. (A good translation would be a paradigmatic form of good interpretation in this regard.) But an inappropriate interpretation, precisely because of its impropriety, is obtrusive. What is forced and wooden is obtrusive in this sense, but there are far worse forms of obtrusiveness. Quirks, mannerisms, excesses, idiosyncrasies, are all telltale characteristics of false, inappropriate interpretations that violate our shared sense, the *sensus communis*, of what is suitable and customary. Such things draw attention to the interpretation itself and to the subjectivity of the interpreter. In contrast, true interpretation, like good translation, would bring only what is meant, our common traditional world, to the fore, thereby allowing the interpreter and the act of interpretation as such to recede from view.

Appropriateness can also be thought of in another way. Gadamer speaks of a *Sich-Bewähren* of any appropriate interpretation, a kind of being borne out, or self-confirmation, as one proceeds from the parts of the interpretation to the whole. Coherence and congruity are the test here. The "of-courseness" of the appropriate interpretation emerges in this context as what is fitting. What fits, namely, blends with the whole as opposed to what is obtrusive in the sense of "sticking out." In this regard Gadamer stresses what he calls the tone of the work (HL). A poem, for instance, is a unity of tone and significance, and tone not just as *melos* or a certain sonority, but as an overall quality and character that pervades the whole. When violence is done in the interpretation of a work of art, that tone is disrupted. The interpretation that seemed valid for a verse, a passage, a phrase, a movement, and that went unnoticed for a time now obtrudes. Our attention is jolted away from the world presented, and we become conscious of the interpretation as such.

Again, it is not coincidental that the word tone, in the sense Gadamer means it here, has its principal use in the realm of practice and behavior, a use more common in German than in English, but not altogether unknown to English speakers. The expression *guter Ton*, good tone or form, refers to the quality of one who is well-mannered and cultured. Such a person "fits in," not because his or her behavior is studied—in that case it would only "stick out" all the more—but because of an unaffected graciousness acquired in long familiarization with what is customary and proper. Without effort he or she quite un–self-consciously avoids the faux pas, as a valid interpretation does. (And here, it might be remarked, the unconscious background behind any conscious decision made becomes plain and, with it, the indispensability of the right *hexis*, as Aristotle calls it, and Aquinas, following him, *habitus*.)

To be sure, these considerations of propriety and especially of "good tone" do seem to be matters less of ethical concern than of mere etiquette. Thus the question persists as to just what relevance, if any, Gadamer's theory of truth in interpretation has for ethics. In the hopes of answering it, let us now inquire specifically how the theory of interpretation of artworks that we have been elaborating might be extended into a theory of interpretation of ethical principles.

As a matter of fact, we have already had indications that Gadamer's theory of interpretation might have applications in ethics. It will be recalled, for instance, that we began our investigation of Gadamer's critique of aesthetic consciousness with a passage in which he argued that an artwork was not to be taken as a discrete presence excerpted from its proper embeddedness in the continuum of history: the work was not a "great moment" given to worldless aesthetic consciousness as a single, discontinuous experience (*Erlebnis*). It does not take a particularly keen ear to detect elements of Kierkegaard's *ethical* critique of the aesthete in such an argument. And as a matter of fact Gadamer explicitly states that he has appropriated this Kierkegaardian theme (WM 91). For Gadamer the key to distinguishing between Kierkegaard's aesthetic stage on life's way and the ethical stage that supersedes it lies in the difference between the *Erlebnis* of the former and the *Erfahrung* of the latter. The aesthete cultivates the particular, discontinuous moment of rapture in any aesthetic impression while the ethical man or woman builds temporal continuity.[11] And if the starting point for Gadamer's hermeneutics is in fact the ethical realm, as this passage and the repeated considerations of ethical themes elsewhere in his works would indicate, we have every reason to expect that what we have established in elaborating Gadamer's critique of aesthetic subjectivity and the theory of interpretation that he builds upon this critique would have a correlate in the ethical realm. There too the anarchic gratuitousness of Kierkegaard's aesthete is to be avoided and historical continuity maintained. There too one's choices are to be based on interpretations of traditional principles which, though not the eternal essences of mathematical science, are not the ephemeral fictions of the whimsical romantic either.

As a matter of fact, we do find in the ethical interpretation of a customary ethical principle the very same structure we uncovered in our analysis of the aesthetic interpretation of a work of art, which is to say, the *hermeneutical structure*. The interpretation was seen to be the concretization of the work, in which alone the work is "there," in which alone it exists. And such is also the case in the interpretation of ethical principles. These too, it may be argued, exist only as the history of their interpretive applications. Consequently, the interpreter of an ethical principle cannot be said to intuit its essence behind its appearances in the tradition of its interpretations.

Here is where W. D. Ross, for one, makes a fundamental mistake.[12] He fails to see what the ontological status of ethical principles is, that is, what sort of being or reality they actually have, and as a consequence he misunderstands the cognitive relationship between the interpreter and the principles to be interpreted. His tacitly accepted mathematical model of absolute knowledge of timeless, self-evident verities is inappropriate, for interpreters of an ethical principle know this principle only in its temporal concretizations. And far from having absolute knowledge of it, they know it as part of the inherited tradition to which they themselves belong and which effects their very understanding of it. (See above on *Zugehörigkeit* and *Wirkungsgeschichte*.) As in the case of aesthetic interpretation, interpreters of an ethical principle are not autonomous reasoners apart from the history of that principle; rather, as historically effected-effective (*wirkungsgeschichtliche*) consciousnesses, they themselves are constituted by the tradition of the very principle which, in their own interpretation, they continue to constitute.

The hermeneutical structure is thus circular. There is no fully determinate "essential" principle that could precisely define the interpretation ahead of time. The interpretation, in fact, gives determination to the principle just as the principle gives determination to the interpretation. Like the artwork, which exists only in the history of its interpretations, the ethical principle defines itself, comes into being, in the tradition of choices made in interpreting it.

But as the critique of aesthetic consciousness has demonstrated, this fact does not make ethical choice gratuitous. Although one has a certain latitude in one's choice, one cannot choose arbitrarily. One is obligated to give priority to the communal tradition over one's private inclinations. Indeed, we are as far removed here from an existentialist "act" ethics, on the one hand, as we are from a post-utilitarian rationalism that speaks of an "original position" (Rawls), on the other. One chooses on the basis of what one "always already" knows to be right, though this knowledge remains indeterminate until one has made a choice that concretizes it. The good is, it exists, only in its instantiations, and someone is good only insofar as he or she makes, and has been making, good choices.

We see, then, that one can choose the good only when one is "always already" under way within the tradition of right choices. To be ethical one must "always already" (*immer schon*) have an ethical sense of what is appropriate. (See above on *das Anständige*.) Put another way: a hermeneutical ethics is ultimately an ethics of good tone, not as mere good manners, but as ethical discretion founded on an inherited sense of what is fitting, on a sense of what is proper and customary that one shares with others, a *sensus communis* (see WM 16ff.). The circularity here lies in the fact that one acquires and defines this traditional common and communal sense—Aristotle would call it *phronēsis*—in making choices according to it, though one cannot choose according to it without already having it. It is a circle that reinforces itself once one is under way within it and if one continues within it, but that one can fall out of by entering a pattern of actions that are self-centered. Thus the task is a *Sich-Hineinhören*, a faithful "listening" to the tradition in which what is merely "mine" is subordinated to what is historically "ours."

It follows that the truth or falsity of any interpretation of a customary ethical principle—just like the truth or falsity of an interpretation of an artwork—cannot be the same as truth and falsity in the mathematical sciences. For given the hermeneutical structure of ethical choice, given our *Zugehörigkeit* to the tradition of applications of the principle, we are never in a position where we could know an ethical principle clearly and distinctly, that is, with precision and certainty. An ethical sense of what is appropriate is very different from a mathematical insight. In the latter case, as has been shown in Chapter 1, we stand unaffected, apart from our historical circumstances and intuit an eternal, ideal reality that presents itself with no indeterminacy attaching to it. In the case of knowing what is appropriate, on the other hand, we are effected and affected by an evolving, partially indeterminate reality which precedes us and within which we find ourselves under way. We know and understand this reality only as it displays itself to us within our historical situation.

Hence, like the criterion for true interpretation of an artwork, the criterion for right choice as true interpretation of a customary ethical principle cannot be a criterion that guarantees the correspondence of a judgment to a transcendental invariable ideal. Rather, it must be immanent to the historical situation within which the individual chooses one way or the other. We saw that Gadamer proposed *Anständigkeit* as just such an immanent criterion of truth in the interpretation of artworks, and we observed at the time that the word actually has its primary role in the realm of practice. *Anständigkeit* is, in fact, an ethical criterion. And if we take that as our guide, we could say that like the appropriate interpretation of the artwork, the appropriate interpretation of the ethical principle, the true interpretation of it, is characterized by its "of-course-ness" (*Selbstverständlichkeit*) and proves to be consistent with the tradition (*sich bewährt*). The true interpretation of an ethical principle is in keeping with what is customary and with what is fitting for the occasion. Thus it does not draw attention to the interpreter or the interpretation as such. (See above on the opposite case of over-interpretation, which has its correlate in the inappropriate choice made on the basis of idiosyncratic volition.) On the contrary, in allowing the interpreter and the interpretation as such to recede from view, the valid interpretation of an ethical principle brings to the fore the principle itself as a part of the ethical world that the interpreter shares with the community— just as the true interpretation of an artwork brings a segment of world into view rather than asserting itself as an interpretation.

False, inappropriate interpretation of the ethical principle, on the other hand, results when interpreters place themselves above the custom in which it is transmitted to them and exploit it for their own purposes. Their actions then become objectionable (*unanständig*) and obtrusive, for these are neither customary nor fitting. Thus in calling attention to themselves as the ones who are acting in this way, they violate the "tone" of the community.

We see, then, that if extended to ethics, Gadamer's theory of interpretation leads in one respect to a modified form of Kant's deontologism: as in Kant individuals are obligated to rise above their merely egoistic inclinations and to act according to communal principles that provide the basis for their ethical judgments. However, in contrast to the familiar versions of Kantian deontological theory, say in Ross, these principles emerge in

Gadamer not as insights of pure reason, but as an ethical inheritance from time out of mind, whose never wholly determinate truths continue to define themselves in the history of its applications. And since these principles are not immutable realities, but become what they are in the tradition of interpretations of them, the emphasis shifts from insight into the essence of the principle to understanding how it is to be applied in the particular circumstances. The paradigm becomes finite interpretation, hermeneutics, rather than absolute mathematical knowing.

Here, as is so often the case, Aristotle plays a paradigmatic role for Gadamer; indeed, it is Aristotle's emphasis on *prohairesis* or choice that provides the link we are seeking between an ethical and a hermeneutical theory. What we see in *prohairesis* and the *bouleuesthai* (deliberation) that leads up to it is the ethical instance of the hermeneutical problem of interpretation, namely, the application of the general to the particular. "It is necessary," Aristotle says, "not only to have stated this general [*katholon*] point but also to show how it applies to the particular cases [*ta hekasta*]" (EN 1007A 28); and again, "Ethical reasonableness [*phronēsis*] requires knowledge not only of what is general but also of particulars, for it is practical knowledge, and practice is concerned with particular matters" (EN 1141B 14). Thus for Aristotle the problem of the good is the hermeneutical problem of interpretive application and concretization. And as Gadamer puts it, "human life under the guidance of practical reason contains the good only insofar as it concretizes the good in its actual practice as the choice of one thing in preference to another" (IGPAP 122). The question, then, is not what the principle is in itself—for as Aristotle's critique of the idea of the good shows, there exists no such *eidos para touto* here—but what the true application of it is on the given occasion.

In this, too, ethical interpretation proves to be like interpretation in the arts. To interpret a piece of music truly one must always already be a participant in the communal tradition of its interpretations, and drawing upon the precedents of this tradition, one brings the piece to bear upon the occasion at hand in a manner that is appropriate, which is to say, fitting and unobtrusive. Analogously, to interpret an ethical principle truly one must be, and remain, under way within the communal tradition of its interpretation. I am a translator of the principle; "I" carry it over from "our" past into "our" present. In this way, in interpretation the "I" becomes "We."

It goes without saying that such a theory of ethical understanding and interpretation is problematical. At first sight, it seems that Gadamer would be proposing totally uncritical conformity to accepted ways of doing things, no matter how exploitative or unjust these ways may be. One ought, it seems, simply to fit in with whatever a society's practices have been. However, if one keeps in mind that exploitation and injustice concern what Hegel calls "persons" and raise issues of abstract right and Legal Status that we, in following Hegel's distinction, must keep separate from what is ethical, one sees that it does not follow that Gadamer's theory of *ethical* interpretation implies indifference to the need for critical reasoning in matters of Legal Status or the Condition of Right as it is variously called.

Furthermore, it is obvious that faithfulness to any tradition presupposes a community secured in *philia* and one not ravaged by each individual's unrestrained pursuit of his or her own advantage at the others' expense—a point we must consider in some detail subsequently. Suffice it to say here that the criterion of appropriateness obviously obtains *only* where an ethical world with a genuine tradition of ethical principles remains intact. Where the *sensus communis* has collapsed, where, as in Socrates' Athens, "no one does what is right voluntarily" and individuals habitually pursue only their private gratification, the self-evidently "appropriate" thing to do *is* to seek one's own advantage, and the sole assurance that the powerful will not trample under foot the legal rights of the individual in the process is the coercive force of external law applied to persons as equals. In this circumstance where the ethical has been displaced, whoever would still be ethical, for example, Socrates, appears merely naïve. Like Socrates, it is he or she who will obtrude as the exception to what is accepted.

It follows that a hermeneutical ethics must be developed in two stages, and that in beginning with the theory of interpretation of customary ethical principles, we have tacitly presupposed the first of these stages: before proceeding to a theory of interpretation of ethical principles a hermeneutical ethics must have treated the subordination of egoistic inclination (Kant: *Neigung*) to communal obligation (*Pflicht*). Where there is no longer a sense of community, where as in the case of Kierkegaard's aesthete, no sense of *Zugehörigkeit* exists, there can be no ethical choice. The "I," as Hegel has put it, must be raised to the "We" if there is to be anything like valid interpretation of a customary ethical principle. Hence ethical understanding and interpretation as we have elaborated it here has as its prerequisite the transcendence of unlimited selfish desire or cupidity. Hegel's word is *Begierde* (compare PhG 139–40). We will return to this point specifically in our considerations of the *sympasa aretē* or comprehensive virtue in Part 3. But for the moment, acknowledging that an essential component remains to be built into the argument, let us continue with our elaboration of the idea of ethical understanding, that is, of the application and interpretation of ethical principles in our deliberations and choices.

2. THE NATURE OF ETHICAL REASONING

And here are we, living in an age in which science to an ever greater extent is expanding its mastery over nature and directing the management of our human co-existence with each other. And this science—the pride of our civilization, which indefatigably works to remedy the deficiencies of its successes and which thereby constantly generates new research projects for itself upon which new progress, planning, and preventative measures ensue—now acquires a truly dazzling power over us. In rigid persistence on the course of progress and of scientific restructuring of the world, a system is perpetuated in which our practical consciousness [of what we ought to do] either blindly resigns itself to its fate and gives up or seeks to defend itself—and no less blindly at that—in rebellion.

. . . only a science lured to myopic self-infatuation could fail to see that the debate concerning the true goals of human society, that our sense of our historical past and our future, depend on a kind of knowing that is not that of science, the knowing, namely, that guides practice in all human affairs [KS IV 118].

Genuine conservative thinkers such as Gadamer have often turned to Aristotle in seeking support for their ideas, for they have shared his aversion to any purely ideal ethical and political theory and his common-sense approach to ethics. Aristotle's emphasis on the distinction between ethical and scientific knowing, between *phronēsis*, on the one hand, and *epistēmē*, on the other, has always appealed to those like Edmund Burke, to take an example from the tradition of English-speaking thinkers, who were of the conviction that anything that might be reasoned out in the abstract about politics and ethics will never coincide with the actual course human events and actions take. Hence, they argue that what is called for in practical matters is not so much pure reason as a sense of traditional precedent or what Burke, in rendering Aristotle's *phronēsis* and the Medieval *prudentia,* called prudence. In his response to the "Appeal from the New to the Old Whigs" (1791) Burke writes:

The lines of morality are not like ideal lines of mathematics. They are broad and deep as well as long. They admit of exceptions; they demand modifications. These exceptions and modifications are made, not by the process of logic but by the rules of prudence. Prudence is not only first in rank of the virtues political and moral, but she is the director, the regulator, the standard of them all.[13]

And just as Burke distances himself from his rationalist contemporaries with such an argument, Gadamer, in similarly following Aristotle and developing the latter's idea of *phronēsis*, may be said to have laid the foundation for an ethical theory that differs dramatically from the modern rationalist schools of deontological and utilitarian thought with their various contemporary advocates and critics, in particular the new contractual theorists, Rawls, Nozick, and others. While Gadamer stresses interpretative deliberation (Aristotle: *bouleuesthai*) based on authority and tradition, these, as I will again emphasize here, all stress autonomous reasoning.

Gadamer thus offers something outside the mainstream of contemporary Anglo-American moral thought, to be sure, but, given its proximity to Burke, something not without precedent in the English-speaking tradition, and, furthermore, something that might well respond to the disquietude felt by many reflective contemporary Anglo-American thinkers. In a perceptive article, "Why Is the Search for the Foundations of Ethics So Frustrating?" MacIntyre, for instance, argues convincingly that analytically trained moral philosophers falsely presuppose "that the set of rules whose status and justification they are investigating provide an adequately demarcated subject matter for investigation, provide the material for an autonomous field of study."[14] He maintains that the results of such "piecemeal" research conducted on this premise inevitably lack convincing underpinnings, and thus, for instance, one could just as easily accept either Robert Nozick's conclusions about justice or John Rawls's or neither's. To be sure, if the tenets of either are accepted, one may well go along with their argument, but precisely these tenets lack sufficient justification. (At the outset of our investigations we saw Rorty making a quite similar argument.) What is missing in their considerations, MacIntyre asserts, is the context, historical and social, from which they have arbitrarily removed themselves, from which they have excerpted the object of their inquiry, and which alone, were it brought into view, could support their conclusions. MacIntyre is on the verge of making a most significant point here: the epistemological model of the timeless, uninvolved, reasoning subject surveying an "adequately demarcated" field of objects simply does not work for ethics.

It is probable that the pervasive uneasiness regarding the foundations of moral theory in contemporary Anglo-American philosophy, to which I alluded at the beginning of this book, may well result from applying the wrong epistemological model and expecting the wrong kind of results. The problem might well be that in ethics most English-speaking philosophers continue to cling to an inappropriate ideal of "rational" inquiry derived from seventeenth- and eighteenth-century science; they go in search of ethical principles as if they were autonomous reasoners looking for timeless self-evident truths only to discover that "the Good" eludes them. For any objective certitude revealed by this mode of investigation proves to be value neutral, that is, neither good nor bad in itself. Consequently, anything one might propose as objectively good and as a principle or principles for making ethical decisions is fair game for analytical and positivist philosophers, who, in relying on the same model of valid science, are quick to show that something has been assumed somewhere which in fact, given the presupposed criteria of what scientific justification and demonstration should be, has no justification itself and provides none for anything else.

As MacIntyre points out (AV 22ff.) and as even the briefest review of Anglo-American ethics over the last seventy-five years or so suffices to demonstrate, the likely response to such criticism is to propose that value judgments are actually not to be taken as demonstrable assertions, that is, propositions, at all, but only as utterances of how I feel about something, as in the "emotivist" theory, or how I would like you to act, as in the "prescriptivist" theory. The fact that Charles Stevenson[15] and the advocates of emotivism allow that we can reason with each other about my attitude and yours, if they are at variance, is cold comfort, for on his emotivist premise there are no cognitive grounds underlying either my position or yours, and thus though we might argue logically about improperly drawn conclusions, the best I could do in regard to my position as a whole would be to persuade you to accept it. I could not get you to see, to know, that it is right, for no one could ever be said to *know* what the moral truth is. It is non-cognitive.

R. M. Hare's prescriptivist theory,[16] on the other hand, would seem to imply that there is some non-relative, objective standard of the Good upon which evaluative statements are based, for it insists on a principle of universalizability and reasonableness. But in point of fact one cannot extend the prescriptivist theory to include such a principle without introducing an ingredient of either naturalism or non-naturalism, both of which Hare wishes to avoid. The prescriptivist account implies only that I *hold* that there is a rational, universalizable criterion to justify my assertion that something is good, but it does not say that there actually is such a criterion or how I could know it if there were. And again, in the absence of such a test, moral disputes would have to end in mere persuasion to belief and not in knowledge.[17] (And nevertheless those who maintain these positions and who must conclude that there are no objective standards of good and bad but only attitudes go on making ethical decisions much as Hume went on shooting one billiard ball into another after having "invalidated" the concept of causality.)

We can only conclude, it seems, that "X is good" is a subjective, not objective, judgment, much as for aesthetic consciousness "X is beautiful" appears to be subjective. Not only intuitionalism but also descriptivism is shown to rest on some unwarranted assumption, for, as G. E. Moore points out,[18] an empirical "demonstration" of the good is not at all like the demonstration of a fact; it can be verified that "an orange is yellow," but it cannot be demonstrated in the same way, for instance, that maximum pleasure (either quantitative or qualitative) is good. And yet Moore somehow comes up with a list of "non-natural" goods he claims are more than matters of personal sentiment.

Or again, if one looks at Ross's table of *prima facie* duties,[19] most "moral" people would agree that they are indeed *prima facie* duties, but clearly there is no objective test, intuitive or empirical, that can demonstrate that they are, and as Ross himself admits, there is certainly no objective test for deciding how in various circumstances the priority of one *prima facie* duty over another is to be established.

Although it goes against the grain—as ethical human beings we sense that a mistake is being made somewhere—we are led to conclude reluctantly that Nietzsche is right (and MacIntyre as well): all tables of values seem to tell us nothing about the world, but only something about the person who proposes them. But has not an *epistemological* mistake in fact been made here? Is it reasonable to expect that ethical human beings could objectify their ethical principles, which exist for them from time out of mind and within which they find themselves under way?

Significantly, the models for these attempts of autonomous reason to found ethics upon an objective basis are provided by Descartes' *Discourse on Method* and Hume's *Treatise of Human Nature*. Method here is either deductive or inferential in the sense that one proceeds either from clear and distinct insights and shows what can be strictly deduced from them or, as in Hume and the more skeptically inclined, from statements about empirically given "facts" and shows what can, or, more often, cannot be legitimately inferred from them. Whether deductive or inferential, such a method depends on the self-evidentness of the premises: to be clearly and distinctly ascertained these premises must be *entirely* in the open, in front of one, as it were, with no trace of obscurity or dubiousness attaching to them. We learn from Gadamer, however, that no such method as this can be applied in ethics, for a truth of ethics is never "clear and distinct" in this way, but always partially unclarified and indeterminate. As traditional–historical, it exceeds the horizons of any individual's consciousness of it. What comes to mind remains embedded in time out of mind; *anamnēsis* and *lēthē* are indissociable. Hence, one can never completely formulate one's ethical principles; there is always a background of what remains unsaid and unformulated in any argument one might make in thinking things out for oneself or in justifying one's position to another. Since we never have ethical principles entirely in front of us but instead always find ourselves within them, with the foundations of them exceeding the horizons of our limited perspective, there can be no proceeding *more geometrico* here. There is only what Aristotle calls *bouleuesthai*—deliberating on the basis of what remain inexplicit, immemorial, traditional truths.

Gadamer brings the problem here into focus using Plato's (Socrates') dispute with sophism as his example:

> He who asserts that promises must be kept, for that is the moral precondition of our living together as human beings, and he who seeks to justify this assertion must certainly present evidence. . . . Even so there is no means of compelling someone to see the truth who does not want to see it. Not only is it possible for him to point to what "everybody" says or does in order to evade unpleasant obligations. He can justify his evasion theoretically by placing moral obligation as a whole in question, as Thrasymachus and Callicles do. He who has no sense of propriety and obligation, he from whom no response is drawn when recourse is had to these concepts, will never understand what they are about. But worse than that, he will in fact be of the opinion that he knows better than anyone else and will seem to be the one who sees through the naïveté of all those inhibited by such "morality" [DD 115–16].

Someone who places moral obligation as a whole in question places himself precisely in the position of a Cartesian autonomous subject who makes judgments about objective states of affairs that he views before him. But this, Gadamer argues, is not how we know ethical truths. Indeed, to put ourselves in that position of autonomy is to make ethical understanding impossible. We have a "sense of propriety [*Anständigkeit*] and obligation" only as long as we continue to be under way within the ethical tradition, which is to say, only as long as we submit ourselves to the authority of what takes precedence over us— the authority of this tradition. Ethical truths, in other words, are not given to an autonomous intellect removed from the influences of tradition and culture. Instead they are inherited by individuals, whose task is to apply them with discretion in the circumstances in which they find themselves. What is called for is not autonomous reasoning but rather the very different ability to deliberate appropriately on the basis of what precedes and founds one's individual thought.

In this argument Gadamer once again proves astonishingly close to Burke, and it is certainly this conservative, Burkean thread in the tradition of English-speaking philosophy that best enables the interweaving of it with Gadamer's thought, best enables, that is, the "merging of horizons," that I am seeking here. Burke writes in his *Reflections on the Revolution in France*:

> We wished at the period of the Revolution [of 1688], and do now wish, to derive all we possess as an *inheritance from our forefathers*. Upon that body and stock of inheritance we have taken care not to inoculate any cyon alien to the nature of the original plant. All the reformations we have hitherto made, have proceeded upon the principle of reference to antiquity; and I hope, nay I am persuaded, that all those which possibly may be made hereafter, will be carefully formed upon analogical precedent, authority and example (RRF 43).[20]

The key phrase at the end, "carefully formed upon analogical precedent, authority and example," is reinforced a few paragraphs later when Burke speaks of the guiding "spirit of philosophic analogy" (RRF 46). The tradition here is a long one extending back through the idea of the *analogia entis*, or analogy of being, in Medieval philosophy to Aristotle's critique of Plato. Aristotle introduces the idea of analogy precisely to avoid hypostasizing whatever it is that existent things (*entia, ta onta*) might have in common. A general is good and a doctor is good, but there is no good in itself that exists besides the general and the doctor; rather, "good" only indicates an analogousness between the two in what they do, *allo allou,* the one in one way, the other in another (compare IGPAP 155). Consequently in one's reasoning about what is good, or for that matter about anything that is, any *ens* or *on,* one does not start with some abstract idea and reason from it to the particular circumstances. Rather, as Gadamer puts it, one starts with the fact "that," with Aristotle's *tode ti* or this something.

In ethical reasoning this means that one reasons from within one's situation in relationship to what has preceded it, or, as Burke says here, in relationship to precedent and example. For there is no abstract right or wrong independent of our historical experience to which we might turn in removing ourselves from the latter, but only an analogousness of what is right and wrong in the present circumstances to what was right and wrong in the historical circumstances that have led up to the present. Hence in deciding what to do in regard to the present, the standard is not some abstract idea of right or wrong *para tauto,* by itself, in Plato's somewhat misleading language, but the authority of the past, of precedent.

Here again, obviously, Gadamer, despite his proximity to Burke or perhaps on account of it, places himself sharply at odds with most moral theory in the English-speaking world today. To take a first example: William Frankena begins his general introduction to contemporary ethical thought with a reference to a passage in Plato's *Crito,* to which Gadamer also refers—the scene where Socrates, though offered the chance to escape his death sentence, chooses not to accept it and, instead, to abide by the decree of the state.[21] Frankena, who would be challenged on his reading by only a few contemporary Anglo-American thinkers, takes this passage as an example of what engenders *autonomous* moral reasoning. "Moral philosophy arises," he writes,

> when like Socrates we pass beyond the stage in which we are
> directed by traditional rules and even in which the rules are so
> internalized that we can be said to be inner directed, to the stage

in which we think for ourselves in critical and general terms (as the Greeks were beginning to do in Socrates' day) and achieve a kind of autonomy as moral agents.[22]

In commenting on this same passage Gadamer writes,

> In Socrates he [Plato] encountered in living reality how a person could steadfastly hold to what he viewed as right—unerringly, unconditionally, in self-reliant independence from all external influences. Plato's *Crito* provides perhaps the most impressive monument to this fact: on the eve of his execution Socrates refuses the escape which had been readied for him, an escape which might well have been greeted with relief by the broad circle of the Attic public. And he refuses it solely because it seemed right to him, after having acknowledged the laws and customs of the *polis* for so long and having enjoyed the protection of his rights which they afforded him, to submit to even an unjust verdict [DD 3–4].

To be sure, Gadamer adds that the justice to which Socrates adheres must clearly transcend "all behavior established by social convention and all of a society's beliefs [*doxai*]" (DD 4). That seems to be precisely what Frankena is saying, but a closer examination reveals some very important differences.

Gadamer by no means argues that Socrates' choice goes against tradition. On the contrary, his choice "seemed right to him, after having acknowledged the laws and customs [*nomoi*] of the *polis* for so long and having enjoyed the protection of his rights which they afforded him." Socrates, Gadamer tells us, breaks with convention and current opinions (*doxai*), to be sure, but not with tradition. This distinction is crucial. At the time he made his choice, the accepted thing to do was to seek one's own advantage. We know from the *Republic*, Books I and II, that the principle of self-interest had become the unchallenged dogma of Plato's society. No one, it was held, does what is just voluntarily, for justice "is accepted and approved, not as a real good, but as a thing honored in the lack of power to do injustice"

(607B). It is not tradition but precisely this sophist thinking which places reasoning in one's interest ahead of tradition that Socrates abjures when he breaks with what is "conventional." Thus "critical," "autonomous" thinking is not at all the basis of his choice—consider in this regard his reliance upon his *daimonion*—but allegiance to what transcends him as an individual, the "parent" *polis* with its written and unwritten laws, its *nomoi*. To justify his apparently "naïve" decision to stay in jail, he tells his listeners how he would be refuted had he declared himself ready to leave and the *nomoi* themselves were to cross-examine him:

> When you were born and raised and educated, could you say, first, that you were not our [the laws'] progeny and slave, both you and your progenitors? And if this is how things stand, do you believe that what is right [*to dikaion*] for you and what is right for us is equal? And do you believe that whatever we undertake to do to you is right for you to do in response? . . . Or are you so wise [*sophos*] that you have forgotten [*lelēthen se*] that your country is more to be valued than your mother and father and all your other progenitors, more to be honored and revered . . . [*Crito* 50Eff.]?

Indeed, as Gadamer sees it, the choice Socrates makes is precisely between his *Zugehörigkeit*, his belonging to the historical traditional community, and the free thinking of "wise" (*sophoi*) individuals who in severing themselves from the tradition, forgetting it, reason out on their own what is advantageous—even if "advantage" here might be construed as social utility and not merely egoistically. It is clear that in Socrates fidelity to the tradition takes precedence over his own autonomous reasoning.

Hence, in contrast to Frankena, the issue for Gadamer when he appeals to the *Crito* is not that of uncritical acceptance of current practices *vs.* critical, autonomous reasoning. The line is drawn in a very different way. On the one side is the range of sophist thinking that extends from its moderate (Protagoras, Gorgias) to its extreme advocates (Thrasymachus, "Callicles"). Here, to be sure, individuals must depend upon themselves when making decisions. In choosing they must seek what is advantageous—for all or for themselves, as the case may be. On the other side are the individuals who make their choices (Aristotle: *prohaireseis*) after deliberation (*bouleuesthai*) and in applying the traditional principles (*nomoi*) within which they find themselves under way. Such individuals act as is fitting (*hōs dei*). Gadamer argues for this second approach, which he finds common to Plato and Aristotle. What is ethical, he maintains, is like a language and, as we have seen, is transmitted in language. And like language, consequently, someone cannot invent it on his own, privately. He cannot think it up autonomously. Instead he is initiated into it in guidance by those who precede him.

To make this point a second comparison with a contemporary American thinker is useful—John Rawls, who, like Frankena, serves nicely to illustrate an opposed, and, from Gadamer's point of view, mistaken approach. In his *A Theory of Justice* Rawls proposes that "we should strive for a kind of moral geometry with all the rigor which this name connotes." "Unhappily," he adds, "the reasoning I shall give will fall far short of this, since it is highly intuitive throughout. Yet it is essential to have in mind the ideal one would like to achieve" (TJ 121).

The concession he makes here is of particular interest, for it reveals sensitivity on his part to the discrepancy between the methodological exactitude (Aristotle: *akribeia*) he would like and the indeterminacy of the actual subject matter of his investigation. Aristotle, it will be remembered, cautions that we must not expect more exactitude than the subject matter, in this case moral theory, allows (EN 1094B 15). Rawls, however, despite his reservations about it, proceeds with his project of "moral reasoning." As is well known, in seeking a substitute for a traditional sense of what is good he resorts to a contractual theory. According to this theory a group of reasonable individuals would be able to work out among themselves what is just and to contract to abide by it. But precisely here the perpetuation of the myth of the autonomous moral reasoner can be seen to undercut the project. Any assembly of people who would remove themselves from all tradition and precedent and put themselves in what Rawls calls an "original position" (TJ 118–92), from which they propose to reason their way to what is just, faces precisely the familiar problem of Russell's hypothetical Council of Elders who in inventing language would agree to call a sheep a sheep and a wolf a wolf. Obviously they could not arrive at such conventions if they did not already have a language to begin with. For if they could not talk to each other in ways that followed previously established, accepted ways of speaking without thinking about it, how could they possibly get on with the process of talking about how to name things? Any invention of language presupposes an already existing inexplicit language with its accepted usages (see p. 131 above).

And if the argument concerning the indissociability of language and ethical principles is valid, if, that is, ethical principles concerning what is *dikaios* are given in language bequeathed to us from time out of mind, any "invention" of the principles of justice can only follow on the basis of standards already transmitted to us in the language we use to speak of them. Any invention, that is to say, is a process of getting clear about new dimensions of what we always already know. Invention, as in the Latin *invenire*, is a "coming across" what is already there.

Thus the same objections brought against any invention of a language from scratch can be brought against contractual theories concerning justice, at least to the extent that they purport to be "moral reasoning" and not just legal reasoning at the abstract level.[23] Except for the totally a-moral individual (Nietzsche's *Übermensch* or Kierkegaard's aesthete, for example) there is simply no such thing as an "original position," a position where we would not "always already" be bound by established principles. Pre-existent principles from time out of mind would be presupposed by any council of human beings who would set about drawing up further principles that were to govern a society—which, moreover, is precisely Burke's argument against those Frenchmen who set out to draft "the rights of man" as a foundation for their revolution.

To be sure, Rawls is not arguing that his "assembly" is anything more than a thought construct to be used by an individual in reasoning out what is just. But even if it is only a single individual who must carry out the hypothetical debate by himself or herself, he or she will have to do so starting with precedential accepted norms that provide the background for the debate. Neither a group nor an individual can invent a language in which to reason *ex nihilo* about the right thing to do. Even Plato's "dialogue of the soul with itself" is "always already" under way, as Gadamer and Heidegger like to say, within pre-given principles and values as these are passed on in words such as *kalos* and *aischros*.

It is striking in this regard that Rawls, like Locke before him and Nozick after him, comes out exactly where he wanted to: the contract theory is used to justify what one always already believes, and for that reason it can easily be exposed as circular and hence declared a rationalization rather than the justification that it pretends to be. From Gadamer's point of view, however, there is nothing wrong at all with argument based on unquestioned assumptions, and consequently nothing wrong either with circular reasoning. Indeed the nature of ethical argument is such that it inevitably tacitly presupposes what is to be demonstrated. Demonstration, reasoning, argument, here is a showing, an *apophainesthai*, that makes an aspect of what is inexplicitly accepted explicit. Contract theorists are not to be faulted for doing exactly this, but only for their failure to acknowledge openly the inevitable circularity of their reasoning and for disguising it in the garb of reasoning *more geometrico*.

In sum, ethical principles are like rules of language usage. "New" ones can be arrived at only on the basis of pre-existent ones and are in fact an elaboration of the latter, an explication *and interpretation* of what we understand them to mean in our circumstances now. In regard to language and the ethical principles bequeathed in it, there is no getting around all given rules to an "original" pre-linguistic or pre-ethical condition. For precisely as language, as ways of saying something, ethical principles are given from time out of mind. Or, as Gadamer puts it, they are *unvordenklich*. The German—literally translated, unprethinkable—indicates that any thinking (*Denken*) in these matters rests upon that which itself is never completely brought into awareness and which, in sustaining thought and being partially "recollected," remains partially inexplicit and un-thought-of. Any talk of an "original position" overlooks the fact that conscious ethical deliberation always takes place on the basis of tacitly accepted principles which themselves are not raised to the level of consciousness, and that any truth (*alētheia*) that becomes clear remains embedded in that to which we remain oblivious (in *lēthē*).

In pursuing the consequences for ethics of Wittgenstein's and Austin's understanding of language as rule-governed practices, Rawls himself comes close to acknowledging that the rules do precede the reasoning of an individual.[24] Arguing against a "summary" conception of rules that arrives at a rule by gener-alizing from particular cases, he points out that the rules exist prior to any particular case and define the practice the case is an instance of. Rules, in other words, are what make a practice as such possible in the first place. Consequently, if one is engaged in a practice, one cannot alter the rules as one sees fit, for that would be to stop engaging in the practice constituted by them (just as one cannot arbitrarily decide to use "slab" in a different way from that defined by the language game of building without ceasing to play that game). To this extent, then, rules may be said to have a certain authority over reasoning individ-uals, who, if they are to follow a certain practice, must abide by the rules that define it.

If being ethical is such a rule-governed practice, it too would seem to imply the subordination of one's reasoning to the constitutive rules of the practice. Indeed the argument here begins to sound like the one the personified *nomoi* make in the

Crito. Rawls, however, balks at drawing any such conclusion. In heading off those who would like to think that his argument implies such subordination, he insists that "There is no inference whatsoever to be drawn with respect to whether or not one should accept the practices of one's society. One can be as radical as one likes . . ." (TJ 132). And how is the acceptance or rejection of practices to be decided upon? By surveying and assessing the practices from outside them, from the "original position." Rawls, it turns out, is arguing on a very different basis from Gadamer's: for Rawls the entire body of practices can become the explicit object of conscious scrutiny. There is no necessarily inexplicit foundation for one's ethical deliberations.

We have a curious ambivalence here. Like Austin, Rawls would turn to an existent practice in seeking to ascertain the rules that define it, Austin to a language practice, Rawls to a social one. And in each case the practice would seem to take precedence over the participants engaged in it. But even so it is assumed throughout that the rules defining practices are to be subjected to the critical reasoning of the individual. (Austin resists radicality here only insofar as he concludes that the time-tested will most likely work better than that which you and I might think up in our armchairs. See Chapter 2, note 4.)

As we have learned from Gadamer, however, language usages are not at our disposal in this sense: a "whole" of unquestioned usages is presupposed in the questioning of any particular usage, which is to say that given language usages are the precondition of our reasoning about any one of them and these given language uses cannot be raised as a whole into consciousness for critical evaluation. And if my extension of Gadamer's thesis—specifically, that language is the medium (*Mitte*) of understanding—to our ethical understanding is valid, the same is true of ethical principles: in any ethical deliberation we are bound by a body of usages and meanings within which we are "always already" under way and which remains at least partially unthought-of in any thinking we might do. Of course, like a Callicles or Nietzsche, I may reject the ethical altogether, in which case communal obligation (Kant's *du sollst*) gives way to private volition (Nietzsche's *ich will*). Then I am free indeed, but not to make ethical choices. For I have forfeited the precondition of being ethical much as when I decide to use "slab" privately, that is, in any way I want (*ich will*), I have forfeited the precondition of language.

The inappropriate epistemological model that persists in Austin and Rawls alike turns out to be that of an Enlightenment science, which, at least prior to the recent upheavals in physics, thought of the knower–known relationship in terms of an unprejudiced rational subject surveying states of affairs from somewhere "above it all." But clearly this model does not fit when we are in among the facts, conditioned by them, and can attain no position outside them. And this is certainly the circumstance in ethics: we ourselves are "effected" by an ethical tradition or history of effects (*Wirkungsgeschichte*) that transcends us as individuals. Any ethical theory constructed on the basis of a rational subject objectively surveying supposed universal moral essences or moral empirical facts therefore spins itself out in a vacuum of abstract reflection, and its arguments will inevitably fall to those of its critics, be they the sophists with whom Plato saw himself confronted or positivist and analytical philosophers. For such a theory has removed itself from that which alone could sustain it in any reasoning about it, removed itself, that is, from what Hegel calls ethical substance, and Gadamer, our sense of "propriety and obligation."

But if ethical reasoning must be based on tradition rather than pure intellectual insight, and ethical choices, upon discretion (*phronēsis*) and a "sense of propriety and obligation," rather than scientific knowing (*epistēmē*), what sort of justification, what sort of argument, *can* be given in ethical matters? The question is inevitable, for it is plain that justification indeed must be given once any society has lost its innocence and becomes vulnerable to sophistic manipulation; our reasoning must be able to assist us in holding steadfastly to what is right. The importance of rational justification, Gadamer argues in his *The Idea of the Good*, is made evident by the whole of Plato's dialogues, which in large part are concerned with *logon didonai*, with giving a justification or grounds to oneself and to others for the choices one makes and thereby justifying one's choices against sophistic refutational techniques and the sophistic cajolery of the senses. But what form can such justification take? What sort of thing is ethical argumentation?

Plato himself leaves the way open for a serious misunderstanding here. In the *Meno*, where the issue is whether knowledge of the good can be demonstrated and taught, he takes a *mathematical* example of teaching, demonstration, and learning to illustrate his theory of "recollection." The slave in the dialogue is asked to "solve the problem" of how to double the area of a square. It is demonstrated (taught, *memathēmenon*) to him why a second square constructed on the diagonal of the first will have double the area, and the problem is solved when he attains this *mathēma* (insight or teaching). If this example is supposed to have anything at all to do with the good, it would appear that in ethical matters too we have problems to solve, that we can be taught the answer—even if only by the inducement of a recollection—and that what we are taught, the insight, will enable us henceforth to give grounds, the "reason why," for the "right" solution. We would be able to demonstrate the conclusion from the grounds we are now able to give for it.

But as we have seen, and as Plato himself obviously knows all too well, this sort of argumentation *more geometrico* gets nowhere in ethical matters. We do not draw conclusions about ethical choices in the way we infer conclusions in mathematical demonstration. And where we pretend to, ethical argument simply relapses into idiosyncracy (MacIntyre: "disquieting private arbitrariness" [AV 8]). If, however, ethical cognition, ethical understanding, is of a different sort from mathematical knowing, if *phronēsis* is to be distinguished from *epistēmē*, its argumentation must be different from *episteme*'s demonstration (*apodeixis*). Giving grounds, reasons, or justification here would take a different form. What would that be?

Despite the appearance the *Meno* gives, the answer is to be found in Plato, specifically in the model of Socratic *discussion* that pervades the dialogues as a whole.[25] The choices one makes are to be justified to others, or even to oneself in the "dialogue of the soul with itself," in discursive exchanges. In overcoming idiosyncratic dogma, these exchanges bring into the open shared ethical principles we have in mind from time out of mind. In discussion individuals get clear about a limited segment of the ethical discourse in which they participate together and which, in connecting them in community with one another, makes it possible for them to rise from their isolated physical and natural existence to the "life of spirit," from the "I" to the "We." The *anamnēsis* or recollection here is that of the recovery of language usages belonging to the tradition which have lapsed, or are on the verge of lapsing, into oblivion. (See Chapter 2, Part 4 on Socrates' discussion with Polus in the *Gorgias*.)

What happens in discussion is thus quite different from what happens in mathematical demonstration. In demonstration one proceeds logically from clearly established premises to consequences or, in explanation, vice versa. And thereby one achieves definitive incontestable results. In discussion, as we have already seen, we circle within a range of significance that becomes clearer to us as we proceed, but never completely clear. Hence unlike mathematical truths, the ethical truths arrived at in discussion do remain vulnerable to sophistic refutation and unconvincing to someone utterly lacking a sense of "propriety and obligation." Plato's point, even in the *Meno*, is actually not at all that *logon didonai*, giving justification, in ethical matters should proceed in the manner of geometrical demonstration, but that understanding and knowing, precisely in ethical matters, means getting clear about what we already know. It is recollection of foreknowledge—foreknowledge to which ruined souls may well have become fully and incorrigibly oblivious.

If that is so, the contemporary idea of autonomous "moral reasoning" that would "solve problems" is spurious, and attempts at such reasoning are bound to miscarry. MacIntyre is right, it seems, when he adduces the interminability of moral debate as evidence of its uselessness and finds emotivism to be the inevitable result of it. But his objection would not hold for ethical justification as we have characterized it here since it proceeds in the very different manner of discussion. Discussion is indeed "interminable" (Gadamer: *unabschliessbar*), but, as we have seen, that is not a fault in discussion though it would be in mathematical demonstration. Accordingly it would be better to speak of inconclusiveness here rather than of interminability, and, above all, better to recognize that ethical reasoning is an unending dialogical task of getting clear about what is right and not "problem solving" at all.

The *Gorgias* illustrates this point nicely. As opposed to Callicles, who is indeed a ruined soul wholly oblivious to the good, Polus preserves some "sense of propriety and obligation," to use Gadamer's words, for he does not hesitate to call injustice *aischros* though he is reluctant to call it bad. Socrates brings him to see that the understanding he already has of *aischros* as indecent, ignoble, ill-formed, disfunctional, implies "bad" and, conversely, that justice, which he knows is *kalos*, meaning honorable, noble, well-formed, functional, implies "good." The ethical reasoning Socrates pursues here makes no pretence of demonstrating something new; it only brings out what is "always already" presupposed and known ahead of time.

3. THE *Sympasa Aretē* OR UNDERLYING VIRTUE

This difference between mathematical and ethical argumentation makes clear in yet another way that the model of rational thinking unfettered by past authority and prejudices cannot be carried over into ethical deliberation. On the contrary, ethical deliberation, we now see, depends on what Burke calls the wisdom of the species, and Gadamer, the authority of the past.

Thus a hermeneutical ethics would presuppose what Gadamer calls a "rehabilitation of authority and tradition" (WM 261ff.), this in sharp contrast to the stress put on individual autonomy by Western moral thought at least since Kant. Gadamer accepts that, as Kant proposes, individuals do give themselves the law, but he would severely restrict the sense in which we are to understand this "legislative" act. We must gain self-control over our sensuous inclinations. Autonomy (*autarkeia*) in this sense—in Plato's and Aristotle's sense of freedom from the tyranny of the passions—is presupposed in any ethical life. But as Plato and Aristotle teach us, we are dependent on authority for the disciplining that initially gives us this self-control. To begin with, our souls must be put in a certain state or condition. They must be predisposed to respond in the right way if they are to deliberate rightly (*dikaiōs*) and choose what is right (*ta dikaia*).

With that, an implication of ethical understanding's dependence on authority comes to the fore which we have touched on before but to which we must pay closer attention from now on: as opposed to mathematical thinking, ethical thinking, deliberation (*bouleuesthai*), occurs against the background of what is not thought about at all. Indeed, it is grounded in pre-conscious dispositions, or *hexeis*, as Aristotle calls them. We have seen that the individual cannot be said to invent autonomously the content of the custom that guides deliberation and choice and sustains the justification given for it. Rather he or she inherits this content in the form of traditional precedent—precedent, however, not only in ways of thinking but also in ways of acting. To be ethical we must "always already" be under way in the tradition of applications of what is customary and have a proper "sense" of what is appropriate. And as such a simple expression as "He hasn't enough sense to come in out of the rain" suffices to make evident, having a "sense" of the appropriate thing to do extends from what is consciously and explicitly thought of into what remains inexplicit and unconscious, and thus it is a blend of what one thinks *and* of what one is accustomed to do without thinking.[26]

Aristotle provides a number of apt illustrations of this phenomenon of having good sense (*phronimos einai, nous echein*). In regard to the virtue of even-temperedness (*praotēs*), for example, he tells us that an individual who displays it feels anger against the appropriate people, *hois dei*; as it is appropriate, *hōs dei*; and when it is appropriate, *hote dei* (EN 1123ʙ 32). In the case of temperance, he tells us, the temperate person desires what is appropriate, *hōn dei*; in the appropriate way, *hōs dei*; when it is appropriate, *hote dei* (EN 1119ʙ 16). What defines appropriateness, propriety, here? The appropriate thing to do is, of course, the "mean between the extremes," but that serves only to define the appropriate negatively in opposition to the excesses of self-indulgence. It establishes a loose schema that defines the *in*appropriate, defines, as it were, what is beyond the pale. The content of the appropriate itself is not given thereby. Indeed, the actual content of any reasonable appropriate action is given only in the ethical substance of the tradition inculcated as an habituated disposition (*hexis*) that predisposes us to think and act in accustomed ways.

The deliberately indefinite use in Aristotle of *hōs dei, hote dei*, and so forth makes clear that he relies, not at all on something that someone as an autonomous consciousness might conclude by himself or herself in "critical" reasoning, and not merely on socially predisposed *thinking* by itself, but also, and to begin with, on an unconscious predisposition to do what is traditional and customary, to do what is fitting, *to deon*, or, as Gadamer calls it, *das Tunliche*, what is supposed to be done.

The unconscious disposition or *hexis* thus provides the indispensable grounding for any ethical reasoning, and any reasoning by itself removed from this grounding could not provide the specific content of the appropriate thing to do. Ethical understanding is, therefore, a function not just of mind but also of who we *are*. There is no *logos* without *ergon*, which is to say, no reason and reasoning without deed; that we have already learned from Plato's *characters*, Socrates and Callicles, whom he uses to present his argument for the choice (*prohairesis*) of the philosophical life over the life of pleasure and the pursuit of power. And now we see that there is neither *logos* nor *ergon* without a *hexis* or predisposition to choose the appropriate course of action in reasoning or deliberation.

In Part 4 of Chapter 1, we considered the special nature of the reasoning or deliberation (*bouleuesthai*) that leads to an ethical choice, and the faculty of *phronēsis* or reasonableness on which it is based. We saw then that *phronēsis* is to be distinguished, on the one hand, from *epistēmē*, for which mathematics is the paradigm, and, on the other, from *technē* or artisanship insofar as in the choices that *phronēsis* makes, it is the one making the choice who is effected or brought into being and not something else, namely, the table, or ship, or healthy body, or whatever else an artisan (*technitēs*) might produce. As we have also seen, there is a circularity here: to be ethical one must have already been ethical; to make ethical choices one must have already been making them. The question to be asked here is just what sort of being is this "self" or soul (*psychē*) that is presupposed in making ethical choices yet at the same time is brought about or effected by making them? Put another way: what is the excellence, the virtue, of the soul that is effected by the right choices one makes and has been making and, circularly, is needed to begin with in order to choose rightly?

For all the differences that modern interpreters have found between Plato and Aristotle, or at least between the young Plato and the mature Aristotle, in addressing this question Gadamer asserts that these two consistently provide the same, and, for that matter, the best, answer to this question, insofar as both build their answer on the premise of human finitude. Their common concern is with *to anthrōpinon agathon*, the good for human beings as such, and this is a good very different from what might be good for a god. For gods are not temporal, finite existences. But human beings are. On that Plato and Aristotle are in full agreement. Thus in truth Plato is not at all the mystic "idealist" who experiences some transcendental "idea of the Good" in a flash of divine insight, while Aristotle, the "realist," contents himself with giving us loose guidelines for acting in our human situation. Despite any appearances to the contrary, if we look closely enough, we see that Plato too never goes beyond a *dialectical* ethics and that he, just like Aristotle, always acknowledges human contingency:

> Plato's philosophy is dialectical not only because in conceptualizing it remains under way to the concept, but because in conceptualizing in this manner it sees the human being as just such an under-way and in-between. The Socratic character of this dialectic lies precisely in the fact that it carries out and exemplifies that very thing which it recognizes as characteristic of human existence. Hence the name of philosophy: philosophy is not *sophia*, knowledgeable disposing over something; rather, it is striving for *sophia*. As such it is the highest possibility. . . . That implies, however, that human existence includes an element of non-disposing-over, non-control-of, itself, and that as a human possibility, philosophy carries itself out within the dialectical questionableness it recognizes as part of human existence [PDE 3].

And for its part, Aristotle's ethics is to be viewed as a "conceptual projection" of precisely this Socratic insight (PDE 7).

For both Plato and Aristotle the human being *is* and *is not* good, *is* and *is not* wise, brave, temperate, and so forth; the positive and the negative are "equifundamental" (Heidegger: *gleichursprünglich*) in him. He *is* authentic, but as Heidegger's *Being and Time* makes clear, equifundamental with his authenticity is his inauthenticity, his *not-being* authentic. This dialectical tension is expressed here in the emphasis on his being *in-between*: he is neither a god who *is* good nor some sort of sea creature (for example, the oyster alluded to in the *Philebus* [21c]) that *is not* good. He is between being and not-being, between pure *nous* and vegetative torpor. Since human beings always carry with them a "remnant of earth" (Goethe: *Erden-rest*), they can never be said to have attained full divine being, but instead are always under way toward it, always in the temporal–historical process of attaining it. Hence their life remains an ongoing carrying-out (*Vollzug*). It can never be said that a human being is good but only that he or she is becoming good.

Gadamer alludes to this characteristic of human existence not only in emphasizing our being under way, but in stressing questionableness (see WM 344ff.). In regard to a god one could not even say that all questions of existence have been resolved, for in the case of a god nothing ever was unresolved to begin with. A god *is* good; for a god there never were, are, or will be any open questions, any choices. For human beings, in contrast, the course of life is always unresolved. They do not come to the end of it, and thus their existence remains an open question with possibilities to be decided for or against. Compare in this regard Aristotle on the deliberation (*bouleuesthai*) that precedes a choice of what to do: "Deliberation," he says, "is about things that are by and large constant, but unclear in their outcome," indeed even "indeterminate" (*ahoriston*) (EN 1112B 9).

Consequently, though both Plato and Aristotle speak of *sophia* and argue that we should, in *philosophia*, orient our lives toward it, neither goes so far as to say that a human being can finally reach this absolute thinking; no human being can be absolved from the historicity of finite existence.[27] Gadamer thus stresses the structure of *Unabschliessbarkeit* and *Unvollendbarkeit* of human thought and life, their inconclusiveness and imperfection (see DD 153–54). And he is able to uncover in both Plato and Aristotle testimony to this inconclusiveness and imperfection.

Now, it is easy enough to see that Aristotle asserts the ongoing inconclusiveness of human existence. But what can Plato have in mind when he speaks of the "idea of the Good" as something ineffable (*arheton*) beyond existence (*epekeina tēs ousias*) (*Republic* 506D)? That makes it sound as if it could only be the object of a *conclusive*, trans-discursive insight. Plato speaks this way, Gadamer answers, because for him the good is a structural principle of existences—the most important of these existences for our considerations here being the soul—and though this structure is immanent in the structured existences themselves, it is to be distinguished *qua* structure from them. This argument is known to us already from the *Phaedo* where, as we have seen, *auto to kalon*, for instance, means, not "absolute beauty" as some thing, but "beautiful itself" as a characteristic to be thought of in distinction from things that may be spoken of as "beautiful." The good is to be distinguished from this idea and any of the other ideas, and is "ineffable" only because it is a *first* principle, a principle before all distinctions and differences that are the precondition of any speaking. *The good is the structural principle of unity or self-identity*, and since one can speak only of what is self-identical, of what, in being identical with itself is different from something else and distinguishable, in a strict sense one cannot "speak" of the good, which is self-identity itself. In contrast—to take another example from the *Phaedo*—one can speak of fire itself, *auto to pyr*, namely, as something in which a higher principle or form, heat, is present and which, in being one with itself, is different from both snow and cold.

In being the precondition of speaking of anything the good is peculiar, but this by no means implies that it is unknowable. One must keep in mind that Plotinus takes a completely new step when he calls the One *epekeina noēseōs*, beyond knowing, as opposed to Plato's *epekeina tēs ousias*, beyond existence, and sees all existence, like all thought, as a cipher of transcendence (IGPAP 28). The good in Plato is neither more nor less than a structure that can be known and recognized in existent things. It is certainly not Plotinus' One, which alone is, and is beyond existence; rather, it is that which makes it possible to bring any multiplicity to a condition of unity. The idea of the good emerges as the principle of all conditions of order, as the unity of the unified, the unity of the Many (IGPAP 31). The good, then, is the "integer," which is to say, that which integrates any one thing and provides it with its integrity, this in the good cosmos, the good state, and, most important for us, the good soul.

And now the relationship of Plato's idea of the good to the *aretē* or excellence of the soul becomes clear: the soul of someone who submits to the flattering influences either of the senses or of sophistic opportunists seeking to ingratiate themselves with it is a soul that dis-integrates, a soul that loses its harmony and ceases to be at one with itself. In contrast the good soul, the excellent soul, maintains its unity. That we learn from both the *Republic* and the *Philebus*. Ultimately it is the cosmos that instructs us here, for it above all displays the principle of self-identity maintained in difference. The cosmos is a one that, in preserving the rhythmic order of the cycles of nature, prevails over difference and diversity (the Many) and prevents the disintegration of itself into lawless chaos. The *Timaeus* and the *Republic* teach the same thing: the good is the structure of unification that constitutes and preserves the life of any good thing (DD 191–93).

But in what sense, then, can Socrates be said to "look to" (*apoblepein pros*) the good (IGPAP 28)? There may seem to be a problem here if, as Gadamer maintains, the good is not a thing but a structure of things and indeed something that we might identify with the *aretē* or excellence of a thing. For how could one "look to" a structure? Essentially the argument is this: those who decide rightly (*dikaiōs*) hold to *one* thing, thereby bringing unity to the many different desires that threaten to distract them. Thus looking to the good means preserving the structure of unity and continuity in diversity. To know this structure is to hold to it, or, as Plato puts it, to know the good is to do it. The model here is the *technitēs*, in particular the doctor. In the *Gorgias* it is pointed out that, as opposed to those who only have a mere knack (*tribē*, *empeiria*), those who have a true *technē* are concerned with bringing order and harmony, which is to say, unity, to the different parts of the thing they are working on (503E–504A). For this reason they are always looking to something, *apoblepon pros ti* (503E–504A), namely, the ordered whole of the parts they wish to effect. Consequently, as opposed to mere cooks whose concern is flattery (*kolakeia*) of someone's tastes with no regard to whether this be good or bad, doctors do what they do *with an eye to* the good of the patient's body, namely, its health. And precisely this good consists in a right ordering of the different parts in a unity. Similarly, as opposed to sophists who are concerned only with gratifying the desires of their audience, the philosopher Socrates, the doctor of the soul, always has an eye to the soul's health and excellence (*aretē*), and it is this excellence that he strives to effect in what he says. In other words, he says what he does, whether it be pleasant or painful, gratifying or not, in looking to the idea of the right order of the soul, in *apoblepein pros ton agathon*, looking to the good.

Obviously, in doctoring our own souls our task is the same, namely, not to give in, in sophistic rationalizations, to our desires for gratification with no regard to whether these contribute to the right order and good of the soul, but rather to reason with ourselves in making choices, always in regard to, always with an eye to, the good we seek to effect in ourselves. Thus the idea of the good we look to, far from being something transcendent and separate (*chōriston*), is indeed the structure of unity in diversity, the structure of integrity we seek to effect *in* ourselves and others.[28]

What we see in Plato's discussion of the good in the *Gorgias* is in fact an exemplification of Plato's unwritten doctrine of the One and the indeterminate Two, of determination within indeterminacy. *Symmetria*, *metroitēs*, and *kallos*, symmetry, measuredness, beauty, are, as the *Philebus* tells us (64E), the structural characteristics of the good as it shows up in human life. Each of these implies a number (*arithmos*), an integer, a so-and-so many taken together as one, a limited segment established in an infinite continuum. And as number they exist *in* what they constitute and not as some sort of "transcendent" idea: ". . . εὑρήσειν γὰρ ἐνοῦσαν (for we will find it existing therein) (*Philebus* 16D).

What is to be learned from this concerning the excellence of the soul that effects, and is effected by, our ethical choices?

From Plato and Aristotle alike we learn that the human being is "composite" and, more specifically, if good, may be said to be a balance of two tendencies and if bad, an inbalance of them, the tendencies, that is, toward integration or disintegration, toward oneness or manyness, integrity or duplicity. These tendencies in us are set forth by Plato as the principle of unity, the One (*to hen*), and the principle of indeterminacy, the *ahoristos duas* or indeterminate Two. In Plato, whose expositions are largely metaphorical, the nearest thing to a conceptual formulation of the relationship of the One to the good and, correspondingly, of the indeterminate Two to the bad is found in the *Philebus*. There the good soul is portrayed with the poetic metaphor of a mixture (*mixis*) of two ingredients: intelligence and pleasure. Pleasure is by nature indeterminate; it is an "unlimited urge" (IGPAP 111). Furthermore, like hot and cold or wet and dry, it is a "two" in the sense that it exists in an unlimited continuum of more or less (*to mallon te kai hetton*) (*Philebus* 24A). At one extreme is pure and infinite pain, and at the other, pure and infinite pleasure, for with the exception of pure and intellectual pleasures, any pleasure is dialectically tied to its opposite. The more extreme a pleasure is, the *more* extreme and *less* pleasant the pain that precedes or follows it. Thus in human existence the infinite continuum of sensation ranging from the one extreme of intense pleasure to the other of intense pain is the indeterminate two, the indeterminate two that shows up in all unlimited continua, for example, the more and the less hot and cold, fast or slow, and so forth. What is good, and not only in the soul, but "analogously" in the state and cosmos as well, is what is marked off and raised out of the undemarcated streaming past of mere *genesis* (becoming) and raised up into *ousia* (being) (IGPAP 117). This is to say, in the language of the *Philebus*, that in what is good, *to peras* is brought to *to apeiron*, limit to the unlimited or indeterminate. In the cosmic realm the *metriotēs* or measuredness that results is the cyclical pattern of the universe, its beauty (*kallos*) and balance (*symmetria*) of synchronized recurrences established against the background of potential chaotic excesses—of hot and cold, for example (see *Timaeus* 29D–40D). In the human realm *metriotēs* is moderation imposed upon excesses of seeking pleasure or on the always wanting still more (*pleon*) of a "Callicles." Thus human life is ordered, one-ified, against the background of the chaos of debauchery.

Gadamer points out that the good is thought of in just this same way in the *Republic* too. If one extracts the conceptual content of the metaphor of the well-tuned instrument, it can be seen that the *Republic* teaches us that "all health [of the soul and of the state] is harmony against the background of possible disharmony" (DD 88), that is, a unity against the background of indeterminacy. The fact, for instance, that Plato cannot and does not stop at the idyllic vision of the "city of pigs" (369B–374E), in which pacified human beings would content themselves with satisfying physical needs, indicates his clear recognition of two "equifundamental" ingredients in the human being that must be put in an ordered relationship by cultivation (*paideia*), training (*askēsis*), and disciplining (*kolazesthai*). The human being is not just pacific; he "must cultivate the philosophical nature in himself while at the same time reconciling that nature with the violent drives in himself of self-preservation and the will to power" (DD 56). *Paideia*, consequently, is necessary to produce the proper harmony—the *Philebus* would say mixture—of the drive for power and the love of knowledge: "It is the shaping of an inner harmony in the soul of a person, a harmony of the sharp and the mild, the willful and the philosophical, . . . the bestial and the peaceful" (DD 57).

To be sure, the emphasis in the *Republic* is not so much on the unbounded desire for pleasure as on the unbounded will to power (*pleonexia*). But we know from the *Gorgias*, for instance, that these two "indeterminacies" are indissociable and that together they constitute the tyrannical personality, the individual who fails to bring unity, oneness, measure, to the indeterminate urges in himself or herself. Where the *Philebus* speaks of bringing limit to the unbounded (*apeiron*) in the human being, the *Republic* speaks of *paideia* that brings harmony to the soul. And for Plato harmony means the tuning of a dissonance inherent in the human being (*Republic* 375C) (DD 54). Thus in both cases the good and our excellence, our *aretē*, consist in restraint, that is to say, in measure that is brought to what otherwise is boundless.

To show the correlation with Aristotle here we need only carry this line of thought one step further: if one approaches the *Philebus* with that art of measurement in mind of which the *Statesman* speaks, one sees that what the *Philebus* refers to as the good mixture is in fact *das Angemessene* (IGPAP 123), that is, what is measured to fit the situation, the appropriate, or, in short, "the mean between the extremes" (see the *Statesman* 253Bff. where Plato himself speaks of *to meson* or mean). Hence Gadamer concludes that one finds in the mytho-poetical images of the *mixis* and *harmonia* the very same phenomenon as Aristotle formulates conceptually in his ethics. *Metriotēs* as measure and restraint in Plato is the same thing as Aristotle's *mesotēs*, that is, holding to the *meson*, the mean between excesses or extremes. What Aristotle calls the excessive soul is that same dissolute soul Plato sees dissipating itself in the indeterminate "streaming" from pain to pleasure and pleasure to pain. In Aristotle this soul, because of either its *akolasia* or its *akratia*, its lack of discipline or lack of self-control, is unable to hold to a measured life.

It is worth noting in this regard how *to kalon* and its opposite, *to aischron*—as we have treated these in Chapter 1, Part 3 in reference to the deliberate openness and lack of specificity in Aristotle's *kalagathia*, and in Chapter 2, Part 4 in our discussion of Plato's *Gorgias*—figure in nearly all Aristotle's discussions of the particular *ēthikai aretai* or ethical excellences. It is *aischros* (shameful), Aristotle tells us, to succumb to boundless fear for one's life and to flee one's comrades in battle; it is *kalos* (noble, a fine thing), he says, to be measured, moderate, in one's sensuality; and so forth. Measuredness is the key to what is *kalos* in virtues and ethical obligations quite as much as it is the key to what is *kalos* in any product of true artisanship (*technē*).

In regard to a product of *technē*, *kalos* would be easily translatable as beautiful, an English word that unlike the German *schön*, for instance, in *"Das war gar nicht schön von dir"*— "That wasn't a bit decent of you!"—cannot really render *kalos* in any of its ethical applications. Since "beautiful" cannot render *kalos* in this sense, we have been led to overlook the ethical implications of the "Beautiful" in Plato's *Symposium* and *Phaedrus*, for example, and this oversight has introduced considerable puzzlement concerning Plato's linking of *to kalon* and *to agathon* (the good) in the *Republic* and *Philebus*. There should be no problem here either in understanding Plato or in understanding Aristotle's extension of Plato's line of thought in his own concept of *kalagathia*. For what is *kalos* is measured and proportionate, insofar as all its components are "harmonized," which, as the Greek *harmottein* makes clear, means fitted and joined together in such a way that there is no deficiency or excess that would cause the whole to come apart. Like *hylē*, which originally meant wood, the meaning of *harmonia* and its intrinsic ties to *technē* go back to the art of woodworking and joining, for instance, in building a chariot (*harma*), and it is applied in music only in a transferred, secondary sense.[29] What "harmonized" means in matters of human feelings and passions (*pathē*) is as accessible as it is in the architecture of a temple. As Aristotle puts it, it is *kalos* to establish rational proportions not only for the stuff out of which we build something, but for any raw fear or desire so that it does not become excessive or deficient and bring our souls into inbalance and instability and so that it does not thereby cause us to lose our composure and harmony and to "go to pieces" or "come unhinged." And it is *aischros* (ugly) not to have established these rational limits, for instance, to have fled out of overwhelming fear for one's life.

We find virtually the same argument toward the end of the *Gorgias*, where Socrates, given Callicles' intransigence, has to bring the discussion to a conclusion by himself. At 506D he raises the question in what virtue (*aretē*) in general consists and answers that the virtue of "a tool or of a body, or, on the other hand, of a soul or any living thing, does not come about in it in the most beautiful and noble way [*kallista*] by chance, but through an ordered placement [*taxei*], a rightness of arrangement [*orthoteti*], and an art [*technēi*]." The reference to *technē* here in considerations of what properly speaking are matters of *phronēsis* or at least matters of who is *sōphron* (of sound mind) as opposed to *aphron* (senseless) (507A), goes back to 503E where it is said that one has only to look at any of the artisans to see "how each one of them puts each part, whichever he places, in a certain order and forces the one to be fitting [*prepon einai*] for, and to join [*harmottein*] with, the other until the whole is put together as a composed and ordered [*kekosmemenon*] thing."

The usefulness of the *technē* analogy in ethics derives from the fact that this condition of *aretē*, of the excellence or virtue of something, that results from *technē* is precisely the condition that must be brought about in the self or soul of someone who would do the right thing. It will be remembered that *phronēsis* parallels *technē* save for the fact that what is brought about or effected by *phronēsis* is the self itself and not something else; in *phronēsis*, as opposed to *technē*, effectuation is self-effectuation. But if it is good, the product, as it were, has the same nature in both cases: the excellence of what is harmonized. Aristotle's *dikaiosynē* (see above, Chapter 1, Part 3) and Plato's synthesis of *sōphrosynē* and *dikaiosynē* (Gorgias 504D, 507D), this virtue of integral harmony, is the precondition of all the others, the *sympasa aretē*, the comprehensive excellence of the soul. And only the one who has it will, as a consequence of having it, do what is seemly or appropriate (*ta prosekonta*) and what is right (*ta dikaia*):

And, indeed, by doing what is appropriate in regard to human beings he would do what is right, and in regard to the gods, what is pious. But in doing what is right and pious it is necessary that he be just and right. That is the way it is. And he will of necessity be brave. For it is not the role of a man of sound reason [*sōphronos andros*] either to pursue or to flee what is not appropriate, but rather to pursue or flee what it is fitting to [*ha dei*], be it things or people or pleasures or pains, and to remain steadfast where it is fitting [*hopou dei*] [*Gorgias* 507Aff.].

The reference to remaining steadfast (*karterein*) points up the link between this view of the ancients and Kierkegaard. The task for human beings, surprisingly enough, has remained essentially the same: namely, to transcend aesthetic immediacy with its discontinuous "great moments," and to hold consistently through time to what is ethical. Put another way: the *sympasa aretē*, the comprehensive underlying excellence or virtue of the soul that makes such steadfastness possible does not change, whatever the historical variation in the particular *aretai* may be on which MacIntyre, for instance, focuses.[30]

The opposite condition to the soul's *sympasa aretē* of *dikaiosynē* and *sōphrosynē*—the latter meaning soundness of mind, or, as Aristotle perceptively glosses, keeping (*sōzein*) one's wits, (*phronēsis*) about one—is *akolasia*. The usual translations, licentiousness, profligacy, and intemperance, leave out a dimension of the word crucial to Plato's and our own considerations: namely, its relationship to *kolazein*, meaning to punish, but, more to the point, to discipline in the way that one might discipline an insolent or shameless (*aischros*) child. *Akolasia* is the state of needing to be punished, of *deisthai tou kolazesthai* (*Gorgias* 507D), which is to say, the state of being undisciplined. This makes clear that it is a state of the soul which extends well beyond the level of anything we are conscious of and into the pre-conscious patternings of our existence. *Akolasia* is what Aristotle would call a *hexis* or disposition to respond in a particular way in thought and action, word and deed, to the feelings we have. Compare too the *Philebus* 11B, where Socrates proposes that the good, be it the life of pleasure (*hedonē*) advocated by Philebus, be it the life of reasonableness (*phronē-*

sis) he advocates, will in any case consist in a *hexis psychēs* or fundamental disposition of the soul. Accordingly Plato speaks here in the *Gorgias* (509E) of the need for training (*askēsis*) to correct (*kolazein*) undisciplinedness, and he even warns of the danger in imitation or *mimēsis* of the tyrannical personality (511E). *A fortiori* we may conclude that since conscious insight into what is wrong would not suffice by itself to correct us had we been imitating those who *do* wrong, so conscious insight into what is right would not suffice had we from the start not been imitating those who *do* what is right.

With that in mind we can see just why Plato fears imitative art. For Plato the right mixture or harmony is, as we have learned, a precarious balance and must be secured against the sophistic flattery of either other people or our sensuous inclinations. That, however, is something neither an imitative actor is able to accomplish nor his audience, once it is drawn vicariously into the imitation (see *Ion* 533cff.). Where the ethical community (Gadamer: *sittliche Gemeinschaft*) remains intact, poetic dramatization presents no danger. On the contrary, role-playing of this sort is a valuable educational tool insofar as it initiates the actor and audience into the traditional *ēthos* or ethical patterns of their society. But in a state where the common sense of what is proper has weakened and each "person" has been thrown back from the social world into a private life where the best one can do is to seek one's own advantage—in a state, in short, where "no one does what is right voluntarily"—dramatic poetry is reduced to a mere stimulus of the passions. And as Plato saw, those who imitate, not in order to learn but for the sake of imitation itself, lose themselves, lose their composure, and dissolve themselves in the experience (Gadamer: *Erlebnis*): "The charm of imitation and the joy taken in it are a form of self-forgetfulness which is most pronounced where what is represented is itself self-forgetfulness, i.e., passion" (DD 64). Instead of the self relating itself to itself as a measured "one," it abandons itself to its "many" indeterminate passions. *Phronēsis*, which in essence is self-knowledge, that is to say, an integration and unification of the self with itself, can no longer be maintained (*sōzesthai*) and loses its hold on the soul, leaving it to unrestrained excesses of pleasure and the inevitably concomitant pain. What was measured and a self with integrity thus relapses into the unlimited, and the one self dissipates in the indeterminate two of pleasure and pain. Here the one-ifying power of the good ceases to obtain, and the soul has forfeited its excellence.

Precisely this phenomenon is what Plato has in view in his treatment of *akolasia*, which for him and Aristotle alike is the primary vice (*kakia*) and dysfunctionality of the soul. And where Plato stresses *mimēsis* of the right things as essential to the excellence of the soul, namely, of his own philosophical dialogues (see DD 71–72), Aristotle stresses the relationship of ethical virtue, *ēthikē aretē*, to habit, playing as he does upon the Greek words *ēthos* (character) and *ethos* (habituation) (see note 5 above). His point too is that seeing what is good, knowing it, does not suffice to make someone do what is good. For that a disposition (*hexis*) is also necessary, and it is acquired through habituation and being accustomed to act in certain ways.

4. *Logos, Ergon, Ēthos,* AND *Ethos*

It will be recalled from our contrasting of the aesthetic *Erlebnis* with ethical *Erfahrung* earlier than the good soul establishes consistency through time. Instead of yielding, now to this desire, now to its opposite, it holds to what is right (Plato: *ta dikaia*) and to the right thing to do (Aristotle: *to deon*). It holds steadfastly to one thing that endures throughout various, shifting circumstances. Now, holding to one thing means choosing what is good in distinction from what is bad, and this, it now emerges, is the Socratic task of avoiding seduction by the many things that proffer themselves as good, of resisting the flattery of the senses and adhering to the one principle that is to be maintained throughout. In Plato and Aristotle it is *phronēsis* or ethical reasonableness that makes this possible. Of course, in Plato this *phronēsis*, as it is displayed by Socrates, is widened to include the skill of dialectical division (*diahairesis*), and thus it appears to be a function of theoretical, not just practical, intellect. But in fact this widening by no means changes its basic meaning. For even dialectic is at its core the ability to distinguish and, above all, to distinguish right from wrong and to hold to this distinction against all sophistic attempts to induce confusion by blurring the line between the two. And as such it is neither an innate intellectual ability nor a communicable insight. In Plato and not only in Aristotle it is rooted in an *acquired disposition*, that is, the steady disposition of the good soul that stands in sharp contrast to the inconstant and inconsistent inclinations of a diseased soul. If one turns to the *Republic*, one finds that the warriors and guardians hold to what is right and do not allow themselves to be diverted by the seductive power of the senses. This implies that they must be predisposed to choose what is right in distinction from what is wrong. Indeed, says Gadamer, Plato means by dialectic less a method than the practical task of distinguishing properly where confusion threatens (IGPAP 42).

We should note carefully what has emerged here. As Gadamer states in commenting on the *Philebus*,

> Being confronted with choices . . . is the unalterable circumstance of human beings. Their having to make choices removes them from the realm of the rest of living things, which unquestioningly follow their animal desires (*therion erōtēs*) wherever these—like forces of nature—may drive them. To be a human being means always to be confronted with choices. As Aristotle puts it, human beings "have" *prohairesis* (choice). They must choose [IGPAP 109].

As we know, to choose the good, one must have always already been seeking the right thing to do, and this implies in turn that one must already be under way within a pattern of right choices. Put another way: being under way within the good means knowing, seeing, the good, but this seeing presupposes, in turn, an established disposition (*hexis*). Consequently, as we have also seen, adhering to one thing, to principle, in resisting the suasion of the senses, is a form of discipline, not just a form of intellection. That is why "From the beginning [of the *Republic*], Socrates proclaims his program to be an entirely new kind of education [*Erziehung*] (518B), in which the concern is not so much with learning something as with turning 'the whole soul' around (521c)" (IGPAP 82–83). In short, one must be habituated to pursue the good. Otherwise the desire for pleasure will make one blind to it.

Gadamer is not propounding some form of behaviorism here:

> The way in which all living things blindly submit to the immediacy of the pleasure principle—driven as they are by the hidden power of the life urge—is not the way for human beings to fulfill their potential for leading their own life. . . . What makes human beings human beings is the fact that they must ask about the good and must give preference to one thing over another (*prohairein*) in conscious, deliberate decision [IGPAP 110].

Hence, the habits in question are not conditioned reflexes but predispositions of the soul to *reason* in certain ways, *hexeis psychēs* as Plato calls them. Gadamer is saying, however, that as opposed to any mathematical insight, which has all that is relevant clearly in view, an ethical decision is based in part on things that remain hidden and inexplicit in the consciousness of the individual who makes it. Consequently, how one chooses now depends on how one has already been disposed to choose by one's past choices, past choices that although one is not directly aware of them at the moment provide the "unsaid" background of one's present choice. The pattern of one's previous decisions is all-important.

It is significant in this regard that neither Plato nor Aristotle maintains that *phronēsis* or knowledge of the good can be taught. For unlike the things that can be taught—namely, *epistēmē* and *technē*—*phronēsis* does not derive from insight into fixed principles (see Part 1 of this chapter on the interpretation of ethical principles and Chapter 1, Part 4 on the differences between *phronēsis*, on the one hand, and *epistēmē* and *technē*, on the other). Indeed, since its principles are precisely not fixed, an habituated disposition to choose wisely among possibilities that remain open to choice is prerequisite. Hence, just as Aristotle links *logos* with *ēthos* and *ethos*, rational principle with character and habituation, Plato links *logos* with *ergon*, rational principle with deed.

This question of habituation is of crucial importance to our consideration of the ethical implications of Gadamer's thinking. As we know, Gadamer depends in large part on *Sitten* or customs as a basis for ethics. And a custom is obviously something we learn, not through intellectual insight alone or even primarily, but through becoming accustomed to it. For that, apprenticeship under the authority of tradition is essential. Thus, we see why autonomous reason in severance from all traditional influences—in severance, that is, from what is customary—must, if Gadamer is right, fail in its attempts to found ethics on itself.

And is there, we might ask, not a serious oversight in MacIntyre in this regard too, an oversight he shares with the very analytical tradition he would break with? In turning to specific, concrete historical virtues rather than to "rights," he does succeed in bringing our intellectual moral abstractions down to earth, as it were, but even so he does nothing to bring the inexplicit extra-intellectual background of ethical reasoning to light. He overlooks the habituated *hexeis* that underlie any of the individual virtues he chronicles and that are the prerequisite of any ethical reasonableness or *phronēsis*. More than any other contemporary Anglo-American thinker, it is Hampshire who has focused on this indispensable "pre-conscious" dimension of the ethical, as he calls it.[31] And in this he, not MacIntyre, turns out to be the one who comes closest to Gadamer's conception of ethical understanding. But perhaps the easiest way to find access to Gadamer's thinking here is not from anyone in the Anglo-

American tradition—not even Burke who is so like him on this point too (see note 26 above)—but from the Continental, speculative tradition from which, after all, Gadamer's thought derives. I have in mind the tradition of Greek thought as it is transmitted through Medieval philosophy to German Idealism.

In Part 4 of Chapter 1 we saw that, in contrast to Gadamer, it is Hegel's aim to demonstrate that nothing exceeds the reach of consciousness, and this aim seems to entail that Hegel would want to eliminate the immemorial and customary dimension of the ethical, upon which Gadamer so strongly insists. And indeed, Hegel, given his aims, has nothing to say about the preconscious, habitual dimension of the ethical that we have been emphasizing. But the fact notwithstanding, on the way to his goal he does make something like the point Gadamer does in regard to the insufficiency of autonomous reason in ethics: see PhG 301–12, on "Reason Giving Laws" and "Reason Testing Laws," and 423ff., on mere Morality as opposed to *Sittlichkeit*, and for his critique of what he perceives to be Kant's moral intellectualism. We have already considered these matters at some length in Chapter 1.

The question I wish to raise here is whether Hegel's is in fact a fair criticism of Kant's actual argument and if, in fact, Kant could be understood very differently if he were viewed as a continuation of the very Latin speculative tradition to which, in settling accounts with Christian Wolff *et alii* and his own Latin dissertation,[32] he is generally held to have put an end. For in an essay entitled "On the Possibility of a Philosophical Ethics" (KS I 179–91), Gadamer argues that Hegel's critique of Kant is, in fact, not justified, and in making this argument he gives us insights into Kant that those stressing Kant's emphasis on autonomy and his place in the rationalist tradition of the Enlightment, Hegel among them, have obscured. Furthermore, this essay's discussion of Kant and Aristotle *and their concurrence* is Gadamer's most explicit treatment of ethical theory and deserves, if for no other reason than this, to be recapitulated here in conclusion to our exposition of a Gadamerian theory of ethical understanding and the possibility of a hermeneutical ethics.

Gadamer asks what function a theoretical ethics might have in guiding our practice. In his opinion, Kant sees that the modern understanding of the relationship of theory and practice, in which theory is taken to be the "explanation of the multiplicity of phenomena that makes practical mastery of these phenomena possible" (KS I 180), leads to a groundless faith in the progress of morality. For on that understanding moral theory is expected to guarantee ever more complete implementation of the good in practice. Utilitarianism, for example, together with our post-utilitarian contract theories, is based on just this understanding of the relationship between theory and practice. And why does any such faith in progress prove to be a false hope? Because, as Kant astutely perceives, any ethical practice founded solely on a theoretical calculation of consequences fails to shield itself against the seductive influences of pre-conscious inclination on the conscious calculation process.[33] Ethics must have a foundation different from utilitarian calculation if it is to withstand such temptations, a foundation, namely, in the *Sittengesetz* or customary ethical law: "Kant's philosophical reflection about morality . . . presupposes the recognition of customary ethical law" (KS I 183). In other words, Hegel is right "when he . . . finds the essence of customary ethics [*Sittlichkeit*] in ethical custom [*Sitte*]," that is, "in the substantial customary ethical order embodied in the objective family, society, and state" (KS I 183). But, Gadamer maintains, this argument can scarcely be advanced in criticism of Kant as Hegel thinks it can. In resisting self-interest and inclination Kant stresses duty and conscience, and he would never deny that "the alert warning voice of conscience depends on the substance of institutions in which one always stands already" (KS I 184).

The principle of universalizability in Kant's categorical imperative, Kant's focusing on universal law, does not imply an abstraction from particular ethical practices at all. Rather, it is intended solely to protect ethical reasoning from making an exception (*Ausnahme*) for itself, as it might do unconsciously under the influence of self-interest and inclination. One must not succumb to the "dialectic of the exception" (KS I 182) and rationalize a violation of the ethical principle by saying to oneself, "But this case is an exception!" There must be *no* exceptions; and exactly this is meant when Kant insists that the ethical law must be universal.

Theoretical recognition of this universality, it turns out, is necessary to shield us against being led astray in practice. For in truth unreflective adherence to ethical custom, as enviable as it is, gives in all too easily: " 'Innocence is a beautiful thing,' " writes Kant, " 'but at the same time it unfortunately cannot be preserved and is easily led astray' " (KS I 182). The task of ethical theory that Kant sets for himself is to defend ethical custom against the sophistic persuasion of self-interest and thereby to give the previously naïve individual an immunity to that persuasion that he or she did not have. Kant would come to the aid of *Sitten* by providing a theoretical buttressing of them, a "*Grundlegung zur Metaphysik der Sitten.*" (Given the present sense of "morals" in English, the usual translation of *Sitten* here as morals in "The Foundations of the Metaphysics of Morals" tends to obscure the point of Kant's enterprise.)

Furthermore, however much he may have been faulted by Hegel and others, Kant himself fully recognizes that a formal principle of universalizability does not provide the actual content of what is ethical, and in pointing this out he pre-empts the Hegelian criticism. Kant's cases of conflict between duty and inclination, Gadamer maintains, are not intended to be deductions of particular content from the principle of universalizability. Rather Kant has in mind "extreme cases in which a human being is led to consider his *pure* duty as opposed to all inclination, cases that bring home to him, as it were, the power of his moral reason and thereby provide a firm foundation for his character" (KS I 183). In this way the individual is secured against the seductive influence of self-interest and inclination. We have here the theoretical correlate of what Plato would achieve by a *paideia, kolazein,* and *askēsis* that strengthen character and sustain reason to the point where one is disposed to withstand the sophistic flattery of the senses, or, in Kant's terms, to the point where the will (*Wille*) is good. Compare the opening of Part I of the *Grundlegung zur Metaphysik der Sitten*: "There is nothing that can be thought of anywhere in the world, indeed, even outside it, that could be considered good with the sole exception of a good will."

But how are we to tie this Kantian ethical *theory* into actual practice? Here, writes Gadamer, "another approach seems worth trying: a philosophical reflection upon morality [*moral-philosophische Besinnung*] that instead of starting with the extraordinary case of a conflict starts with the ordinary case of following the ethical custom [*Sitte*]" (KS I 184). And in this, Aristotle may be our guide.

Although theoretical considerations such as Kant's or, for that matter, such as Aristotle's ethics, are needed to fortify *Sitten* and our *sittliche* or ethical dispositions, these theoretical considerations presuppose the ethical dispositions they would fortify. Here too the relationship is circular. Aristotle's way of putting this fact is to draw an analogy with archery (EN 1094A 23 and IGPAP 163): just as it helps the archer in hitting the mark to concentrate on a specific point on the target, so too it helps someone who would choose rightly to focus theoretically on what he or she is doing in making such choices. But one can only concentrate on a point on the target once one is accustomed to handling bows and arrows, and, similarly, one can raise theoretical questions about ethical choices only if one is already accustomed to making them. That is why youths, for instance, are not an appropriate audience for Aristotle's lectures on ethics (EN 1095A 2ff.).

For Aristotle "ethical [*sittliches*] knowledge does not fulfill itself in [arriving at] universal concepts of courage, justice, and so forth, but instead, in the concrete application that determines what is the appropriate thing to do [*das Tunliche*] here and now in the light of such knowing" (KS I 187). Gadamer makes two points in regard to this concretization: first, he emphasizes that concrete application in Aristotle does not begin with our cognition but with our predisposition (*hexis*), not with what we think and know but with what we are. For Gadamer, Aristotle raises the question whether in fact something like Kant's "autonomy of practical reason that secures for us the unconditional nature of our duty against the insinuations of our inclinations is not to be taken instead only as a limiting condition placed on our caprice and not as constitutive of the whole of our ethical [*sittliches*] being" (KS I 188).

Second, Gadamer points out that in Aristotle the universal which is to be concretized is given as a loose schema that receives specific content only in application to a particular situation. In other words, ethical theory in Aristotle becomes a theory of *interpretation* (See Part 1 of this chapter)—interpretation conditioned by the context in which it takes place:

> Kant discredited the *raisonnement* of the Enlightenment and its blind and vain trust in reason, by severing unconditioned practical reason from the conditions of human nature and presenting it in its transcendental purity. Aristotle, on the other hand, focuses on the conditioned human situation and singles out the concretization of the universal and application of it to the given situation as the central task of philosophical ethics and acting ethically [KS I 190].

Certainly in Gadamer's case it would be appropriate to ask just what the *Wirkungsgeschichte* or history of effects is that makes his reading of Kant and this fusion of Kant with Aristotle possible? Obviously, in Gadamer Kant is not viewed retrospectively from modernity, but prospectively from the ancients and the reception of them in the Middle Ages. Hence, perhaps the best place to look for traditional origins of this blend of Platonic–Kantian and Aristotelian elements, which Gadamer proposes, is Aquinas—as it was, not coincidentally, for the traditional origins of Gadamer's understanding of langauge (see WM 399ff. on the non-reflectivity of the word or *verbum* in Aquinas).

In questio XCVII, art. 3, of the *Summa theologica*, "Whether custom [*consuetudo*] may obtain the power of law," Aquinas argues,

> I respond that it must be said that all law starts with the reason and will of the lawgiver, which is to say, divine and natural law starts with the rational will of God, and human law, on the other hand, with the will regulated by reason. But in matters of action, just as human reason and will are manifested in word [*verbo*], so too are they manifested in deed [*facto*]. For what anyone chooses as good is to be seen in what he carries out in work[s] [*opere*]. It is manifest, moreover, that the law can be changed and set forth by the human word to the extent that the word manifests an interior movement and concept of human reason. It follows from this that a law may also be changed and set forth by acts that in being done a great many times make up a custom. And it may even come about somehow that a custom obtains the strength of law insofar as an interior movement of the will and a concept of reason are made clear most effectively by repeated exterior acts. For whatever is done multiply is seen to proceed from a deliberate judgment of reason. And from this it follows that custom has the power of law, sets law aside, and is the interpreter of law.

There are a number of things to be learned from this seminal, if equivocal, passage. In the first place it makes the difference between the divine and the human clear insofar as it speaks simply of the rational will of God (*rationabilis Dei voluntas*), but speaks of the will of human beings, in contrast, as regulated by reason (*voluntas hominis ratione regulata*). Implied here is a point made by Aristotle in Book X of the *Nicomachean Ethics*, when he establishes that *ēthike aretē*, ethical virtue, pertains only to humans and not to gods; for any ethical virtue, as opposed to contemplative happiness, requires the regulation by reason of what is amenable to reason in the soul, but is in itself irrational: the virtue of courage, the regulation of fear, for instance, or the virtue of temperance, the regulation of sensuous desire. Ethical virtue is strictly human (*anthrōpinon*), in other words, because it presupposes a mixed (*syntheton*) being (1177b 29) whereas a god is unmixed. The same point is made in Book I where it is said of the human soul, "It appears, then, that there is some other irrational [ἄλογον] nature of the soul that in some way or other participates in rationality [μετέχουσα μέντοι πῃ λόγου] . . ." (1102b 12); "at least it obeys the rationality of the continent man and is perhaps even more amenable to that of the temperate and brave" (1102b 27). (See also Plato's *Phaedrus* on the difference between the "chariot" soul of the gods and the "chariot" soul of humans with one "horse" needing to be restrained.)

From this it follows that human beings, not gods or God, need a pre-conscious *hexis* (Aquinas: *habitus*), for they must be so disposed that their reason does in fact regulate their will instead of their will's being in the tow of their passions. And elsewhere (*Summa theologica*, quaestio XCVI, art. 2) Aquinas does make just this Platonic, Aristotelian, Kantian point: "It is necessary too that laws be imposed on human beings in accordance with their condition. For, as Isidore says, the law must be 'possible according to both the nature and the custom [*consuetudinem*] of the country.' But the power or faculty of doing something proceeds from an interior habit or disposition [*habitu seu dispositione*]."

Thus the word that results from interior movements and a concept of reason is, in individual human beings, not always coincident with what they are disposed to do. And, analogously, the human law, which has its origin in the reason of the lawgiver, is not always coincident with what a people actually does or is supposed to do. *Verbum* and *factum*, *logos* and *ergon*, word and deed, can be discrepant in single individuals just as they can in a number of individuals or a people (*multitudo*). Consequently, Aquinas repeats Aristotle's admonition that new laws which dispense with custom lack the constrictive force (*vis constrictiva*) necessary for a people to abide by them in deed (*facto*) and should be promulgated with the greatest caution (*Summa theologica*, quaestio XCVII, art. 2).

In the passage we have been considering from article 3 there now follows a most remarkable point—on which Aquinas, once again, is not always consistent.[34] Just what a law is *verbo*, that is, in words deriving from rational concepts, is subordinate, he says, to what a law is *facto*, that is, what a people has been accustomed, habituated (*consuetum*), to doing. Hence, the exposition of a law is not only verbal but factual: the exposition follows from a deliberate judgment of reason (*ex rationis deliberatione*), but the law is also set forth in what a people habitually does by custom (*consuetudine*). And Aquinas, who began the passage in question emphasizing the origins of law in the reason of the lawgiver, concludes here by saying that *consuetudo* is the interpreter of the laws (*legum interpretatrix*).

That would evidently mean two things: first, that human law, again as opposed to divine and natural law, exists not as an immutable essence and is not to be understood as we understand the latter, for instance, as a mathematician understands triangularity. Indeed this Quaestio XCVII as a whole is entitled "De mutatione legum humanarum"—on change in human laws. And human law is to be understood as the history of its changing interpretations. Second, it means that what we do habitually and customarily precedes and predisposes what we conceive of, reason, or say, in defining how a law is to be understood. One relies on precedent practices, usages, on *consuetudines*, as much as, indeed perhaps even more than, judgments of reason (*judicia rationis*) expressed in words. Custom, in fact, "sets aside" (*abolet*) laws. Indeed, under certain circumstances— Aquinas is not entirely consistent on this either—"the consensus of the entire multitude of people manifested in an observance of a custom weighs more than the authority of the ruler" (art. 3).

If we were to carry over this discussion of law to the ethical realm in which, as Kant puts it, the individual gives himself the law and is his own ruler, we could see immediately that the process is complex, not simple, for unlike a god, each human individual has two components, one corresponding to the reason of the lawgiver, and the other, to the customs and habits of the people. As we know, as human, our will and what we will to do are not simply rational as God's will and actions are, but regulated by reason. One may now add that this regulation will succeed only if our will is habitually disposed in the right way to begin with. And for that there must be something in each individual corresponding to the *vis constrictiva* in the public realm, something Aquinas calls *disciplina*.

In elaborating why it is that the human being is by nature the political animal (*animal sociale*) Aquinas comments that:

> . . . the human being is aided by the civic community of which he is a part not solely in regard to things of the body—for the service of which there are, to be sure, many, many artifices in the state that a household would not suffice to provide—but also in regard to ethics [*moralia*], inasmuch, obviously, as insolent youths are constrained by public power out of fear of punishment, whom paternal admonition is not strong enough to set straight [*Commentum in X libros Ethicorum ad Nicomachum* I, lect. 1].

With that we have returned to a theme in Plato and not just Aristotle's *Nicomachean Ethics,* the theme, namely of undisciplinedness or *akolasia* and the need to have oneself disciplined (*kolazesthai*) in the event one has forfeited self-discipline in repeated unjust actions (Aquinas: *per exteriores actus multiplicatos*). As preserved in the Italian *insolito* and French *insolite*, "insolent" (*insolentes*) here has in it the dimension of what is unaccustomed, counter to custom, and hence an affront to it, or, in Gadamer's German, what is *unanständig*. And the "setting straight" (*corrigere*) of someone who is insolent requires discipline. Before one can do what is right, one must oneself be righted, set straight. See Chapter 1, Part 2 on Hegel's primary virtue of rectitude or *Rechtschaffenheit*, which, literally translated, we now can see, means the condition of having been made, or set, right. And such, Aristotle tells us too, is the nature of the *ēthikē aretē*, the customary habitual excellence, which is the precondition of what he calls *orthos logos*, or right and righted reason that, in turn, governs the choices one makes in reasonable deliberation concerning a given situation.[35]

NOTES

1. John Stuart Mill, *On Liberty* (Indianapolis: Bobbs-Merrill, 1978), pp. 55–56.

2. At IGPAP 110, Gadamer points out that by itself choosing presupposes commitment to the life of reason rather than to the life of pleasure. Hence, strictly speaking, one cannot be said to "choose" the life of pleasure over the life of reason, as the character of Philebus in the dialogue of the same name makes evident. Philebus, committed as he is to following his desires for satisfaction, is incapable of engaging in deliberation about whether a life of pleasure would be the best choice or not and turns the whole thing over to Protarchus. He has foresworn deliberation, but not deliberately, not *logōi*, but *ergōi*, not in reasoning or by choice, but in deed alone. Much the same thing happens, as we noted, when Callicles backs out of the discussion with Socrates leaving him to finish the deliberations about the best choice of life, rhetoric or philosophy, by himself.

3. Michael Oakeshott speaks of a conservative *disposition* that inclines thought away from possibility and toward actuality, or, as Musil puts it (see Chapter 1, note 6, above), away from thinking in the counter-factual subjunctive, "if only it were the case that . . . ," and toward acceptance of a familiar present expressible in the indicative. A man of this temperament, Oakeshott submits, "will not be an ardent innovator." "For, innovating is an activity which generates not only the 'improvement' sought, but a new and complex situation of which this is only one of the components. The total change is always more extensive than the change designed; and the whole of what is entailed can neither be foreseen nor circumscribed" ("On Being Conservative," in *The Portable Conservative Reader*, ed. Russell Kirk [New York: Viking, 1982], pp. 571–72).

4. Gadamer views the *Republic*'s exposition of the "perfect" state as a satirical inversion or a caricature that exposes *e contrario* the

perversions of the contemporary political reality. Plato's proposals, far from being meant literally as Popper assumes, are provocatively absurd. Hence, Gadamer's emphasis on the "comical" here.

5. The two classical *loci* for the indissociability of character and habituation, *ēthos* and *ethos*, are Plato's *Laws* 792E, ". . . for at that time [when just born] there occurs for all by habituation the most decisive growth in the whole character" (κυριώτατον γὰρ οὖν ἐμφύεται πᾶσι τότε τὸ πᾶν ἦθος διὰ ἔθος) and Aristotle's *Nicomachean Ethics* 1103A 17, ". . . but ethical excellence [as opposed to intellectual excellence] results from habituation" (ἡ δ' ἠθικὴ [ἀρετὴ] ἐξ ἔθους περιγίγνεται).

6. Again, we must always keep in mind that for Aristotle, as opposed to Hegel, the legal and the ethical were not separate. Hence *dikastē phronēsis* or juris-prudence is not distinguished from *phronēsis* or prudence in ethical matters. The task of the *dikastēs* or judge is not at all to apply abstract standards to abstract "persons," each considered alike and equal to all the others, but to decide what is right, *dikaios*, given the particular people and circumstances involved.

7. The ontological foundations of Gadamer's thinking are in large part Heideggerian. And more than the Heidegger of *Being and Time* it is the later Heidegger who, in abandoning the project of fundamental ontology and transcendental phenomenology, influences Gadamer's thinking: not being as it is given in self-consciousness' reflection *about* the world, but being experienced *in* the world as partially disclosing itself from obscurity all the while concealing itself, is the subject matter of Gadamer's hermeneutical investigations, that is to say, the being that the later Heidegger's strange and forced language of *"a-lētheia,"* "disconcealedness," "presencing," and "absencing" struggled to bring into view. In his hermeneutics Gadamer seeks to provide an exemplification and application of Heidegger's insights while for the most part avoiding his unnatural vocabulary. The being of artworks and texts and our understanding of this being display what Heidegger had in mind. Though our Cartesian desire for scientific certainty might make us wish otherwise, in regard to these things there can be no penetration behind shifting, partially indeterminate phenomena to a constant reality exactly defined and fully known. There can be no founding on a "clear and distinct" basis. Artworks and texts are only as they appear to us. Their temporal appearance (and disappearance) is their reality, their being.

8. Hampshire, whose thought is most assuredly the product of a very different *Wirkungsgeschichte*—in part Burke, perhaps (cf. Burke's response to "An Appeal from the New to the Old Whigs," *Edmund Burke: Selected Writings and Speeches*, ed. Peter J. Stanlis [Chicago: Regnery/Gateway, 1963], pp. 518–46)—makes a similar point in contrasting abstract universal right with knowledge of what is right in a particular situation: "The issue is sharply focused by the old eighteenth-century Whig idea of the veil of ignorance: behind the veil is an abstract universal man dressed in neo-classical drapery as in some Reynolds paintings, to indicate that he belongs to no particular place or time. In the unearthly light of the ideal, classical and timeless scene, reason cannot tell him how he should be married or how he should speak to his children or educate them or fit into his community or give one local loyalty precedence over another. For these purposes some Tory history, as in a Scott novel, has to be told of the complex conventions in which he was brought up and which fix him in a certain time and place and constitute an identity for him . . ." (MC 138–39).

In *Law's Empire* (Cambridge: The Belknap Press of Harvard University Press, 1986), a work that would seem to revise some of his earlier positions on universal rights, Ronald Dworkin raises similar questions about interpretation of law as approximation to a timeless, placeless ideal. But in his case there is a direct influence of Gadamer (see pp. 55, 62, and 420).

9. Because the primary concern of Gadamer's hermeneutics is with language, he has comparatively little to say about non-verbal art forms, especially music. Even so, I find some of the best corroboration of what he wishes to say in, remarkably enough, the writings of Igor Stravinsky. The latter's *Poetics of Music* (New York: Vintage, 1947) is particularly useful in displaying the connection I wish to establish here between aesthetic and ethical concerns. On the one hand, Stravinsky is a staunch advocate of order and mathematical rationality: "Art is the contrary of chaos," he proclaims (p. 13), and he accordingly condemns the "individual caprice and intellectual anarchy" (p. 75) which, he says, prevail equally in twentieth-century music and politics. His emphasis on this rationality is most apparent in his rigidly objectivistic theory of interpretation. In an attempt to extirpate any and all subjective caprice, he replaces interpretive discretion with strict execution of the composer's will.

Even so, with respect to his own composing, Stravinsky relates,

". . . I experience a sort of terror when, at the moment of setting to work and finding myself before the infinitude of possibilities that present themselves, I have the feeling that everything is permissible to me" (p. 66). In this condition of existential *Angst* he decides for the "seven notes of the scale and its chromatic intervals" (p. 67), and given the complete uprootedness of the modern composer from the tradition, that choice itself, as Stravinsky admits, is not rational at all but gratuitous. The artist, he tells us, is condemned to be a "monster of originality, inventor of his own language, of his own vocabulary, and of the apparatus of his art" (p. 75), for he is faced with a "complete break in tradition" (p. 76): "Times have changed since the day when Bach, Handel, and Vivaldi quite evidently spoke the same language which their disciples repeated after them, each one unwittingly transforming this language according to his own personality. . . . Those times have given way to a new age that seeks to reduce everything to uniformity in the realm of matter while it tends to shatter all universality in the realm of spirit in deference to an anarchic individualism" (p. 76). And Stravinsky acknowledges that "whether he wills it or not the artist is caught in this infernal machination" (p. 77).

He goes on to point out that this problem of fragmentation and the burden of unlimited, undefined decision that it places on the artist is not only a problem for art. It is an ethical problem as well, he says, for there is no longer a "body of moral principles" that puts "everyone in accord concerning certain fundamental concepts of good and evil, truth and error" (pp. 77–78). Here too autonomous reason, though Stravinsky puts his remaining hopes in it, is, as he himself admits, no substitute for the continuity of tradition. The interpretation of ethical principles, it would seem, is also preconditioned by the authority of the past: established tradition alone gives the interpreter the basis on which to make decisions and choices that transcend what is merely private. Whether the tradition is as shattered as Stravinsky thinks is a question we will return to at the end of our study. There is reason to believe it is not.

10. See my dissertation, *Das Sein des Du: Die Philosophie Martin Bubers im Lichte des Heidegger'schen Denken an das Sein* (Heidelberg: Dissertationsdruck, 1966).

11. In recounting his own philosophical development Gadamer often mentions the importance to him of Kierkegaard's exposition of the ethical stage on life's way and the dialectical destruction of the aes-

thetic stage, which precedes it (see WM 91). The fact that Kierkegaard also subjected the ethical stage to dialectical critique and argued that it too would be forced beyond itself—to the religious stage—is notice-ably absent in Gadamer's reception of Kierkegaard. I suggest that some of the reasons for this omission are to be found in Gadamer's insistence on the insurmountable finitude of the human being, who, as opposed to a god and even as opposed to a being who is one with God's will, must continue to make choices as best he or she can in a situation where matters remain indeterminate. It is one thing to sus-pend the ethical and submit to the will of God, to follow the divine command as does the Abraham of Kierkegaard's *Fear and Trembling*, and quite another, to remain in the ethical and have to make ethical choices. Gadamer's principal concern is with the latter dimension of our experience, and for that reason Aristotle, who argues the inevasi-bility for us finite human beings of *ethikē aretē* or ethical excellence, ultimately takes priority over Kierkegaard for him. See EN 1177B 27ff., "ὁ δὲ τοιοῦτος ἂν εἴη βίος κρείττων ἢ κατ' ἄνθρωπον . . ." (But such a life [of godlike contemplation] would exceed what is humanly possible . . .) and note 27 below.

Seen another way, Gadamer's concern is with the *politeia*, not the *ekklēsia*, with the political community founded in *philia*, not the body of believers bound to each other by faith, hope, and love (*pistis, elpis, agapē*).

12. See his *The Right and the Good* (Oxford: Clarendon, 1930).

13. "An Appeal from the New to the Old Whigs," pp. 522–23.

14. *The Hastings Center Report*, 9, No. 4 (August 1979), 19.

15. *Ethics and Language* (New Haven, Conn.: Yale University Press, 1972).

16. *The Language of Morals* (New York: Oxford University Press, 1964).

17. Plato, for one, would find such an outcome of moral debate wholly unsatisfactory. In the *Gorgias* he argues against sophist rheto-ric precisely because it is a mere *tribē* (knack) which, instead of leading to knowledge regarding what is good, seduces the listener into a mere belief for which he cannot give justification (*logon didonai*) and which he consequently can be talked out of just as easily as he was talked into it.

18. See his *Principia ethica* (Cambridge: Cambridge University Press, 1962).

19. Again, see his *The Right and the Good*.

20. In conformity with Gadamer's hermeneutical principles, we should keep in mind that Burke's text is a decidedly political tract, not a philosophical study such as *Truth and Method*. Put another way: its "performative" function (Austin) and the "occasion" for it (Gadamer) are completely distinct from those of *Truth and Method*. Thus, just as Plato's literary dialogues must be de-mythologized if they are to be compared to Aristotle's lecture notes (see IGPAP 124), Burke's pamphlet must be de-politicized if it is to be compared with Gadamer's treatises.

21. *Ethics*, pp. 1ff.

22. Ibid., p. 4.

23. Of course, if, as Hegel does, one were to distinguish Civil Society with its system of need satisfaction and Legal Status from the ethical realm (*Sittlichkeit*) and to see Rawls's project as dealing *only* with the former, the objections raised here would not be valid. And indeed Rawls does seem to have something like Hegel's Civil Society in mind insofar as he is speaking of a contractual process among individuals with a "minimal morality," who out of no sense of *philia* and obligation to one another but out of sheer self-interest, strike the best deal they can for themselves concerning the distribution of what Rawls calls the "primary goods" of opportunity, power, income, wealth, and so forth. Justice here would seem to be the abstract justice concerning the distribution of property (*res*) among persons (*personae*) equal before the law. But Rawls realizes that such contracting, if it were wholly uprooted from its underpinnings in fairness, would collapse and that fairness (might we say *dikaiosynē*?) has its origins in communal bonds of friendship and trust. See TJ 467ff. on "The Morality of Association." I will have more to say about this point in the Conclusion.

24. In "Two Concepts of Rules," *The Philosophical Review*, 64 (1955), 3–32; repr. in *Ethics*, edd. Judith J. Thomson and Gerald Dworkin (New York: Harper & Row, 1968), 104–35.

25. The *Meno* itself makes quite clear than any teaching of an insight (*mathēma*) concerning what is right or good is far more complex than the teaching of a geometrical principle. Indeed *the* issue of the *Meno* is whether virtue can be taught at all, and if so, who its teachers would be. And in the end Plato takes refuge in "divine dispensation" (*theia*

moira) to account for what remains a most mysterious kind of learning. Compare IGPAP 51 on the unteachability of what is good.

The problem here, as we will see in Parts 3 and 4 of this chapter, is that mathematics is a matter of pure *logos* or intellectual insight. No particular *hexis tēs psychēs* or disposition of the soul, no particular training of character (*ēthos*), is presupposed in grasping a mathematical truth. But, as Gadamer points out, with ethical truths, it is quite a different matter: whoever is not disposed by character to understand an ethical truth cannot be made to understand it by any sort of logical argument. *Ēthos, ethos*, and *logos* are inseparable here. Therefore character-building by imitation (*mimēsis*) of those characters in Plato's dialogues with good character, in particular, Socrates—character-building by the reader's re-enactment in deed (*ergoi*), as it were, of what Socrates is and does—is presupposed in any understanding of what he says in words (*logoi*). Significantly in this regard, Plato could count on the fact that in his day any of what we call his "texts" would be read aloud. Actually they are not texts at all, but dramas, which as the Greek *draō* makes clear, are things done, things acted out.

26. In his *Political Thought from Locke to Bentham* (New York: Holt, 1920), Harold Laski, himself a convinced socialist but succeeded, remarkably enough, at the London School of Economics by Oakeshott, arrives at the following summation of Burke's conservative argument against political and moral intellectualism, an argument astonishingly close to the one Gadamer makes in defense of the authority of tradition over mere intellect: "We render obedience to what is with effortless unconsciousness; and without this loyalty to inherited institutions the fabric of society would be dissolved. Civilization, in fact, depends upon the performance of actions defined in preconceived channels; and if we obeyed those novel impulses of right which seem, at times, to contradict our inheritance, we should disturb beyond repair the intricate equilibrium of countless ages. The experience of the past rather than the desires of the present is thus the true guide to our policy. 'We ought,' he said in a famous sentence, 'to venerate where we are unable presently to comprehend' " (pp. 249–50).

A much-needed tracing of the cross-fertilization of the German-speaking and English-speaking conservative traditions, a cross-fertilization reflected, albeit in a somewhat alien medium, in Dworkin's *Law's Empire*, for instance, ought to include F. A. Hayek, whose economic and political epistemology largely coincides with Gadamer's ethical epistemology. See his *Studies in Philosophy, Politics, and Economics* (Chicago: The University of Chicago Press, 1967), dedicated incidentally, to Karl Popper. Where Wittgenstein's retreat from mathematical logic fits in this interplay of conservative influences is yet another question worthy of pursuit.

27. At EN 1175A Aristotle argues that those who possess knowledge surpass those who are still in pursuit of it—this in defense of *theōria* as the highest activity to which a human being may attain. Here, and indeed throughout his discussion of *theōria*, one might be led to believe that he holds we could indeed transcend the *anthrōpinon agathon*. But he states expressly at 1173B 27 that we cannot: unlike a god, the human being is "composite" (*syntheton*), which is to say that unlike divine reason, which is pure, human reason is mixed with an irrational component. Thus the specifically human good is ethical activity in which the irrational is subordinated to the rational (EN 1102B 15), however "second best" (*deuteros*) this ethical activity might be to the divine activity of *theōria*.

28. Surprisingly, if the good is taken in this way as a structure to be effected in things, Aristotle's critique of Plato's idea of the good ends up illuminating it rather than refuting it. Aristotle draws on the argument used in the *Categories* to differentiate among the many senses of "to be." At EN 1096A 24 the same categorial differentiation is applied to the senses of "good" in order to show that there is no one transcendent, separate (*chōriston*) good in and for itself, and thus to discredit Plato's "idea of the good." But, Gadamer argues, Aristotle is guilty here of reading Plato's mytho-poetical dialogues far too literally, and consequently he overlooks the fact that, just as he (Aristotle) singles out a most privileged sense of "to be" without "separating" it, namely *ousia*, Plato too, if de-mythologized, points to a privileged but immanent sense of "good," namely, the structure of that which is integrated and in harmony with itself (IGPAP 31, 125). As the structure of what is good, such a good is not at all a separate reality in itself. And the way to conceive of it is exactly the way in which Aristotle suggests *ousia* is to be conceived of: as existing *analogously* in the existences of which it is constitutive (see *Metaphysics* 1069A 31ff.).

Gadamer's suggestion here is supported by Aristotle himself. At EN 1096B 12ff. Aristotle asks in what sense we can speak of different things as good. It might be that all good things derive from one good, he submits, or that they all contribute to one good. But then he concludes, "Is it not rather more the case [that they are called good] by analogy [*kat' analogian*]?" Like the argument on *ousia*, this argument on the good is advanced in opposition to Plato, but if we look phenomenologically at the content in Plato's literary dramas, we see that the three major instances of order, that of the soul, the state, and the cosmos, emerge as analogous (IGPAP 155). The good is not an absolute entity removed from the things of the world; rather, it is the analogous structure of unity in multiplicity *in* all of these.

29. I am indebted to Gregory Nagy for this point. See his splendid *The Best of the Achaeans* (Baltimore: The Johns Hopkins University Press, 1979), pp. 298–99.

, 30. Hampshire overlooks the possibility that the good, if defined as *aretē* or the excellence of the soul, if defined, that is, as a *structure* of the soul in the way Plato defines it, could indeed be comparable to health and consequently generalizable in the way health is. He argues correctly that the "stripping down" of local practices called good in various societies reveals no underlying common practice that could be called good in all societies. There is irreducible diversity in "good" practices. In contrast, he argues—again correctly—in matters of health there is a common conception of good health ascertainable behind the variations of it in different societies. He then argues—here I think, incorrectly—that Plato and Aristotle are therefore wrong to treat the good as something like health that could be general or common to all peoples.

Plato and Aristotle do not say what form specific acts of courage, for instance, would take in all societies. Both leave the specifics completely open. And Aristotle, in particular, is not trying to universalize the examples of courageous acts he takes from his own tradition when he comes to discuss courage. What he is trying to show is that these particular acts of courage, like acts of gentleness or magnanimity, display a right relationship of reason in the soul to the soul's *pathē* or feelings, such that the deeds which follow from this right relationship are *kalos* and not *aischros*, decent and not ugly, and such that they are done *hote dei*, *hōs dei*, when it is fitting, as it is fitting, and so forth. He gets no more specific than this. Thus only the right relationship or "health" of the soul, its *aretē* or excellence, is generalizable and not specific practices themselves which follow from it.

31. But see also Chapter 1, note 12 on the *Habits of the Heart*.

32. *De mundi sensibilis atque intelligibilis forma et principiis* (1770).

33. Hampshire points out dangers similar to the ones Kant discerns in any utilitarian thinking divorced from the "customs and rituals that govern, in different societies, relations between the sexes, marriage, property rights, family relationships, and the celebration of the dead . . . this inexplicit morality of ritual and manners" (MC 97). The "computational morality" of utilitarianism, he says, "carries the deritualization of transactions between men to a point at which men not only can, but ought to, use and exploit each other as they use and exploit any other natural objects . . ." (MC 96–97).

34. Michael Foster, in his *Masters of Political Thought* I (Boston: Houghton Mifflin, 1941), p. 242, points out that Aquinas displays, perhaps unbeknown to himself, the tension characteristic of his age between those arguing that the monarch, though constrained by natural law, is absolute, and those arguing that he is subordinate to the customs of his people. This double influence creates an unresolved ambivalence in Aquinas regarding which of the two, natural law given to the reason of the monarch, or custom, takes priority over the other. Our excerpt in particular would seem to reflect this ambivalence. But see also Book III, Chapter 8 of St. Augustine's *Confessions*, where the problem of priority is already implicit.

35. One should not overlook the sense of *orthos* in Aristotle's *orthos logos* that is perpetuated in our orthopedics and orthodontics.

Conclusion: Gadamerian Conservatism

PLATO, ARISTOTLE, AQUINAS, KANT, HEGEL—this is the speculative tradition from which Gadamer derives, and, incidentally, in the first three of whom Edmund Burke's idea of prudence, taken from the tradition of Aquinas' *prudentia* and Aristotle's *phronēsis*, also has its origins. But just this tradition, principally because of its challenge to autonomous reason, has been nearly suppressed in the English-speaking Enlightenment tradition, of which Locke, Mill, and Anglo-American moral philosophers generally are the inheritors and for whom any such thinking as Edmund Burke's is synonomous with *restauration*, reaction, and privilege. (See Thomas Paine's *The Rights of Man*, for example, but also MacIntyre's *After Virtue*, pp. 221–22.) But is theirs a fair assessment?

It is evident by now that in following the speculative tradition Gadamer arrives at a position which in the usual political and ethical parlance would be called conservative. However, in the process he has done a great deal to demarcate the sense of "conservative" from "reactionary" and hence to shield his argument from the objections generally raised against so-called conservative thinking. For, obviously, reactionaries, the sophists of Plato's time and our own, though supposedly teaching conformity to the established ways of doing things, are not conservative in Gadamer's sense at all: their principle, if it can be called a principle, is the "natural" one of self-interest that Callicles advocates in the *Gorgias*.

The reactionaries' acknowledgment of traditional authority thus extends only to those institutions and practices that perpetuate their own advantage, and in regard to those that do not, they are quick to pervert traditional standards in a rhetorical misappropriation of them that twists them to make them serve their own purposes. Gadamer succeeds in demonstrating that this "natural" pursuit of one's "advantage" and authentic faithfulness to what is customarily ethical are incompatible with each other. For faithfulness to tradition presupposes that the I has been cultivated beyond its merely "natural" self and raised to participation in the We of communal custom (*Sitte*). Any individual or group of individuals who appropriate, re-interpret, and revise what is customary to suit their advantage can be seen to annul custom and undo the cultivation of the I to the We upon which custom depends. For just as a game, in order to be a game, must have priority over the players in it, the ethical tradition, in order to be tradition, must have acknowledged priority over those who participate in it. Precisely this point emerges from Socrates' refusal in the *Crito* to evade the written and unwritten laws (*nomoi*) of his country: faithfulness to an ethical tradition means the choice of action according to communal custom, not according to the advantage of any individual.

It follows that we must distinguish sharply between an ethical tradition and many day-to-day practices or what "everybody" does, as Socrates distinguishes between them. Cheating or bribery, for instance, may well be a common practice in a given society, but—and precisely this is *Kant's* point—both are based not on one's sense of participation in the community with others (*Pflicht* or obligation) but on self-interest (*Neigung* or inclination). Indeed, there can be no community where they are pervasive because where they are, the prerequisite of any community, friendship (*philia*), the communal bond of loyalty, has degenerated into a merely reciprocal self-service. In such societies the "friend" is to be helped only because he can be helpful, just as the enemy is to be harmed because he can do harm (see Lysias' speech on love and friendship in *Phaedrus* and Socrates' provocative parodying of the principle of helping friends and hurting enemies at *Gorgias* 440cff.).

Thus if the ethical tradition is taken as it has been defined here—namely, as the We expressed in language usages and in customary practices that takes priority over the I—such practices as cheating or bribery are counter-traditional not only logically but empirically in the sense that they undermine the traditional community by re-asserting the antithetical principle of self-interest. Put another way: though sophism and all that accompanies it can be a "way of life," strictly speaking there is no such thing as an ethical tradition of sophism either as Plato knew it or as we know it today. It is essential for the preservation of the ethical (*sittliche*) tradition that the principle of self-interest be superseded.

Talk of superseding self-interest becomes particularly problematical, to be sure, in regard to societies in which the ethical realm has been drastically reduced by the preponderance of what Hegel has called Civil Society and its system of need satisfaction, by the realm, that is, of contractual exchanges that distribute goods and power. As I have pointed out, Plato and Aristotle knew only the precursor of such a development as this, but, even so, they were alert to the danger of those sophistical manipulators of laws governing the distribution of goods and power, who merely disguise their uninhibited pursuit of self-interest—even to themselves—in the garb of adherence to custom. Gorgias and Protagoras are exemplary of the deceit here, a deceit that ultimately only the invention of a "Callicles" lays bare. In Plato's "Callicles" it becomes clear how Gorgias actually perverts genuinely conservative thought. Behind feigned adherence to a society's customs the pseudo-conservative sophist carries out his attempt to circumvent civil law, the law, that is, that regulates the competition of self-interested individuals to ensure that the distribution of goods and power is just and that one gets no more, *pleon*, than one's fair share, however "just" and "fair," *dikaios* and *kalos*, might be defined. As Callicles shows, it is not adherence to communal custom that sophists want, but rather to evade what Aquinas called the *vis constrictiva*, the constrictive force, of civil law. They do not want to be constricted at all, but instead set as their goal the attainment of the power to do anything they are inclined to do. Only a "Callicles" is willing to say straight out what the others conceal: namely, that *nomoi*, laws and customs, are to him nothing more than "conventional" impediments to his "natural" right to have more for himself should he have the courage and intelligence to get it (see the *Gorgias* 482Eff. for the *nomos–physis* distinction he makes). Thus by undercutting the laws of what we now call Civil Society the pseudo-conservative sophist, far from superseding its principle of self-interest, radicalizes it. Despite cleverly contrived appearances to the contrary, there is no reinstatement of the ethical here whatsoever.

As Gadamer sees it, this sophistical subversion of the ethical tradition by raw self-interest is precisely Plato's concern when he specifies in the *Republic* a philosophical course of study for the guardians of the ideal state. Plato's utopia responds to the political reality of his Athens, in which the communal "life of spirit" threatened to degenerate completely into the animal conflict of every individual will with every other, into what Hobbes would call the "war of all against all" and endless "pursuit of power after power." So, Gadamer writes, "When Plato opines that such a person [who has been trained in philosophy] is more suited than anyone else to direct public affairs, he is exposing what seductiveness there is in having power: power wants only itself. The education of the guardians has the purpose of making them immune to this seduction" (IGPAP 72). And it is not mistaken, Gadamer adds, to see Plato's requirement of immunity to the seductiveness of power reflected in the modern ideal of the honest and incorruptible public official (IGPAP 72).

(We might note that in thinking these things through, as he does in the *Republic*, Plato is undertaking his own version of a Kantian *Grundlegung zur Metaphysik der Sitten*. As in Kant, theoretical reflection here is intended to fortify us against sophistical attempts to undermine our loyalty to the *ethos* or *Sitten*, the ways and customs, of our society.)

To sum up, in any conservative ethical and political theory we might hope to generate from Gadamer's hermeneutics, the danger of sophism is to be combated for two indissociable reasons: using Hegel's distinction, we may say, first, that sophism undermines the distributive justice of Civil Society with its Condition of Right, and, second, that it undermines the sense of community presupposed by *Sittlichkeit*. We know from Hegel, if not from Plato and Aristotle, that *both* the Condition of Right and *Sittlichkeit* must be conserved. We need now to consider their interrelationship in a Gadamerian conservatism.

The inclusion here of the Condition of Right or Legal Status as the necessary counterpart of *Sittlichkeit* poses a problem given what we have seen regarding not just ethical understanding, but practical understanding in general: namely, what basis could Legal Status have other than the critical autonomous reason that Gadamer has called into question? After all, right *seems* to be like mathematical reality insofar as it is universal and insofar as any understanding of it abstracts from any particular ethical (*sittliche*) circumstances in treating *all* individuals indifferently as "persons," alike and equal (Hegel: *gleich*) before the law. And mathematical reality *is* known by autonomous reason freed from the prejudices of any historical and local perspective that Gadamer argues are the precondition of any practical knowing. Exactly this characteristic of mathematical knowing makes it so attractive as a model for critical reasoning that would identify and rectify the violations of right perpetuated in any ethical tradition. Indeed, since Gadamer rules out mathematical knowing in practical thought in both its ethical and its *legal* dimensions (see WM 292ff.), he seems to eliminate any basis for right and, consequently, any possibility for criticizing an ethical tradition and remedying its inherent injustices. There seems, accordingly, to be no place after all in Gadamer's thinking for Legal Status as a check on the injustices of *Sittlichkeit*.

For without critical, autonomous reasoning would not Thrasymachus be right in Plato's *Republic*? Would not justice as traditions define it always be nothing other than the interest of the stronger, the acceptance of which has been coerced by skillful control of discourse? And how, if this is so, could precisely *language*, which is rigged from the start by those in power, be trusted to transmit what is really just? It seems clear that if right is to have a basis, if, for instance, the traditional unjust patterns of exploitation of women by men, of one class, race, or nation, by another, are to be found unjust and a violation of right, one must have recourse of some sort of system-transcendent reasoning, to autonomous reason of precisely the sort Gadamer has placed in question. If Gadamer's attack on autonomous reason is correct, in justifying ethical understanding as the special kind of knowing it is, he has, it appears, at the same time precluded the Condition of Right that I have argued here— with Hegel against MacIntyre—is *Sittlichkeit*'s indispensable counterpart. How is this objection to be met?

The very failure of Rawls's project, I suggest, points toward a possible way out of the apparent impasse here. A most difficult problem for Rawls, certainly, is to what extent legal status and abstract right applied to equal persons develops not in abstraction from, and apart from *Sittlichkeit*, as Rawls, following his mathematical model of understanding, his "moral geometry," would like to argue it does, but *within Sittlichkeit*. Despite Rawls's monumental effort to think through a universal system of right from an "original position" in complete abstraction from any particular ethical codes, he ends up finding that system sustained by what he calls the "morality of association." And "the content of the morality of association," he says, "is given by the moral standards appropriate to the individual's role in the various associations to which he belongs" (TJ 467). He goes on to mention such things as family, school, neighborhood, and society "in which each member has *certain* rights and duties" (TJ 467; emphasis added). Here, quite clearly, we are in the realm of the ethical. This raises the question whether any abstract legal system or system of right (Hegel: *Rechtssystem*) can be developed apart from *Sittlichkeit*, from which it abstracts to begin with, and if not, in what way legal and ethical understanding, jurisprudence, and prudence actually remain continuous with one another.

Suppose Rawls had abandoned the system-transcendent project of "moral geometry." Could he have come to any conclusions about universal justice precisely on the basis of the morality of association and not in transcendence of it? Aristotle and Hegel, I think, show us how he could have.

Aristotle, whose epistemological model is not mathematics but life science, shows us that not only mathematics but reasoning that begins and stays with growing particulars can arrive at insight into universals; as Medieval Aristotelianism puts it, he shows us that universals (*universalia*) are also to be discovered *in rebus*, in the experience of particular developing things, and not only in abstraction from them in pure mathematical knowing. Hegel, in his "Logic of the Concept," the last stage of his *Logic*, takes over precisely this Aristotelian epistemological model. And he then proceeds to put it to use in his ethical and social expositions. He shows, for instance, that the universal underpinnings of any system of right, Kant's moral imperative that a human being is never to be treated only as a means but always as an end in him- or herself, is uncovered *in rebus*, specifically in the *res publica* as we experience it. Consider, for example, Hegel's dialectic of recognition, which explicates the self-destruction of inequality and exploitation (see PhG 141ff. on the master and servant, to which Gadamer, not coincidentally, devotes a chapter of his *Hegel's Dialectic* [HD 54ff.]). We see that, quite apart from any perspective "for us" philosophers with absolute knowledge *above* the experience which consciousness undergoes here, the universal idea of freedom emerges in this consciousness, "for it," and entirely *within* its experience. The relationship of master and servant is *experienced* (*erfahren*) by those who participate in it to be non-viable and self-canceling. Freedom, the concept of no one person's exploiting another

and the acknowledgment of each by the other as an end in him-
or herself, works itself out in the self-unfolding of the inherent
self-contradictoriness of traditions where it does not yet exist.[1]
Freedom, to use Aristotelian language, is the formal *entelecheia*,
the *telos* or goal residing in any tradition. To be sure, as formal,
the idea of freedom will need ethical content if it is not to
degenerate into anarchy (see PhG 414ff. on "Absolute Freedom
and Terror"), and it is precisely this danger that conservatives
like Burke seize upon. But it is possible to argue along with, and
not against, conservatives that conversely any ethical content
will inevitably come to be measured against the universal form
of freedom as this form has developed within a particular ethical
tradition. In this way it can be seen that universal right is not
primarily to be envisioned *by* autonomous reason *outside* a
tradition, but instead, like the ethical truth and the "morality of
association," within which it develops, is displayed *to* finite
reason *within* a tradition. It is experienced, *erfahren*, experienced by the consciousness undergoing the experience of it, and
we are returned here to Aeschylus' *pathei mathos*, of "by
suffering learned." Gadamer's acknowledgment of human finitude, of the inevitability of our being under way within truth that
we come to understand only limitedly in the language we have
to speak of it, does not, therefore, preclude consciousness of
universal right at all.

Of course, as Aeschylus knows and Gadamer points out, our
learning is finite and never concluded, and as opposed to Hegel's
projected synthesis of all antitheses, the contradictions we experience, especially between universal right and particular *Sitten*
or ways of doing things, are never entirely resolvable (see
Chapter 1, Part 4, above). In fact, as Hampshire shows, the cost
of eliminating an injustice, a violation of formal right, must often
be weighed against the cost of destroying an ethical pattern to
which we are accustomed (MC 6), for, contrary to Hegel's
projection, the contradictions between them are not reconcilable
in anything that would transcend them (Hegel's state). An Antigone and a Creon will always be in conflict. But such irreconcila-

bility does not justify the sacrifice of one side or the other for the sake of consistency. Both must be maintained in whatever degree of tension they might have to co-exist, formal right as a corrective for the potential injustices inherent in any *Sittlichkeit*, but, we should note, also *Sittlichkeit* as the indispensable content for any formal right.

For in regard to *Sittlichkeit*—which has been our principal concern here—whoever would genuinely acknowledge the priority of the traditional We over the I cannot persist exclusively in Civil's Society's *hexis* or disposition of self-interest. Obedience to external constraints placed on the sophistic pursuit of advantage and power, though certainly necessary, is not enough. It is the purpose of all the satirical constructs in the *Republic* to make just this insufficiency clear: there must be a turning of the "whole soul," not just some sort of coercive force that keeps the insolent and shameless (*aischros*) individual in check. Put in a more modern context: the disposition dominant in the realm of "need satisfaction" (Hegel: *Bedürfnisbefriedigung*) not only must be constrained there by abstract right, but, beyond that, must not be allowed to infect and disease the souls of the citizens and thereby destroy the realm of the ethical.

With that, however, we have arrived at the fundamental problem for any hermeneutical, and, indeed, any conservative, ethics in the sense we have defined it: What is to be done in those circumstances where, as Gadamer puts it, we find ourselves disoriented by the "obvious dissolution of convention and tradition" (HL), by the collapse of *Sittlichkeit*? Gadamer indicates his answer in his "Plato and the Poets" (DD 39–72). It is clear, he writes, that in his condemnation of the poets Plato is responding to just such a situation as this, in which the only real basis of ethical education, the authority of traditional laws and customs, seemingly no longer exists. As Plato came to see, in such circumstances direct political action is futile, for "incurably ill states" themselves are not susceptible of improvement. The only improvement that can be sought is in the souls of the citizens, and philosophy as care of the soul becomes the single task (DD 74–76). Accordingly, a hermeneutical ethics would tell us that in these circumstances one must begin with the restoration of measure to the soul, restoration of its overall excellence, the *sympasa aretē*. Each individual must be strengthened in holding to the mean and avoiding excesses and immoderation. The whole of Plato's *Republic* is intended, not to define the ideal state, but by parodying the existent one, to rebuild, if only in theoretical reflections "imitated" by its readers, the *ēthos* or character of the individual citizen and thereby heal the disease of the soul. Thus as we saw, when poetic imitation is attacked in Book X, it is because in such acting out of poetry individuals alienate rather than collect themselves. They turn themselves into *many* things—the thunder, the waves, but, worst of all, the passions—and lose the *one* center that might bring measure and harmony to their souls and continuity through time, steadfastness, to their actions.

Still, no one could have failed to observe that a healing of the diseased soul and a recovery of its excellence would neither succeed nor suffice were there nothing left of the communal good to be "recollected" once the individual had been set free from the tyranny of the passions. The *sympasa aretē* or overall virtue of the soul is a necessary, but not sufficient condition of being ethical, for only he who is guided by foreknowledge of the good will be able to hold to it unerringly (IGPAP 43). That, Gadamer tells us, is the reason for Plato's simultaneous teachings on *anamnēsis* or "recollection." If one de-mythologizes Plato's presentation of this doctrine in his dialogues, if one abstracts, that is, from the "story" of the pre-existence of souls, the phenomenon which comes to light is foreknowledge and preunderstanding (Gadamer: *Vorwissen, Vorverständnis*) as these function in any act of understanding and interpretation. (Compare Chapter 2, Part 4, on ethical recollection in the *Gorgias*.)

It cannot be overlooked that this conception of ethical understanding as *anamnēsis* or being reminded, as a bringing to mind of a tradition from time out of mind, raises an inevitable problem, in particular for Americans. For the United States, committed as it is to adherence to no single tradition and tolerance of them all, committed as it is to pluralism, might seem to be a land that ultimately must dissolve all traditions in a system of mere need satisfaction and the legal status and abstract right that govern it. *Sittlichkeit*, for which Americans do not even have a word, seems to vanish as good and bad degenerate into "values" valid relative only to an ethnic group and then, in the extreme, only to autonomous individuals who arbitrarily choose them for themselves. This degeneration brings with it the necessary concession that as mere "values" good and bad have no claim to communal substantiality whatsoever; they have, it seems, become a matter of personal preference. Even *Habits of the Heart*, which laments the collapse of community and this degeneration of the ethical (see Chapter 1, note 12), proposes only *civic* obligation to democratic government and the abstract right it ensures as an alternative to the individual's pursuit of success, gratification, power, or however else he or she might define happiness. It is as if the United States, unlike apparently more ethnically homogeneous nations with their unified linguistic and literary traditions, offered precisely no *ethical* content any longer, no *ethical* tradition in which Americans might be participants and no ethical consensus about which to get clear in deliberation and discussion. There is, it appears, nothing left to recollect. As we have noted, MacIntyre, for one, views things this way, and sees, in the absence of any tacit *sensus communis*, the degeneration of ethical discourse into interminable debate.

Since any ethical consensus, if it exists, would be transmitted and discovered in the language we speak, it is useful in addressing this problem of the apparent dissolution of *Sittlichkeit* to recall, if only in the briefest manner, something of the evolving history of American English. Let us keep in mind that English itself was an evoving amalgam of heterogeneous languages long before it came to North America, a fusion of Anglo-Saxon with Celtic tongues and Norman French with Anglo-Saxon. And once in America English has continued to receive multiple infusions not only from a proliferation of regional dialects and idioms feeding back into the mainstream but from immigrants initially speaking foreign languages and then an English modified and enriched by these languages and their idioms, vocabulary, and sayings. In this way what we call standard American English has evolved and continues to evolve, a language which is distinctively American, and on whose usages there is provisional agreement, continually in question and changing, but agreement nonetheless. At least in regard to the American *language*, then, it would be patently counterfactual to say that because of the plurality and heterogeneity of influences constitutive of it there is and can be no consensus concerning it. However rough, tenuous, and fringed with disagreement it may be, there is a consensus. So too, I would contend, the plurality and heterogeneity of ethical understandings transmitted in American English, far from precluding any consensus, continue to fuse into something distinctively American, an ethical language enriched by its multiple sources and continuing infusions.

To be sure, the process of assimilation is by no means ensured. Protracted clashes and conflict are indeed possible, as has been the case between English and French in Canada and English and Spanish in the United States. But on the other hand, assimilation is not unlikely either. For mutual accommodation and consensus, not infinite conflict, have in fact been the ultimate result of the thousands of years of evolution of English as we speak it today in North America.

And if this is the course American English has taken, so too, it is reasonable to assume, is it the course of the evolving ethical patterns of good and bad (*agathos* and *kakos*), right and wrong (*dikaios* and *adikos*), fair and despicable (*kalos* and *aischros*), that American English as heir of these Greek words and ways of thinking variously translates and transmits them. Insofar as there is at any point a standard American English, whatever the penumbra of disagreement surrounding it, there are, I would maintain, ethical standards to be discovered in it, ethical standards that are the evolving amalgam of initially conflicting influences that fuse and merge with the mainstream altering its course and enriching its substance. Significantly, as in the case of the absorption of Norman French into Anglo-Saxon, the predominant component in the confluence is often *not* that of the ruling class and prevails not because of the political power of its speakers but because of the power of the language itself. Hence it is one-sided to speak as MacIntyre often does in terms of "rival points of view." For in the end one ethical point of view transmitted in language does not so much drive its "rivals" from the field as embrace and merge with them. (Compare the critique of MacIntyre in Chapter 1, Part 3 above.)

What occurs here is exactly what Gadamer has in mind when he speaks of a *Horizontverschmelzung* or merging and fusion of horizons that occurs in the discursive interchange between two interlocutors who are initially foreign to each other. Though Platonic dialogue between two or more people is his paradigm, Gadamer, of course, is referring primarily to the dialogue of the interpreter and the text. Still the hermeneutical structure here is universal: in the interpretive interchange between *languages*, even if it is at first hostile and fraught with misunderstanding and non-comprehension, a fusion eventually evolves in which each, in translating the opposed language into his or her own and translating his or her own into the opposed, comes to see things in a wider perspective incorporating something of the standpoint of the other. This coming to see things from the other's point of view is what we have called *synesis*. Over centuries we continue to talk our differences out in talking them through (Plato: *dialegesthai*) and eventually coming to an understanding (Gadamer: *Sichverständigen*). Ethical understanding too (*sittliches Verstehen*) is the result, always provisional, of just this process—*Verständigung*.

And fortunately even in the most degraded societies there still remains some foreknowledge of the good, some trace of ethical substance from time out of mind to be recollected, a sense of community that takes each person beyond the pursuit of advantage in Civil Society's competition for satisfaction of needs, and back into the ethical realm of community and custom in which you and I are joined in the *Gespräch* (discussion) which *we* are. While Burke would speak of "the license of a ferocious dissoluteness in manners and of an insolent irreligion in opinions and practices" (RRF 50), Gadamer is decidedly more optimistic. "The changes," he writes,

> that spread through the ethic [*Sitte*] and way of thinking of a given time and that tend to give the frightening impression, particularly to those who are older, that ethical customs [*Sitten*] have totally dissolved, take place against an unperturbed background. Family, society, nation, are the constitutive essence of human beings all the while its *ēthos* fills itself with changing contents [KS I 191].

These three, family, society, nation, which, it will be noted, are the very instantiations of *sittliche Substanz* named by Hegel, remain as a fund on which our ethical recollection may draw.

But, as we might expect, it is not the modern thinker, Hegel, but the ancient thinker, Aristotle, on whom Gadamer builds at the end of his Heidelberg Lectures, specifically Aristotle's conception of *synesis*. In the first place *synesis* is that sort of understanding that distinguishes an ethically sagacious (*phronimos*) person from someone who is doctrinaire. It is a necessary adjunct of *phronēsis*, for it is that proper blend of principledness and flexibility that allows one to be sensitive to the singular quality of each situation without falling into either ideological rigidity on the one side or unprincipled opportunism on the other. But *synesis*, as we saw early in this investigation of ethical understanding (Chapter 1, Part 4), is not just understanding *of* a situation, but also showing understanding *for* someone. The basis of it is that one "wishes what is right [*das Rechte*] and that one is linked to the other one in having this wish in common with him" (WM 306). And there are, Gadamer points out, fundamental levels on which such *synesis* as this is still to be experienced even when all community seems lost.

In support of this contention he refers us to the German "Das ist gemein!'' meaning roughly, "That's despicable," though, like the Greek *aischros*, the German "gemein" is much more broadly used than the English "despicable," and extends even to minor things as "That's mean." Whatever the level, we all have an understanding, a *synesis*, Gadamer reminds us, of what is meant when such an expression is used: in some way the individual, of whose action it is said, has, in pursuing his or her own advantage, violated our sense of decency and the community between people known to us from time out of mind. But if that community can be violated, it still exists. Something, however diminished it may be in our consciousness of it, is still there to be "recollected," to be understood like valuable usages that have somehow vanished from our speaking, but that nonetheless have not fallen so far into disuse that we might not recover them.

Thus a hermeneutical ethics would avail itself of philosophy to win the soul back from its dissipation in the self-indulgence of aesthetic consciousness. And having sought, in theoretical reflections like Kant's *Grundlegung zur Metaphysik der Sitten*, Aristotle's *Ethics*, or Plato's *Republic* to assist in fortifying the soul against flattery and in restoring its measure and unity, a heremeneutical ethics would return the individual to the tradition of community between us, in which, however shattered our society might be, we as human beings always continue to under way.

NOTE

1. See Gadamer's "Hegel's Philosophy and Its Aftereffects Today," in *Vernunft im Zeitalter der Wissenschaft* (Frankfurt: Suhrkamp, 1976), pp. 32–53. Since I have avoided the contemporary Gadamer-Habermas-Derrida debate in order to pursue a fusion of Gadamer's thought with English-language tradition, I chose to build my elaboration of a Gadamerian ethical epistemology not upon this work, which largely responds to contemporary issues with recourse to Heidegger's

critique of technology and language as information, but upon Gadamer's expositions of Plato and Aristotle. Still there is much in it that would have been relevant to my argument. For instance, in regard to the transition from the idiosyncratic I to the communal We, see pp. 45ff. on the objectivity of *Geist* that transcends anything subjective and private; or pp. 69–70 in regard to Aristotle's distinction between *phronēsis* (Gadamer: *praktische Vernunft*) and *deinotēs* (Gadamer: *Findigkeit*); or pp. 103–104 in regard to the difference between reaching a psychoanalytic diagnosis and reaching a discursive understanding.

In his *Political Hermeneutics: The Early Thinking of Hans-Georg Gadamer* (University Park: Pennsylvania State University Press, 1990) Robert Sullivan turns similarly to Gadamer's work on Plato, albeit not to the later studies, as I have done primarily, but to the earlier ones. Still it is not this, but Sullivan's quite different intent, that leads him to results quite different from mine. To be sure, I would follow Gadamer's rejection of "developmental" theories generally, e.g., in Werner Jaeger *et alii* (see IGPAP 7–10) and seek to avoid any distinction at all between the "early" and the "later" Gadamer even if it were only to say in the "earlier" works" one finds prefigurations of themes in the "later" works.

BIBLIOGRAPHY

Austin, J. L. "A Plea for Excuses." In *Ordinary Language*. Ed. V. C. Chappell. Englewood Cliffs, N.J.: Prentice-Hall, 1964. Pp. 41–63.

Bellah, Robert, et al. *Habits of the Heart*. New York: Harper & Row, 1986.

Bernstein, Richard. *Beyond Objectivism and Relativism: Science, Hermeneutics, and Praxis*. Philadelphia: University of Pennsylvania Press, 1983.

Burke, Edmund. "An Appeal from the New to the Old Whigs." *Edmund Burke: Selected Writings and Speeches*. Ed. Peter J. Stanlis. Chicago: Regnery/Gateway, 1963). Pp. 518–46.

———. *Reflections on the Revolution in France*. Garden City, N.Y.: Doubleday, 1973.

Cornford, Francis. *Plato and Parmenides*. New York: Liberal Arts, 1957.

Dworkin, Ronald. *Law's Empire*. Cambridge: The Belknap Press of Harvard University Press, 1986.

———. *Taking Rights Seriously*. Cambridge: Harvard University Press, 1978.

Essays on Aristotle's ETHICS. Ed. Amelie Oksenberg Rorty. Berkeley: University of California Press, 1980.

Foster, Michael. *Masters of Political Thought* I. Boston: Houghton Mifflin, 1941.

Frankena, William. *Ethics*. Englewood Cliffs, N.J.: Prentice-Hall, 1963.

Gadamer, Hans-Georg. *Dialogue and Dialectic: Eight Hermeneutical Studies in Plato*. Trans. P. Christopher Smith. New Haven, Conn.: Yale University Press, 1980.

———. *Hegel's Dialectic: Five Hermeneutical Studies*. Trans. P. Christopher Smith. New Haven, Conn.: Yale University Press, 1976.

———. "Heidelberg Lectures on Aesthetics." Summer Semester, 1979. Unpublished.

———. *The Idea of the Good in Platonic-Aristotelian Philosophy*. Trans. P. Christopher Smith. New Haven, Conn.: Yale University Press, 1986.

——. *Kleine Schriften* [*Shorter Writings*]. 4 vols. Tübingen: Mohr, 1967–1977.

——. *Platos dialektische Ethik* [*Plato's Dialectical Ethics*]. Hamburg: Meiner, 1968.

——. *Vernunft im Zeitalter der Wissenschaft*. Frankfurt: Suhrkamp, 1976.

——. *Wahrheit und Methode* [*Truth and Method*]. Tübingen: Mohr, 1960.

Gross, Barry. *Analytic Philosophy*. New York: Pegasus, 1970.

Hampshire, Stuart. *Morality and Conflict*. Cambridge: Harvard University Press, 1983.

Hare, R. M. *The Language of Morals*. New York: Oxford University Press, 1964.

Hayek, F. A. *Studies in Philosophy, Politics, and Economics*. Chicago: The University of Chicago Press, 1967.

Hegel, Georg Wilhelm Friedrich. *Grundlinien der Philosophie des Rechts* [*Outlines of the Philosophy of Right*]. Hamburg: Meiner, 1955.

——. *Phänomenologie des Geistes* [*Phenomenology of Mind*]. Hamburg: Meiner, 1952.

——. *Wissenschaft der Logik* [*Science of Logic*]. 2 vols. Leipzig: Meiner, 1951.

Heidegger, Martin. *Platons Lehre von der Wahrheit* [*Plato's Doctrine of Truth*]. Bern: Francke, 1954.

——. *Sein und Zeit* [*Being and Time*]. Tübingen: Niemeyer, 1960.

Jaeger, Werner. *Paideia* II. Berlin: De Gruyter, 1959.

Kierkegaard, Søren. *Concluding Unscientific Postscript*. Trans. David Swenson. Ed. Walter Lowrie. Princeton, N.J.: Princeton University Press, 1941.

Laski, Harold. *Political Thought from Locke to Bentham*. New York: Holt, 1920.

MacIntyre, Alasdair. *After Virtue*. 2nd ed. Notre Dame, Ind.: University of Notre Dame Press, 1984.

——. *Whose Justice? Which Rationality?* Notre Dame, Ind.: University of Notre Dame Press, 1988.

——. "Why Is the Search for the Foundations of Ethics So Frustrating?" *The Hastings Center Report*, 9, No. 4 (August 1979), 16–22.

Mill, John Stuart. *On Liberty*. Indianapolis: Bobbs-Merrill, 1978.

Moore, G. E. *Principia ethica*. Cambridge: Cambridge University Press, 1962.

Musil, Robert. *Der Mann ohne Eigenschaften*. Hamburg: Rowohlt, 1952.

Nagy, Gregory. *The Best of the Achaeans*. Baltimore: The Johns Hopkins University Press, 1979.

Nozick, Robert. *Anarchy, State, and Utopia*. New York: Basic Books, 1974.

Oakeshott, Michael. "On Being Conservative." In *The Portable Conservative Reader*. Ed. Russell Kirk. New York: Viking, 1982. Pp. 567–600.

Pears, David. *Ludwig Wittgenstein*. New York: Viking, 1971.

Rawls, John. *A Theory of Justice*. Cambridge: The Belknap Press of Harvard University Press, 1971.

——. "Two Concepts of Rules." *The Philosophical Review*, 64 (1955), 3–32. Repr. in *Ethics*. Edd. Judith J. Thomson and Gerald Dworkin. New York: Harper & Row, 1968. Pp. 104–35.

Rorty, Richard. *The Consequences of Pragmatism (Essays: 1972–1980)*. Minneapolis: University of Minnesota Press, 1982.

——. *Philosophy and the Mirror of Nature*. Princeton, N.J.: Princeton University Press, 1979.

Rosen, Stanley. *The Limits of Analysis*. New York: Basic Books, 1980.

Ross, W. D. *The Right and the Good*. Oxford: Clarendon, 1930.

Sartre, Jean-Paul. *L'Etre et le néant*. Paris: Gallimard, 1943.

Smith, P. Christopher. *Das Sein des Du: Die Philosophie Martin Bubers im Lichte des Heidegger'schen Denken an das Sein*. Heidelberg: Dissertationsdruck, 1966.

Stevenson, Charles L. *Ethics and Language*. New Haven, Conn.: Yale University Press, 1972.

Stravinsky, Igor. *Poetics of Music*. New York: Vintage, 1947.

Sullivan, Robert. *Political Hermeneutics: The Early Thinking of Hans-Georg Gadamer*. University Park: The Pennsylvania State University Press, 1990.

Toulmin, Steven. *An Introduction to Reasoning*. New York: Macmillan, 1984.

——. *The Uses of Argument*. Cambridge: Cambridge University Press, 1958.

Warnke, Gloria. *Gadamer: Hermeneutics, Tradition, and Reason*. Stanford: Stanford University Press, 1987.

Weinsheimer, Joel. *Gadamer's Hermeneutics: A Reading of* TRUTH AND METHOD. New Haven, Conn.: Yale University Press, 1985.
Wittgenstein, Ludwig. *Philosophical Investigations*. Trans. G. E. M. Anscombe. Oxford: Blackwell, 1958.
——. *Tractatus logico-philosophicus*. Trans. D. F. Pears and B. F. McGuinness. New York: Humanities, 1961.

INDEX

Aeschylus, on *pathei mathos* (by suffering learned), 175*n*9, 190, 274
aesthetic consciousness, 189–92, 198–99, 213
agathon, to (adj. *agathos*) (the good), xiv, 47, 57, 85, 111, 139, 147, 157, 158, 162, 164
ahoristos duas (indeterminate Two), xx, 237–44; SEE *to apeiron*
aischron, to (adj. *aischros*) (the ugly, unfair, shameful), xiv, 130, 147, 162, 165–71, 177–78*n*15, 180, 222, 228, 239, 242, 265*n*30, 275, 278, 281
aisthēsis (perception, comprehension, sensitivity), 57, 71, 74, 86–87; SEE *synesis*
akolasia (undisciplinedness, licentiousness, intemperance), 239, 242–44, 256
akratia (powerlessness over oneself, incontinence), 82–83, 184, 239
analogy, reasoning by, 48, 56, 58, 82, 140, 216, 237, 264–65*n*28
anamnēsis (being reminded of something, recollection), xxvi, 76, 91, 102*n*21, 139, 165, 169, 190, 214, 223, 226–27, 276, 281
Anaxagoras, xiii, 142
Anständigkeit (adj. *anständig*) (decency, propriety, appropriateness), 25, 177*n*15, 180, 200–201, 204–206
apeiron, to (adj. *apeiros*) (the indefinite, indeterminate, unlimited), 90, 186, 237, 238, 244
apodeixis (demonstration), 56, 58–60, 72, 82, 154–55, 226–27
apophansis (showing forth, displaying), 125–30, 133–34, 137, 152–53, 155–57, 164, 174*n*7, 222
aporia and *euporia* (logical impasse and felicitous outcome), 150, 153, 155–56
Aquinas, Thomas, 175*n*11, 188, 202, 252–57
aretē (excellence, virtue), xxvii, 10, 24, 57, 58, 98–99*n*13, 156, 265*n*30; SEE *sympasa aretē*
Aristotle, xiii, 2, 11, 15–16, 21, 25, 26, 56, 58, 127, 135, 138, 141, 170, 183, 192,

207, 220, 256–57, 258*n*5, 261*n*11, 264*n*27, 264–65*n*28, 267, 273, 282*n*1
and Kant, 100*n*15, 251–52
and Plato, 231–34
on analogy, 216–17
on *hexeis*, 229–30
on justice, 44–52
on *philia*, 29–30, 99–100*n*14, 154
on *phronēsis*, 70–76, 78–84, 101*n*18, 205, 210, 258*n*6
on *synesis*, 169, 280–81
Augustine, 60, 66–67, 266*n*34
Austin, J. L., xvii, xxv, 8, 10, 114, 118, 124, 126, 133, 155, 172*n*4, 223–25, 262*n*20
authority, xvi, 67, 197–98, 215, 217, 223, 228, 247, 260*n*9, 263*n*26, 265*n*30, 269
autonomous reasoning, xv–xvi, 19–20, 27, 49–51, 53, 60, 154, 180–86, 197, 204, 212, 215, 216–21, 228, 229, 230, 248, 252, 260*n*9, 267, 271–72; *see* external reflection

Bach, Johann Sebastian, xxviii*n*3
Bedürfnisbefriedigung, see need satisfaction
Berlin, Isaiah, 15
Bernstein, Richard, xxvii–xviii*n*2
bouleuesthai (deliberation, taking counsel), 21, 49, 56–58, 62, 80–81, 85, 130, 183, 207, 211, 220, 229, 231, 233, 257*n*2
Burke, Edmund, xvi, 172*n*4, 185, 210–11, 216–17, 222, 228, 248, 258*n*8, 263*n*26, 267, 274, 280

Civil Society, 14–16, 69, 93, 97–98*n*12, 101–102*n*19, 104*n*24, 173*n*6, 177–78*n*15, 182, 184, 262*n*23, 269, 275, 279; *see* need satisfaction, *Rechtszustand*
community, xvi, 25, 27, 37, 45–46, 85–87, 93, 95–96*n*6, 99*n*13, 102*n*19, 129, 219, 227, 243, 268, 270, 277, 279; SEE *polis, sensus communis*
consuetudo (what we are accustomed to do), 188, 253–55; *see* custom, *habitus, hexis*